MILLWARD, R 7112
LANDSCAPES
OF NORTH WALES

942.
91

Hertfordshire

−3 DEC 2008

Please renew/return this item by the last date shown.

So that your telephone call is charged at local rate,
please call the numbers as set out below:

	From Area codes 01923 or 020:	From the rest of Herts:
Renewals:	01923 471373	01438 737373
Enquiries:	01923 471333	01438 737333
Textphone:	01923 471599	01438 737599
L32	www.hertsdirect.org/librarycatalogue	

1985
6
86

Landscapes of
NORTH WALES

Landscapes of
NORTH WALES
Roy Millward and Adrian Robinson

David & Charles

Newton Abbot · London · North Pomfret (Vt)

To Eileen and John
at Hafodty

British Library Cataloguing in Publication Data

Millward, Roy
   Landscapes of North Wales.
   1. Wales, North – Description and travel
   I. Title II. Robinson, Adrian
   914.29'1   DA740.N6

ISBN 0–7153–7713–2

Phototypeset in V.I.P. Garamond by
Western Printing Services Ltd, Bristol
and printed in Great Britain
by Biddles of Guildford,
for David & Charles (Publishers) Limited
Brunel House Newton Abbot Devon

Published in the United States of America
by David & Charles Inc
North Pomfret Vermont 05053 USA

CONTENTS

INTRODUCTION

North Wales, as part of Highland Britain, portrays many of the features which we associate with mountainous areas, an irregular skyline of high peaks, bare rock outcrops, steep precipitous slopes and deeply carved valleys often with finger lakes. This description applies particularly to the core region of Snowdonia. In the more subdued, upland country which surrounds this mountain heartland the setting softens and thus stands out in great contrast. With its lower elevation it provides the right scale for the foreground out of which the highest mountain tops rise so majestically. It is these differences of scale as well as the major contrasts of mountain and coastal scene which distinguishes North Wales from many of the upland areas of Britain. Within its borders there is a multiplicity of landscape types and these are explored in the first part of the book. Another distinguishing feature which sets it apart from other upland areas like the Lake District or the Pennines is the unique cultural heritage enjoyed by North Wales. This is especially so of the language which has survived to a remarkable degree in Gwynedd and to a lesser extent in the interior country farther south where it gives the region a distinct sense of unity which otherwise might be lacking.

Man arrived very late on the scene, long after the forces of nature had created the basic outlines of mountain and valley, sea and shore. Yet within a span of only five thousand years his influence has been so great that much of what we see today in the present landscape is the result of his endeavours. The clearing of the woodland which formerly occupied all save the highest lands, the creation of great upland sheep pastures and the forging of new routes through the mountainous heartland, quickly and radically altered the whole natural landscape. In a predominantly hostile environment, the available resources of the region were exploited to the full. The working of the lead and copper lodes in the old hard rocks provided a short-lived period of prosperity while from the late eighteenth century onwards slate quarrying was to have a profound influence on the livelihood of thousands in the string of newly created villages on the north-west fringes of Snowdonia.

The events of history have also made a lasting impression on the present landscape as witness the girdle of castle towns which Edward I built in the closing years of the thirteenth century in his attempt to finally wrest control from the Welsh Princes occupying the moun-

6

tainous heartland. After the Act of Union which finally brought about more peaceable conditions, attempts were made to introduce English ideas, especially with the creation of landed gentry and their finely laid out estates. The newcomers were often responsible for developing the available resources of the area for they had the necessary capital and ideas. The pace of change quickened considerably after roads and later railways penetrated even the most rural parts so that the Victorian traveller, the forerunner of the present day car excursionist, could satisfy his appetite for the grand and unusual. Men of idealism like William Madocks moved into the area and attempted great schemes of reclamation as their own individual contribution to the age of improvement. The art of urban planning, which had largely lain dormant for five hundred years since the creation of Edward's castle towns, was now suddenly revived and found expression in Madock's own Tremadog as well as the later Victorian seaside resorts of Llandudno and Colwyn Bay.

The past fifty years have seen even greater man-made changes to the landscape of many parts of North Wales. It is a period which has seen the setting out of great dark and forbidding conifer plantations, the development of huge water storage schemes in some of the most remote valleys, the harnessing of water for power and the concrete symbolism of the present age as expressed in the atomic power stations of Trawsfynydd and Wylfa. Apart from obvious blemishes like the rash of caravan sites which now seem to occupy nearly the whole of the lower stretches of the North Wales coastline, the landscape has absorbed many of man's past excesses to a remarkable degree. But it was a landscape always under attack or threat. Fortunately the creation of the Snowdonia National Park and the designation of areas of outstanding beauty in other parts of the region, came only just in time to save a living landscape which could so easily have succumbed to the pressures of the present age.

Throughout the book emphasis is laid on evidence still to be seen in the present landscape, even though this sometimes calls for a detective approach in searching out details on the ground. To this end maps are essential, especially in covering the individual studies which make up the second part of the book. For identification of individual features National Grid four-figure references are given in relation to the appropriate Ordnance Survey maps listed for each of the individual areas covered by the detailed studies. A suggested itinerary has also been added as an aid to enjoyment and exploration of the landscape, both by car and on foot.

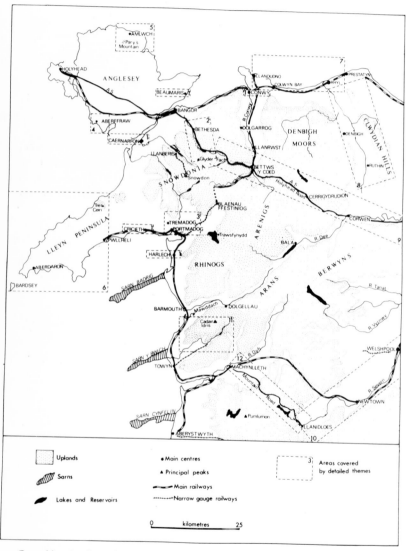

General locational map showing regional sub-divisions and the areas covered by the individual themes

8

LANDSCAPE AND MAN
IN NORTH WALES

Although to many North Wales is simply equated with the mountainous region of Snowdonia, the true identification is with a much larger area. The boundary of the old Welsh kingdom of Gwynedd, now happily restored as an administrative unit, gives a much closer approximation but even this excludes considerable tracts of country in the east and south-east, in the new counties of Clwyd and Powys. On historic and cultural grounds it seems desirable to include the whole area of the principality north of the Dyfi-Severn valley line. Such a large canvas inevitably takes in a rich variety of scenery, often a reflection of the control exerted by the character of the underlying rock whether this is a sandstone, shale, slate or tough uncompromising granite. Although having an overall unity, North Wales consists of a number of regions, each with their own special physical attributes which, in turn, are reflected in their cultural heritage. But even within a single region like Snowdonia there are the inevitable stark contrasts of relief, vegetation patterns and land use which serve to add a welcome diversity to the landscape. Anyone entering the area from the east along the route which hugs the North Wales coast is immediately aware of this contrast between the rich, lush pastures of the well-farmed lowlands around Aber and the rock-strewn summits of the neighbouring Carneddau. There, within the compass of a few square kilometres, is ample proof of the way in which nature exercises an over-riding control over the environment even though man has attempted to tame it over the centuries.

Snowdonia

This heartland of mountainous peaks tucked away in the north-west corner of Wales has a complicated rock structure. The relationship between the rock sequence and the individual mountain masses of Snowdonia can best be understood if the area is likened to a gigantic pie dish with its long axis extending in a north-east to south-west direction. The centre of the pie dish is occupied by Ordovician volcanic beds but its rim is fashioned out of the older Cambrian slates. The slate belt, lying on the north-western side of the main mountain mass, is the most important commercially, taking in the foothills of the Carneddau and then skirting the outer peaks of the Glyder range at Penrhyn, across the Llanberis valley at Dinorwic and then to the Nantlle valley (5053) with its cluster of biblical-sounding quarrying settlements. Much of the country of the Cambrian rim consists of the coastal plateau of Arfon where higher sea levels in the Late Tertiary Period created a series of platforms, a staircase to the inner recesses of the mountain core of Snowdonia. Everywhere the Cambrian beds are steeply inclined due to the presence of even older and more resistant rocks of the Padarn ridge against which the folding took place. On the inner side of the slate belt the Cambrian strata are dominated by a thick slab of grit, over 400m thick, and it is this formation which is responsible for the high sharp ridge of Elidir Fawr (6161), the outer bastion of the Glyder Range.

The rock succession and associated relief of the central core of Snowdonia is well displayed by following the A5 road through the Nant Ffrancon valley from Bethesda (6266) and then across the watershed into the Llugwy basin around Capel Curig (7258). The steeply dipping Cambrian slates of the Penrhyn quarry and the overlying bed of coarse grit quickly give way to the lower sedimentary beds of the Ordovician formation which occupy the centre of our pie dish. These beds are responsible for the prominent peaks of Foel Goch (6260) and Y Garn (6359) where lava beds afford greater resistance to erosion. Between Y Garn and Glyder Fawr (6457) the pronounced downfold which forms the centre of the pie dish is well seen in the beds of lava and volcanic tuffs occurring in the backwall of Llyn Idwal (6459). Both Glyder Fawr and its near neighbour, Glyder Fach are composed of lavas. On the top of Glyder Fawr the beds form a mass of jumbled rocks with great monoliths lying at all angles. The traveller Richard Pennant, who came here in 1781, left a description of the scene while his artist companion faithfully recorded the strange overhanging cantilever stone which still excites the present day hill walker. Nothing has altered during the past two hundred years for Pennant's 'groupings of columnar stones, of vast size, from 10 to 30 feet [3 to 9m] long, lying in all directions' are immovable. From the rock-strewn summit of Glyder Fach, it is but a short trek to the north-east to reach the top of Tryfan, one of the famous climbing peaks of the Snowdonia range, perhaps more impressive from below than on its crest ridge. Again the main mass of the mountain is formed of a succession of lava flows separated by beds of shale, a combination of rocks which give it a distinctive character and appearance. The lava has a tendency to break off along contraction joints and this can give rise to columns of rock, like the 'two stones' of the summit, often mistakenly taken for climbers. Tryfan is the most eastern limb of an upfold, the compliment of the Idwal syncline. One result of the upward roll of the strata is that the lava beds of Tryfan again make their appearance on the slopes of Gallt yr Ogof (6959). Between the two the upward arching of the rock strata can be seen in the backwall of Cwm Tryfan (6658).

The double fold of Cwm Idwal and Cwm Tryfan involving Ordovician beds provides a clear illustration of the way in which the various rock types have been compressed into a number of subsidiary folds within the major regional syncline of Snowdonia, our main pie dish analogue. The Glyder peaks also show the way in which the hard lava beds are responsible for the most impressive elements in the scenery. On the opposite side of the Nant Ffrancon valley the highest peak of the Carneddau, Carnedd Dafydd (6663), also has a capping of the same lava beds. Its near neighbour, Carnedd Llewelyn, only a few metres higher, owes its prominence to a thick sill of intrusive dolerite rock which affords great resistance to the forces of erosion. The presence of the dolerite here and the widespread occurrence of lavas, ash beds and tuffs, throughout the central mountain core of Snowdonia, indicates that volcanic activity must have been intense and widespread in this area about 600 million years ago. The eruptions of that age, mainly taking place on the sea bed and therefore often giving rise to individual lava flows separating marine sediments, have left their mark in the present rugged character of much of central Snowdonia, though the detailed fashioning of the rocks is of much more recent date.

Snowdon or Eryri (possibly meaning high land rather than the more usually accepted 'land of eagles'), lies close to the centre of our pie dish downfold, and it, too, has been fashioned out of volcanic rock. The peak and highest point at 1085m (6054), represents the culmination of a number of convergent ridges and is formed of volcanic tuff ejected from submarine eruptions in a series of cataclysmic explosions. On the sea bed of the time, during periods of relative quiescence, ordinary marine sands and muds accumulated so that today sedimentary rocks with their mollusc fossils occur close to the summit. The lava capstone which we find on the topmost peaks of the Glyder Range is not present but similar beds make a considerable

11

impact on the lower slopes of the mountain. They occur however, on the corrie walls of Maen d'ur Arddu (5956) and again there is a marked downfold in the rock strata, the south-west continuation of the Idwal syncline discussed above. On the eastern side of Snowdon, in the great coombe hollow which contains Llyn Llydaw (6654), the lava beds have been arched up into an anticline, yet another example of minor fold ripples which occur within the broad regional syncline of Snowdonia.

In other mountainous tracts of Britain like the Cairngorms or Cuillin Hills of Skye, granite forms an important element in the rock sequence but this is not so in Snowdonia, a fact all the more surprising when lava flows and tuffs cover such large areas. The volcanic vents from which the outpourings took place are usually represented by crystalline igneous rocks and although many of these have been located they do not give rise to particularly impressive landscape features. Foel Fras (6968), the lofty tract of country in the northern Carneddau, probably represents one such ancient volcanic vent. Only along its northern edge does it give rise to a topographic feature of note, the well-known Aber Falls (6670) where the small stream of the Afon Goch tumbles over the edge of the granite and encounters the more easily removed shales. On the other side of Snowdonia, in one of the less frequented but nevertheless attractive parts of the mountain area, the distinctive hornblende granite of Mynydd Mawr (5454) gives rise to an imposing bluff overlooking Llyn Cwellyn. On the north side of the mountains an igneous rock outcrop forms the great headland of Penmaenmawr (7076), for so long a major obstacle along the coastal route. The crystalline rock, a porphery, has been extensively quarried for over a century and the whole face of the mountain trimmed back as gallery after gallery have bitten deeply into its northern face.

While the basic outline of Snowdonia was fashioned by Late Tertiary time, the onset of the Ice Age during the past million years has led to a detailed sculpturing of many of the mountains. In place of the earlier formed dome the ice created a fretted upland as it gouged out huge corrie basins and chiselled deep valleys along the lines of the former river routes. In some of the higher parts the work of ice sculpture was never quite completed so that even in the present mountain landscape there are a few remnants of the original flat top of the broad dome. Elsewhere the efficacy of ice as an eroding force has left an indelible impression on the present landscape which is perhaps not surprising when it is realised that it is a mere ten thousand years since the last corrie glaciers finally melted away in some of the deeper north-east facing hollows (see Study 2). The whole Snowdonian region, because of its height and westerly situation, was plenteously supplied with snow to nurture active and long-lasting valley and corrie glaciers. This was especially the case in the main Snowdon and Glyder ranges so that today much of the original plateau surface has been hollowed out. The main mountain mass of Snowdon was attacked on all sides as six separate corrie basins developed. Between the corries, narrow arête ridges, often of knife-edge proportions like Crib Goch (6255), radiate from the summit peak. At various times during the Ice Age the active high level corrie glaciers fed the neighbouring streams of ice occupying the valley floors and considerable overdeepening by erosion occurred. The result is that the characteristic U-shaped trough rather than the more usual V-shaped cross profile of a normal river valley is found throughout Snowdonia, being typified by Nant Ffrancon (6362), Nant Gwynant (6350) and the main lower Conwy valley from Bettws y Coed to the sea. The overdeepening brought about by erosion along the sole of the glacier has left its mark in the many rock basin lakes which occupy valleys like Cwellyn (5654), Nant Peris (5959) and Nantgwyryd (7058) to name but a few. The depth of these ribbon lakes varies considerably depending on the efficacy of the glacier and the resistance afforded by the bed rock. Llyn Peris for example, descends to a maximum depth of 35m, slightly greater than its neighbour Llyn Padarn which reaches to 29m in one place. While these two lakes might once have been a single sheet of water they occupy two separate rock basins with a distinct rock bar in between. Sediment brought down by a side valley stream has led to the development of a broad lake flat but this in itself seems insufficient to account for the two distinct lakes. Some of the glacially formed lakes are remarkably shallow, Llyn Ogwen, for example, being less than 5m deep. Many former lakes have disappeared altogether since the Ice Age, only a very flat valley floor like that of Nant Ffrancon remaining as an indication of past conditions. Possibly two lakes formerly existed in the upper part of the Lledr valley around Dolwyddelan (7352). Their disappearance has left behind a thin covering of lake sediments, the basis of today's fertile soils. The area now forms an oasis of fertility set within the barren, mountainous countryside around and inevitably proved attractive to early settlement.

Compared with the valley lakes, those occupying the corrie basins are surprisingly deep considering their smaller size. Llyn Dulyn

(7066), for example, set within a deep recess below the main ridge of the northern Carneddau, descends precipitously to a maximum depth of 57m within a very short distance from the backwall of the corrie. Similarly Llyn Llydaw, situated on the eastern flanks of Snowdon has a maximum depth of 57m and thus provides further evidence of the selective and intense erosive power of the corrie glacier. Rotational slipping, possibly resulting from a greater accumulation of snow close to the backwall of the corrie, seems to be the most effective means of gouging out such pronounced hollows in solid rock. Most of the corrie basins tend to lie on the north-east side of the main mountain ridges where accumulation went on steadily in the lee of the highest peaks and where melting would be at a minimum because of the lower intensity of insolation from this quarter.

The valley glaciation of the past has also had a profound effect on the present landscape of Snowdonia. Actively moving ice had little respect for pre-existing features like cols and watershed barriers and in suitable circumstances lowered them or even removed them altogether. Through valleys, like that used by the present A5 road through the mountains, were made possible by the great erosive power of a former glacier. The whole of the mountain mass has been split up into distinct blocks of country so that it no longer presents a real barrier to communications. Thomas Telford appreciated this fact when he embarked on the route of his Holyhead road in the early years of the nineteenth century (Study 9). The railway engineers, for the most part, left the area alone but this was largely dictated by economic circumstances rather than unsurmountable difficulties of the terrain. One late arrival to the scene, the narrow gauge Welsh Highland Railway did cross the whole width of the mountain mass running from Portmadog to Caernarfon by way of the through valleys of the Colwyn and Gwyrfai. The most difficult section of the route was not at the watershed between the two opposing valley systems even though it had to make a steady climb to reach its highest point at Pitt's Head (5751). Instead it was found necessary to tunnel alongside the Pass of Aberglaslyn where the gorge section of the valley had not benefited from the erosive powers of ice. The Welsh Highland Railway only began operating in 1923 and lasted less than twenty years. In recent years various schemes have been put forward to re-open at least certain sections of the line as a tourist attraction. The only other line which completely traversed Snowdonia was that of the LMS from Llandudno Junction to Blaenau Ffestiniog built in the 1890s to provide an outlet from the slate mines. The route chosen involved a long tunnel at the head of the Lledr valley (6850) in order to reach Blaenau Ffestiniog on the opposite side of the watershed.

In spite of the through valleys left behind as a result of glacial erosion during the Ice Age the central part of Snowdonia was long regarded as an impenetrable mountain fastness where local Celtic influence persisted and could be largely ignored. This was the view even in the late thirteenth century when Edward I built his system of peripheral castle towns to contain the Welsh in the mountain heart rather than attempt complete subjugation. The Romans, however took a different line, and as more evidence comes to light, it is clear that they were intent on establishing a system of roads and forts running through the mountain area. Their regional centre was Segontium (4862), on the outskirts of present day Caernarfon and on a very different site from that chosen by Edward I for his castle town. Lying on the north-west edge of Snowdonia, Segontium could only be approached by the coastal fringe from the north of by way of a direct passage through the mountains. The apparently easier coastal approach, skirting the mountains around the north, was not greatly favoured for the great rock bastion of Penmaenmawr proved an impenetrable barrier. Instead the main Roman route in this area ran farther inland crossing the Conwy valley at Caerhun (7770) where there was a fort to guard the river ford. From this point the road ran over the northern slopes of the Carneddau through Bwlch Ddeufaen (7171) and then dropped down to the coastal plain near Aber (6572). The route diverged at this point, one limb crossing the northern approaches to the Menai Strait and then on to Anglesey while the other made for Segontium by way of the relatively easy coastal plain of Arfon. The alternative approach ran through the heart of the mountains by way of the Cwellyn valley though its precise course is not known. That the Romans were anxious to maintain a road system throughout Snowdonia is shown by the existence of forts like Tomen y Mur (7038) guarding the southern approach or Caer Llugwy (7457) within the heart of the region. At the head of Nant Gwynant a staging camp was established at Pen y Gwyryd (6555), one point on a major north-south route through the area which also linked Caer Llugwy and possibly the recently discovered Roman fort at Bettws y Coed (7956) before making for Caerhun in the Conwy valley. The exact line of the connecting roads between these forts is not known but many are believed to represent prehistoric routes which the Romans simply adapted to their needs. In the present state of knowledge there is plenty of scope for conjecture. Where, for example, did the route lie

15

north of Tomen y Mur? One possibility is that it crossed the mountains to the east of Blaenau Ffestiniog before making the sharp descent into Maesgwn valley (7349) and thence by way of Dolwyddelan, skirting Mynydd Cribau (7655) to Caer Llugwy.

After the Romans left the area towards the end of the fourth century the area returned quickly to the control of the Welsh princes, the mountains providing a secure retreat so that the events of the next few centuries passed without notice. It was not until the late thirteenth century that any attempt was made by the English to wrest control from the Welsh princes of Gwynedd. Even then the hold on the area was a precarious one and limited to containment through the establishment of a ring of coastal castles. Life in the mountainous interior probably went on much as before, with the grazing lands on the upper slopes providing summer pastures and leading ultimately to more permanent settlement in place of the hafod or summer hut, a name which appears repeatedly on the maps of today. Even the accession of a Welsh Tudor to the English throne after the battle of Bosworth in 1485 did little to alter the isolated role which Snowdonia had long adopted and for a time the area became the heartland of Owain Glyndwr's kingdom of Gwynedd. It was only in the seventeenth century when travellers began to discover the area that its isolation was finally broken down. Naturalists and travellers alike came to search out the unusual and marvel at the horrific beauties of the mountain scene. The first recorded ascent of Snowdon was made in 1639 by Thomas Johnson, a botanist who found 'our British Alps veiled in cloud' but that did not prevent him from collecting rare specimens from the rocks and precipices he met on his way to the summit. The real beginning of exploration came, however, well over a century later when Thomas Pennant published the *Journey to Snowdon* in 1781. This started a cult which attracted painters, antiquaries, poets and those engaged on scientific pursuits, as well as the mere traveller who was content to gaze upon the awe-inspiring grandeur of the mountain scene and contemplate the sublime beauties and experience of a new landscape far removed from the ordered uniformity of the English lowlands.

Travelling in the late eighteenth century was something of an adventure for the area lacked adequate roads and many routes were little more than rough packhorse trails. Fortunately the early hesitating steps of tourism coincided with the rise of slate quarrying which demanded the building of new roads and led to the creation of new settlements. Under the Penrhyn family a group of private scattered

16

workings near Bethesda in the last decades of the eighteenth century was turned into a larger and much more viable industry of which the great Penrhyn Quarry stands as tangible evidence in the present landscape (6265). The Penrhyn family owned considerable areas of land both along the coastal strip near their stately home at Llandegai (6071) as well as in the mountainous interior. It was first to his quarry and then to his inland estates at Capel Curig that Lord Penrhyn built a road along the side of the Ogwen valley and thence by the west side of the Nant Ffrancon, diagonally up the great step at its head and continuing through the great gap under Tryfan before dropping down to Capel Curig. It was never an easy route and later it had to be modified by Telford who built his more evenly graded London to Holyhead road through the same gap in the mountains (study 9).

The impact of slate quarrying on the landscape went much further than improving the road system. As the need for slate increased greatly in the nineteenth century, especially as a roofing material in the industrial towns of the North and Midlands, so Penrhyn quarry was extended, burying deeper into the bowels of the earth and climbing steadily as a gigantic stairway up the adjacent mountainside towards the summit peak of Carnedd y Filiast. A quarryman's settlement of smallholdings was established at Mynydd Llandegai (6065) each with about 0.5 hectares of pasture, sufficient to graze a cow or provide other means of sustenance at times of slack working in the quarry. Each holding was surrounded by fences made of blue slate set about a foot apart, interwoven at the top with briars and sufficiently distinctive to evoke a comment from the Reverend Bingley in his famous tour of Wales in 1798. Much of the common land was enclosed at this time and what had formerly been a waste was now able to provide additional grazing grounds for those who held cottages on the Penrhyn Estate. As if to match the improving spirit of his age, Lord Penrhyn set about planting trees to add diversity or act as shelter belts in the more exposed areas. He was conscious of the need to tame the wilderness he inherited and make it profitable for farming. To this end he built Pen-issa-nant as a dairy and poultry farm near the Penrhyn quarry. Even his outlying estates in the upper Conwy valley were improved and expected to make their contribution to the income of the family. It was in the slate industry that he made his greatest contribution, building a new port at the mouth of the Aber Cegin in 1790 'capable of admitting vessels of 300 tons burden, for more conveniently exporting slates from his quarries, about six miles distant'. A railway of a '1 foot $11\frac{1}{2}$ inch gauge' was built for use by horsedrawn trains and when completed in 1801 it facilitated the export of slates from Port Penrhyn. The former track of the railway is still traceable as it follows the contours in making the descent down the side of the Ogwen Valley to the massive stone quays of the harbour.

In the neighbouring Peris valley the family of the Assheton-Smiths of Vaynol were active in developing the slates in the neighbourhood of Llanberis at the Dinorwic Quarry. Thomas Assheton-Smith assumed the right of ownership in 1809 after agreeing to pay compensation to squatters who had built cottages around the quarry on Llandeiniolen Common and quickly attempted to rationalise the enterprise on the lines adopted by the Penrhyn family. The main outlet was at Port Dinorwic by the side of the Menai Strait (5267) where an artificial harbour had been built as early as 1793. The connecting tramway from the quarries was not completed until 1824 and because of the incised nature of the Menai Strait a steep incline was necessary for the final descent to the slate wharves of the port. Although it is some years since the quarry and railway closed, there are sufficient remains to give a striking picture of the whole enterprise. At the quarry itself the former working sheds have now been turned into an industrial museum, complete with the great water wheel which supplied much of the power needed for sawing and preparing the slate. Part of the railway track, as it runs alongside Llyn Padarn, has been re-opened as a tourist attraction while at Port Dinorwic itself the harbour, with its quay walls carefully faced with slate, has been turned into a yachting marina. What was once a working concern for hundreds of people engaged in the slate trade has thus successfully adapted itself to the needs of the present. The same can be said of the slate mines of the Blaenau Ffestiniog area where the Llechwedd and Oakley quarries have now become a tourist attraction.

It was in the creation of new settlements that the slate industry made its other major contribution to the changing face of the landscape during the nineteenth century. The dark grey houses strung alongside the main Holyhead road near the Penrhyn quarry became Bethesda, named after the chapel built in 1820 when the nonconformist hold on the area was very strong. Similarly Deiniolen (5863) grew up in the shadow of the Dinorwic Quarry with the church being built from money given by the Assheton-Smith family. In the other great slate-quarrying area along the north-west fringes of Snowdonia around Nantlle (5053) a whole rash of settlements with biblical names like Nazareth, Nebo and Carmel, grew up as the demand for

1 *The Carneddau with the great cleft of Nant Ffrancon cut along their outer edge and the galleries of Penrhyn Slate Quarry forming the opposite slope*

slate reached its peak in the middle of the nineteenth century. The use of biblical names for chapel villages was, in one sense, carrying on a tradition, for many of the primary settlements of the area were designated many centuries earlier after Celtic saints like St Tegai (Llandegai) and St Peris (Llanberis). For the most part these quarry villages were built without much thought of planning, often simply rows of terrace houses strung along a road. Lord Penrhyn did, however, attempt to create a model village community at Llandegai (6070) partly to serve his own estates. Around the old church neat rows of cottages were built together with a saw-mill using the power of the Ogwen river which ran alongside. Together with his nearby castle home, almost completely rebuilt at a cost of nearly £500,000 between 1827 and 1841, Lord Penrhyn attempted to add a new element to the landscape, perhaps in compensation for the disfigurement which his slate quarrying was leaving in its wake.

Anglesey

As a region Anglesey stands apart from the rest of North Wales not only in the shapes and colours of its landscape but also through its experience in history. Among the islands of the Irish Sea basin, Anglesey ranks second only to Man, and it is the largest island adjacent to the Welsh coastline. Anglesey took on its present shape only eight thousand years ago when the rising sea level of the post glacial centuries that caused the loss of so much land off the coast of Cardigan Bay, resulted in the flooding of the narrow winding valleys which were to form the Menai Strait. Holy Island too became isolated from the main mass of Anglesey. In its physique the island is at one with the Lleyn peninsula and the narrow coastal platform that separates the high mountains of Gwynedd from the Menai Strait. A dominant feature in the landscape of all three tracts is an undulating surface lying between 70 and 100m above sea level. It has been called the Menai Platform and in Anglesey it takes up almost a half of the island's area. Similar and higher erosion surfaces, dissected by the present streams and rivers, may be detected at 130m and 180m above present sea level.

Isolated hills, monadnocks, rise sharply from the boulder-clay covered surfaces that make up the lowlands of North Wales. In the Lleyn peninsula the long line of monadnocks, etched against the sky in soft blues when seen from south-west Anglesey or across Tremadog Bay from the heights of Harlech Castle, contribute the most essential element to the character of that local region. Anglesey's isolated hills are far less impressive than the shapely mountains that rise suddenly from the monotonous platforms of Lleyn. Nine monadnocks lie scattered about the island; among them, Bwrdd Arthur reaches 160m encircled by the rampart of an Iron Age camp. Parys Mountain, once Europe's most prolific source of copper, touches 155m while the narrow hummocky ridge of Garn Bodafon heaves itself above the featureless lower surfaces of Anglesey to a height of almost 200m. Holyhead Mountain, carved out of the ancient pre-Cambrian rocks of the Mona Complex, falls in sheer cliffs to the Irish Sea from a summit at 230m. It has been explained as a lone surviving fragment of a still higher and older erosion surface than those that now compose the bulk of Anglesey's landscape. Whatever its geomorphological origins Holyhead Mountain reveals itself, in clear weather, for miles across the Irish Sea, a natural beacon, clear-cut in outline and violet-hued when the mountains of Snowdonia are lost beneath a motionless belt of cumulus cloud.

Anglesey has always been reckoned a dull island, but the dullness is only relative. Because it lacks the grandeur of the mainland mountains of Gwynedd, its own attractions have always been undervalued. Apart from the bays and sandy beaches that have drawn too many bungalow builders and summer caravans whose only interest seems to be the sound of the sea and some of the highest sunshine averages of western Britain, the island, in its small compass presents a great variety of coastal scenery. The high cliffs of Holy Island from South Stack to North Stack and beyond must rank among the finest specimens of wild coastline in Britain. By contrast Newborough Warren, a complex of dunes in the south-western corner of the island, stirs vague images of desert landscapes under the high suns of long June days. The shoreline of the Menai Strait reveals still another aspect of Anglesey. Here the gently broken surface of the Menai platform with its varied, multi-faceted skin of glacial deposits has been shaped over the past three centuries into one of the quietest and most attractive of pastoral landscapes in the British Isles. Green hedged fields, lush plantations of beech, oak and alien conifers, deep lanes that lead to nowhere but the stony water's edge are characteristic of the southern part of the strait.

The variety of Anglesey's coastline is offset by the superficial dullness of its interior landscape. For the traveller on the way to the Irish ferry at Holyhead the last miles of the A5 from Menai Bridge foreshadow the countryside of lowland Ireland with its quilted patterns of green fields and an absence of any outstanding topographical features. The solid geology of Anglesey is varied enough, as one can see when the pre-Cambrian foundations are exposed in the cliffs of Holy Island or where the Carboniferous Limestone stands open to view at Penmon, but for the greater part the basement rocks lie concealed beneath boulder clays of the Ice Age. The individuality of the landscapes of interior Anglesey rests upon an alignment of its main valleys in a north-east to south-west direction. These shallow corridors, widened and straightened no doubt by the passage of Irish Sea ice some 15,000 years ago, follow similar alignments in the major structural features of the largely buried solid rocks. For instance, the long corridor occupied by the Malltraeth Marsh is limited to the south by the line of the Berw faults. North-eastwards from Newborough the line of this ancient fault is etched out in the present landscape as a tiny ruler-straight escarpment never more than 60m high. To the south of the escarpment the gently rolling landscape is underlain by the ancient rocks of the pre-Cambrian Mona Complex. Here the rocks that compose the wild forbidding scenery of the higher parts of Holy Island are planed across by the Menai Platform and buried in boulder clays. This is pastoral Anglesey, a landscape that was first tamed 5,000 years ago when Neolithic colonists made their settlements at favoured sites in the bays and lowlands around the Irish Sea. To the north of the line of the Berw faults much younger sedimentary rocks of Upper Carboniferous age have been preserved in the corridor of the Malltraeth Marsh. Coal seams, thin and steeply dipping, outcrop between Llangristiolus and Bodorgan. A nineteenth-century estimate of the resources of Anglesey's coalfield placed them at five million tons. Coal has been worked from time to time and keen industrial archaeologists ferret out the remains of Berw colliery, but like so much of the island's solid geology its riches and variety pass unmarked in the present landscape. Only at Parys Mountain, where mineral-rich dykes were injected into the older rocks of the Mona Complex at the time of the Caledonian mountain building, did the exploitation of the foundation rocks transform the historic landscape. An avid half century of copper mining in the decades about 1800 has left behind an unreclaimable wilderness.

The oldest man-made objects in Anglesey's landscape date back to the Neolithic epoch of prehistory—a long period of time that extends from the fourth millenium BC until as late as 1600 BC in the island's chronology. The most striking features of this primal period when the first farming communities established themselves were the burial places, dank passages and chambers built of huge roughly hewn stones. In Anglesey sixteen chambered tombs still survive, though the writings of topographers and antiquarians who visited and researched in the island during the eighteenth and early nineteenth centuries show that many more existed only 200 years ago. They were broken up for building materials in walls and barns at a time when the new evangelism of Welsh nonconformity was able to dispel the dark aura of fear that perhaps invested these pagan communal burial places. Despite the incompleteness of the present pattern of megalithic tombs in Anglesey, there is little doubt that their distribution reveals something of the settlement geography of Neolithic times. They are notably absent from the interior of the island. Several occupy coastal sites; others, such as the most famous Bryn Celli Ddu, lie only a short distance from the sea. A second theme that emerges from the location of the megalithic tombs is a relationship to the areas of Carboniferous Limestone in the south-west and east of the island. Here light and easily drained soils seem to have attracted Neolithic farmers; their communal burial sites suggest a concentration of settlement at the southern entrance to the Menai Strait and again in the north towards Benllech and Moelfre.

The Neolithic geography of Anglesey was also coloured by the island's location in the Irish Sea. Historical geographers and prehistorians have long argued for the cultural unity of the Irish Sea basin at many periods of its history. The seaways of the Irish Sea have not only joined together Man and Anglesey, Wales, Scotland and Ireland, but they have established longer links with Cornwall, Brittany, Iberia and Nordic Europe. Twenty centuries of links with Neolithic settlements suggest the role of the Atlantic seaways in the cultural evolution of Anglesey. For instance, the first phase of Neolithic settlement, representing colonists who imported the earliest techniques of grain-growing and stock-rearing, may be commemorated in the simple Passage Graves. There are three of them in the island, Bodowyr, Ty-mawr and Ty Newydd—all lying close to the southern coast and the Menai Strait. The very location of these monuments might point to colonists who approached Anglesey from the south making their first landfalls on that smiling south-west coast with its wide sandy bays and low cliffs. Valleys, such as those of the Crugyll and Braint, led inland to acceptable places for settlement.

Another kind of megalithic tomb, the Court Cairn that is widespread in Ireland, suggests a different phase of Neolithic settlement in Anglesey about 2500 BC. The most impressive of these long cairns, a gallery of small square compartments framed in big stones, is Trefignath, on the outskirts of Holyhead. The gallery of three of four chambers runs for 12m. But the finest of this series of tombs, Barclodiad y Gawres, stands magnificently placed some 15m above the sea on a cliff top of the south-west coast. The passage, more than 6m long, was set inside a circular mound almost 30m in diameter. Some of the great stones of the burial chamber are inscribed with abstract patterns that are reminiscent of the geometrical art of the series of burial cairns at New Grange in central Ireland. The settlement history of the builders of this succession of burial chambers has been sketched from a study of sites in Ireland and Wales. The finest tombs lie about the mouth of the River Boyne and it is believed that these represent the burial grounds of the earliest settlers who reached the Irish Sea from southern Brittany. The Anglesey graves are looked upon as the work of a secondary migration that began in Ireland, a migration that might well have been induced by the search for copper ores.

The most famous of Anglesey's chambered tombs, Bryn Celli Ddu was one of the last to be built. It dates from about 1600 BC. Bryn Celli Ddu is unique among the relics of Neolithic Britain because it was raised over the foundations of a stone circle, a 'henge' monument of Late Neolithic date. Bryn Celli Ddu is also remarkable for its state of preservation. The enclosing shell of turf, clay and stone has long since vanished from almost every chambered tomb of western Britain. At many places the fallen capstone lies amid a shapeless heap of megalithic rubble; at others the great stones of the central chamber stand intact—a skeleton structure bared to all weathers. But at Bryn Celli Ddu you can still make your way to the central chamber through a passage that burrows for almost 10m through the cairn. And in the heart of the burial chamber, an artificial megalithic cavern 3m across, a central stone obelisk that reaches nearly to the roof calls the mind to the mysteries of a long-lost Stone Age religion.

Bryn Celli Ddu is only one of a number of prehistoric objects among the quiet pastures in the valley of the Afon Braint. In the next field there is a Bronze Age barrow and a few hundred metres away to the north one finds a standing stone. The area about these monuments has also yielded a large number of stone axes. It seems as if Bryn Celli Ddu and its surroundings have formed a core of settlement over many prehistoric centuries. Two other sites in south-western Anglesey, close to the placid channel of the Menai Strait, point to the long occupation of this quarter of the island. Castell Bryn Gwyn probably originated as a stone circle of Late Neolithic times. More than two thousand years later its simple ringwork was reshaped and elaborated as an Iron Age defensive site. Another megalithic tomb, Bryn yr Hen Bobl, now standing in the landscaped park of the Marquis of Anglesey, Plas Newydd, occupies a site that has revealed some clues to the economy of the Middle and Late Neolithic centuries. Close to the monument the site of a Neolithic settlement has been revealed through an abundance of charcoal, broken pottery, animal bones and the waste chippings and flakes of stone working. This stone debris was composed almost entirely of Graig lwyd dolerite, a rock from the summit of Penmaenmawr Mountain used for the making of stone axes that have been found at Neolithic and Bronze Age sites in many parts of the British Isles. It is believed that Bryn yr Hen Bobl, on a bench above the Menai Strait, was the place where the roughed-out axes from the natural quarry among the screes of Penmaenmawr Mountain were finally worked and shaped for export.

The Bronze Age lasted for a thousand years. Even so it is hard to reconstruct the geography of this long period from the remains that have survived in Anglesey. No dwelling sites, villages or field patterns are known in the island from the centuries of the Bronze Age. The material evidence consists of a dozen heavy stone axe hammers that might have been used as ploughshares, burial mounds, standing stones of which some may date from much later times, and half a dozen hoards of metallic axes and scrap metal. Some general conclusions may be drawn from Anglesey's sparse and imprecisely dated objects of the Bronze Age. It seems likely that settlement expanded after 1600 BC into the previously neglected central and northern parts of the island. The most interesting of Anglesey's barrows, Bedd Branwen at Llanddeusant, has yielded the first clue to the character of the Bronze Age landscape through the application of the techniques of pollen analysis. The barrow, it seems, was built in an open meadow rich with buttercups. Close by cereals were under cultivation and

2 *Bryn Celli Ddu in Anglesey, another burial chamber with its restored covering mound*

there must have been in the neighbourhood woods of oak, hazel and alder. The Bronze Age too provides further evidence of the long abiding importance of the Menai Strait in the trade, settlement and communications of Anglesey. In 1874 workmen quarrying for stone close to the Menai Bridge uncovered a hoard of eight bronze axes. They belong to types known and produced in southern England. Their location, close to the narrows of the strait, suggests that this was the chief ferry port from the mainland as long as 3,000 years ago; already traders or wandering metalsmiths found a frequented crossing place where Telford was to raise his suspension bridge in the early years of the nineteenth century.

Finally our present knowledge of the archaeology of the Bronze Age throws up a few hints upon the changing economic geography of the times between the seventeenth and seventh centuries BC. The Graig lwyd axe factory on Penmaenmawr mountain that played such a dominant role in the economy of Neolithic Britain declined in importance. Its micro-dolerite was not used in the manufacture of axe hammers; instead the grey-blue rock of Preselau in Pembrokeshire seems to have been in favour. Again, the copper and tin-producing regions of western Europe must have been of immense value in the Bronze Age, but there is no direct proof that the rich resources of Parys Mountain were tapped in those times. The discovery of a stone mould for the casting of bronze axes suggests that metal-working went on in Anglesey and the hoard of a bronze-smith found close to the hut circles of Ty Mawr, a Romano-British village on Holy Island, indicates that the copper ores exposed in the cliffs of Holyhead Mountain were already being exploited in the Bronze Age centuries.

The relict features of the Iron Age in the modern landscape of Anglesey are as striking as any of the legacy of prehistory in North Wales. Nine hill-top or promontory forts date from the centuries immediately before the Roman occupation of the island in AD 78. At numerous sites, particularly in the limestone country of the north-east and in coastal tracts, clusters of hut foundations, some circular and other rectangular, point to the settlements of the native population in Roman times. But the most striking archaeological discovery of the Iron Age was the chance find of a hoard of 144 metal objects—weapons, chariot fittings, harness gear—during the levelling of ground in the laying out of runways at the RAF base at Valley in 1943. The Llyn Cerrig Bach hoard, as it is now known, has been explained as a collection of offerings made over a span of two centuries to the god of a tiny lake whose peaty floor was dredged 2,000 years later in the making of this wartime aerodrome. The finds from Llyn Cerrig Bach, splendid richly-decorated examples of Celtic craftsmanship, have thrown some light on the importance of Anglesey in the Iron Age, but they have scarcely led to a clear definition of the economy and society of the island in those times. The earliest interpretation of this diverse collection of riches related the site to Anglesey's role as a centre of Druidism. These were the votive offerings at the shrine of a pagan cult. It has also been argued that these offerings of foreign shields and swords whose places of origin remain largely obscure had been taken as tolls by local chieftains from a lucrative trade that passed across the island between the Welsh Marches and Ireland.

The Llyn Cerrig Bach hoard, the most outstanding discovery of Welsh archaeology in the twentieth century, hints at the social and economic importance of Anglesey in the Iron Age. The landscape of the northern parts of Holy Island is one of the richest in features of Iron Age and Roman times. The summit of Holyhead Mountain is enclosed by a rampart, a dry-stone wall that in places still stands as high as 3m. Caer y Twr (SH 2182), as this hill fort is called, lacks hut circles and any other evidence of extensive occupation. It has been explained as a refuge for the several scattered settlements on the lower ground of Holy Island, perhaps at the time of the Irish raids in the late Roman period. On the south-western slopes of Holyhead Mountain another faint landmark of the same period survives as a collection of hut circles. Here was an extensive settlement, occupied between AD 100 and AD 400, that covered an area of some eight hectares. A score of hut foundations still remain now that the site is in the care of the Ministry of Works, but a survey of 1865 recorded more than fifty at that time. Holy Island and the adjacent shore of Anglesey across the sandy strait has at least three other deserted settlements of the Romano-British Iron Age. Welsh tradition knows them as Cytiau Gwyddelod, the Irishmen's huts; and it was contended that they belonged to the Goidels, an earlier stratum of the Celtic peoples who were submerged or driven westward across the Irish Sea by invading Brythonic Celts in the folk migrations of the Iron Age. The archaeology of Anglesey's several settlements of hut circles, as yet scantily explored, does not bear out this thesis derived from an ancient name. Din Lligwy, for instance, on the north-eastern side of the island and one of the most impressive prehistoric settlements in the British Isles, reveals two stages of development in the Roman period. Here an open village, similar to many of Anglesey's hut-circle settlements, was remodelled in the closing years of the fourth century. A wall, 1.5m in thickness and composed of a double line of vertical limestone slabs infilled with rubble, was thrown around a nucleus of circular and rectangular buildings. It is believed that a local chieftain engineered this conversion of an open village into a fortified settlement at a time when North Wales was exposed to pirate raids from Ireland.

The third object in Holy Island's prehistoric landscape, Caer Gybi, a Roman fort, illustrates the theme of settlement continuity that is so strongly present in the geography of Wales. Caer Gybi has been compared with the forts of the Saxon shore, Roman fortifications at several points along the coastline of south-east England that date from the close of the third century. Holyhead's Roman fortifications were probably built late in the third century or in the early years of the fourth century. Caer Gybi stands on a rocky cliff overlooking the harbour, a small rectangular shaped enclosure with circular towers at the corners. The seaward flank lay open, undefended, but recent investigations have shown that the north wall of the fort continued on to the beach below the cliff and down to the low-tide level. Holyhead, it seems was a fortified ship landing and a base for the Roman fleet in the Irish Sea. Doubtless, too, it was established to secure the trade in copper from the ores of Holy Island and the far richer resources of Parys Mountain. The withdrawal of Roman power from Wales towards the close of the fourth century did not mark man's final use of Caer Gybi. By the middle of the sixth century the enclosing wall of the Roman naval station sheltered the wooden buildings of a monastic community, a *clas* of the Celtic church said to have been founded by Saint Cybi about the year 550. After the Edwardian Conquest of Wales the church, dedicated to St Cybi, was built in the fourteenth century. Enlarged and restored towards the end of the Victorian era, it now dominates the dull, slate townscape of the Irish ferry port. But the site of St Cybi, the wall of its churchyard built by the Romans, must have provided a focus for settlement for almost 2,000 years.

The use and re-use of the site of the Roman fort at Holyhead suggests a long continuity in the major settlement sites of Anglesey. Recent research, particularly by Professor Glanville R. J. Jones, has turned to the difficult problems of cultural continuity from the Iron Age and the evidence that survives in the contemporary landscape. Jones believes that the social and economic structures of late Celtic Wales have exercised a powerful influence over the shaping of settlement and field patterns in later centuries, over the layout of township and parish. The location of the major settlements of Anglesey seems to show a link between the medieval and prehistoric periods. For instance, on the west coast of the island with its low rocky headlands and sandy bays we find the medieval settlement nucleus of Trefadog (2986)—today represented by only a single farm—close to the Iron Age promontory fort of Castell. An even more striking example of the deep roots that Anglesey's settlements thrust back in time may be found in the north-east of the island where the hill fort of Din Sylwy (SH 5881), a single rampart of limestone monoliths that overlooks Red Wharf Bay from a height of 152m, formed the nucleus of a medieval township, Din Sylwy Frenin. The profound changes in settlement structure that accompanied the process of estate building in Wales between the Edwardian Conquest and the beginning of the seventeenth century resulted in the extinction of Din Sylwy Frenin as a nucleated settlement attached to a network of open fields that adjoined the eastern flanks of the hill fort. Today, the chief evidence for the continuing long use of this tract of Anglesey's landscape lies in the tiny early fifteenth-century church of St Michael sheltering close against the eastern rampart of the hill fort.

Anglesey provides much scattered evidence for its importance as a focus of settlement in Dark Age Wales. Giraldus Cambrensis, in his *Description of Wales* written towards the end of the twelfth century, made a famous remark about Anglesey as 'the granary of Wales'. He also referred to the 343 villas of the island—a hint that the settlement pattern of Anglesey was already complete by early medieval times. In fact, in the succeeding centuries scores of townships have been reduced to single farms as the extinction of the practices of open-field farming was accompanied by the emergence of consolidated estates. Earlier still, at the beginning of the eighth century, Bede in the *Historia Ecclesiastica* hints at the population and volume of settlement in Dark Age Anglesey. He notes that the island had 'dwelling room for 960 families'. In contrast, he records that the Isle of Man had living space for 300 families. These Dark Age clues to population distribution around the Irish Sea, statistically obscure as they may be, suggest that Anglesey was one of the focal regions of settlement in the post-Roman centuries. Little tangible evidence has survived from these times. A number of early inscribed stones and a profusion of church dedications and place-names that record the presence of the Celtic saints together with some evidence of their monastic sites makes up the sum total of the Dark Age contribution to the present landscape.

Eleven memorial stones with inscriptions in Latin or the symbolic script known as Ogam have been found in Anglesey; they all date from the sixth and seventh centuries. The oldest of such Welsh memorial stones, dating from about the year AD 530, was found in the churchyard at Llansadwrn, a remote spot of rural Anglesey inland from the Menai Strait and in a countryside rich with the evidence of prehistory. The Llansadwrn stone is now to be found in the chancel of the church; it is dedicated to one Saturnius and 'his saintly wife'. The inscribed stones hint at the distribution of settlement in the post-Roman centuries as well as providing clues to the perpetuations of some elements of Roman culture in the emerging Welsh society. For instance the most famous stone from mainland North Wales, at Penmachno in a tributary of the upper Conwy, points to the survival of an ordered system of government two centuries after the withdrawal of Roman troops. Also in the recording of the name *Veneda* the stone provides a clue to the origin of Gwynedd, the name of the medieval kingdom of North Wales. It seems to be connected with the tribal name of the Venii. One striking feature of the Dark Age inscribed stones of Anglesey is the hint of the survival of Irish settlers, perhaps as aristocratic landowners, in part of the island. The stone now in the church at Penrhosllugwy, dating from the sixth century, commemorates an Irish aristocrat of the Deccheti lineage. But the most famous of Anglesey's Dark Age memorials is now built into the north wall of the chancel at Llangadwaladr (3869). It was shaped about the year 625 and its Latin inscription refers to one of the early members of the royal line of Gwynedd, King Catamanus. The inscription runs *Catamanus rex sapientisimus opiniatisimus omnium regum*—King Catamanus, wisest and most renowned of all kings (lies here). The stone was erected by his grandson Cadwaladr ap Cadwallon who himself is commemorated in the place-name Llangadwaladr.

Llangadwaladr was part of a large Dark Age estate whose core lay at the neighbouring settlement of Aberffraw. The manor of Aberffraw was the traditional seat of the rulers of the Welsh kingdom of Gwynedd. Here Professor Glanville Jones has built up a convincing argument for the continuity of settlement onward from the late Iron Age. He has collated evidence from nineteenth-century estate maps, medieval documents and the findings of archaeology together with astute observations of the present landscape, to outline the evolution of Aberffraw. In the oldest man-made feature of the landscape, the promontory fort of Iron Age date called Twyn-y-parc, Jones locates the first stage in the evolution of the ancient multiple estate of Aberffraw. This earthwork, thrown across the neck of the peninsula at the mouth of the Afon Cefni, probably served as a refuge for the inhabitants of Aberffraw and its attendant hamlets. Of late a fortified bank and ditch, dated to the last quarter of the first century AD, has been discovered in the village of Aberffraw, and this site has been shown to be occupied again in the sixth and seventh centuries. Aberffraw probably housed the royal palace of the Dark Age rulers of the kingdom of Gwynedd. This complex of buildings that included a timbered hall, all contained within an enclosure, was known as the *llys*. In the same period when the *llys* at Aberffraw sheltered the royal lineage of Gwynedd, the churchyard at the adjoining settlement, Llangadwaladr, served as a burial place for members of the royal house. But outside the churchyard of Llangadwaladr, Professor Glanville Jones has recognised another important feature in the evolution of Anglesey's landscape. An eighteenth-century estate map shows a pattern of tiny gardens, between 50 and 76m in length, radiating from the central churchyard. He believes that here we see the fossilised evidence of a period of transition in field structures when a rectangular system of 'Celtic' fields was transformed into a patchwork of open-field strips or 'quillets'. As Jones has written 'the gardens of Llangadwaladr may well be late-surviving relics of the important phase of transition, probably in the early Christian period, which witnessed the subdivision of rectangular "Celtic fields" into arable quillets'.

Aberffraw and its vicinity reveal several landscape elements that have survived through the centuries from a remote past. Elsewhere in Anglesey a link with the earliest stage of Welsh society is frequently made through a church dedicated to a saint of the Celtic world preaching and baptising between the fifth and the seventh centuries. The dedications of Anglesey's parish churches take one back to the lands around the Irish Sea that were bound together by the trade routes of Atlantic Europe. An early Christian missionary from the north, from Strathclyde, was St Kentigern who is reputed to have founded a monastery and churches in North Wales in the sixth century. One of his disciples, St Nidan, is remembered in the parish church at Llanidan among the pastures and prim plantations of Anglesey's sheltered southern shoreline on Menai Strait. Today, the simple fourteenth-century church that represented perhaps the last of several rebuildings since the first foundation by St Nidan early in the seventh century is now a ruin, sunlit and green with a carpet of wild vegetation. Another dedication from the age of the saints, Llanbadrig, the church of St Patrick, joins Anglesey with Ireland. Like so many ancient church sites in Wales it lies remote from today's lines of communication. You come upon Llanbadrig at the end of a narrow lane above Cemaes Bay. The serried ranks of tomb slabs and crosses in its circular churchyard stand full in the face of winter's gales from the Irish Sea.

But the most common dedications in Anglesey remember St Beuno who was born in the kingdom of Powys and educated in South Wales at the monastery at Caerwent. St Beuno founded a monastery at Clynnog, on the further northern shore of Lleyn across Caernarvon Bay. St Beuno was a man of some eminence in the Celtic Church. Alongside him the place-names of Anglesey rank a large number of local worthies of the church and members of the royal house of Gwynedd, descendants of Maelgwyn Gwynedd, who have since received the accolade of sainthood.

Just as three decades of twentieth-century research have revolutionised our views of settlement history and economic structures in Dark Age Wales, so the conventional picture of the role of the Celtic saints in Welsh history has been drastically redrawn. For instance, not all the dedications record directly the missionary journeys of these early Christians. Many dedications belong to the great period of expansion and rebuilding of churches between the twelfth and fifteenth centuries. Again, an older view of the history of the church saw the saints as missionaries to a race of pagan shepherds among the woods and mountains of Snowdonia. Now it seems much more likely that the primary intention of the Celtic church was the service of stable farming communities in lowland and coastal Wales, communities gathered in hamlets and engaged in the shared cultivation of open-field strips on sites that had been settled since prehistoric times. Today there is the growing belief that the new wave of Christianity in the sixth century that is represented by the Celtic Saints and their numerous dedications was mainly a ministering and preaching to already existing Christian communities, descendants of a church that was first planted in late Roman Britain.

Over the span of a millennium and a half that separates the present day from the Dark Ages one can recognise several phases in the shaping of the Anglesey landscape. The earliest was an expansion of the elementary pattern of settlement, first sketched out in prehistoric times. From the coastal sites and tracts of well-drained loamy soils new permanent settlements were founded in the interior of the island at places that already provided seasonal pastures for long-established communities. For instance, Meiriogen (3585), now a lonely farm at the end of a lane in the featureless interior of Anglesey, began its existence as a subsidiary hamlet of the parent nucleus of Cemaes— an ancient primary settlement lying six kilometres away on the north coast. Similarly Trescawen (4581), another remote hamlet in the interior established by Dark Age colonists, looked towards a parent vill, Porthamel, fourteen kilometres away on the shore of the Menai Strait. It is hard to determine the date of the colonisation of much of the land in the interior of Anglesey. By the time of the marking out of parish boundaries in the twelfth century this process of settlement was well advanced, if not complete. It is likely that the conversion of summer pastures in the interior of the island to permanent settlements based on arable farming took place before Bede made his brief comparison of Anglesey with the Isle of Man at the beginning of the eighth century.

Another mode of medieval colonisation that has left its mark on the present landscape arose from expansion into the wastelands that surrounded the primary settlements. Much of this seems to have happened under pressures of population and economic need in the twelfth and thirteenth centuries. Llanfaes (6077), possibly the richest place in Anglesey in the late Middle Ages with some 526 hectares of arable land, established a daughter hamlet, Bodgylched (5876), on the light loams of the plateau at 100m above sea level on the margin of the township. The evolution of Penrhos Llugwy (4886) suggests a similar pattern of medieval development. The old nucleus of the manor lay to the north on the fertile soils of the Castleton Series. The parish church, a medieval building that has been much restored by the Victorians, contains an inscribed stone that dates from the middle of the sixth century—a clue to the age of settlement at this place. On the southern edge of the parish a limestone ridge rises above the shallow valley of the Afon Llugwy. Professor Glanville Jones in his highly original study of medieval settlement in Anglesey has suggested that the poorer, lighter, thirstier lands of the limestone ridge were not permanently settled until the twelfth or thirteenth centuries. He associates the building of the now roofless medieval chapel, Hen Capel Llugwy (4986), with the expansion of population into the wastes and pastures on the southern fringe of the township.

The Edwardian Conquest of Wales in 1282 and the reorganisation of government and the social order that followed has left its mark on the landscape of Anglesey. In the countryside the break-up of the ancient Welsh tribal society and the transformation of its legal codes, especially as they related to the inheritance of land, hastened the dissolution of the hamlets that formed the core of a great number of settlements. The process of estate building continued into the seventeenth century and beyond. It meant that compact farms could be built up by individuals out of the scattered strips of the common fields and by encroachment and enclosure of the extensive common pastures. Lands owned by the Crown were particularly exposed to the radical changes of ownership that could transform a township with a patchwork of arable strips in a common open field into a single farm. The leasing and sale of Crown lands provided the energy for a process that was to wipe out so many hamlets. The sites of some former medieval nuclear settlements are known through the location of substantial farms or mansions that bear the name *Plas*. Plas Llanddyfnan (4878), lost amid the quiet lanes inland from the caravan littered coast of Benllech, occupies the site of the original nucleus of the medieval township of the same name. Again, Plas Llysdulas (4889), in the far north-eastern corner of Anglesey, shows the same pattern of development from an ancient nodal hamlet. Here the ruins of a medieval church are all but lost among the planted woodlands that encompass the Victorian mansion of Llysdulas House.

Perhaps the most spectacular examples of the influence of land-ownership and economic practices on the outward appearance of a landscape may be seen along the balmy southern shore of Anglesey, facing the Menai Strait. Here a succession of estates occupies the coastline westward from the Menai bridges. Plas Llanfair, Plas Newydd, grandest and most famous of the country houses, Plas Mona and Plas Coch have obliterated a landscape of medieval settlement and farming. Not only were compact estates shaped out of the former nuclear holdings of Hendref Porthamel, but by the nineteenth century this coastal site of high natural beauty, one of Britain's finest panoramas in which the changing colours and cloudscapes of Snowdonia's mountains are viewed across the calm mirror of the strait, was subject to the principles of 'landscaping' that were in vogue at that time. The estate of Plas Newydd together with the planted woodland, lawns and lakes of Vaynol Hall on the facing shore of the Menai Strait together form a unique element among the landscapes of Britain where the subtle arts of man blend with the natural elements of sea, sky and mountains.

In his study of Anglesey Professor Glanville Jones has shown how the pattern of large farms in the island was shaped out of the medieval hamlets and their now long-vanished field systems. A study of medieval sources and of the nineteenth-century tithe maps shows that more than 150 medieval hamlets are now represented by single farms, each exceeding 16 hectares. The texture of the island's landscape today owes much to the estate-making process and especially to the ease or difficulty with which consolidation was achieved. We have seen that royal estates were particularly open to the activities of speculating estate builders. Monastic properties that were given over to Tudor speculators after the dissolution of the monasteries are invariably represented by large consolidated farms in the nineteenth century. Change came slowly to some other properties; for instance the estates of the diocese of Bangor tended to remain unconsolidated. One of the most instructive examples of the part played by landowner-ship in the determination of settlement patterns occurs in the south-western quarter of the island at Dwyran (4465). In the Middle Ages two landowners shared Dwyran, the monks of Clynnog Fawr in the Lleyn peninsula and the Bishops of Bangor. The two estates were known as Dwyran Esgob, the part that belonged to the church, and Dwyran Beuno, after the founder saint of the monastery. After the dissolution of Clynnog Fawr, Dwyran Beuno became Crown land. It was let to tenants who later purchased and consolidated their hold-ings. By the early nineteenth century only three large compact farms were left in the 69 hectares of the former monastic estate. A dispersed

3   *The cromlech in the grounds of Plas Newydd by the side of the Menai Strait*

pattern of settlement had succeeded the medieval hamlet and its shared open field. The Bishop of Bangor's property at Dwyran followed a different history. There the medieval pattern persisted well into the nineteenth century. In 1840 the 71 hectares of Dwyran Esgob were still divided among thirty farms and the holdings of each farmer were composed of a number of scattered strips. Here the medieval land-use pattern had remained unchanged; only the strips of the open field had been enclosed. The effect of these divergent histories of landownership may still be read in the present landscape. The string of cottages and farmsteads that make up Dwyran today, the settlement along the lane that follows the left bank of the Afon Braint, occupy the land that first belonged to the Bishops of Bangor. One may even sense the outline of an original girdle settlement that once enclosed an open field. The eastern part of the township on the other hand—the former monastic lands—contains only a few scattered farms, large and distant from each other.

The later Middle Ages saw the beginning of a revolution in land-holding that was to create the characteristic dispersed patterns of settlement in Anglesey. If the mode of settlement in the countryside moved towards dispersion, the introduction of planned castle towns at the Edwardian Conquest was to lead towards concentration at certain favoured places. The founding of Edward I's castle at Beaumaris in 1295 and the inducements given to English immigrants to settle there as burgesses gave Anglesey its first town. But history is never as tidy and clear-cut as the kind of mind that compiles the *Guinness Book of Records* might like. It is far from certain that Beaumaris was the first urban settlement in Anglesey, for it seems that in the making of his castle and the laying out of the grid-iron pattern of a new borough, Edward I extinguished a flourishing Welsh commercial settlement at neighbouring Llanfaes (6077)—a place that had many of the economic attributes of a town if not the formal outward appearance of the new planned boroughs of the later Middle Ages. The inhabitants of Llanfaes were transferred bodily, if perhaps reluctantly, to a new town that Edward laid out for them at the south end of the island. There, Newborough was established on the royal manor of Rhosfair in 1303, practically the last of the long series of freshly chartered towns that fills the history of the twelfth and thirteenth centuries in Britain.

The first quarter of the nineteenth century witnessed the coming of a new element in Anglesey's landscape history that favoured the growth of clustered settlements; it is the steadily rising traffic to

Holyhead and the development of the short sea route to Ireland. The improvement of communications between Holyhead and the mainland in the first quarter of the nineteenth century has left some dramatic features in the landscape of Anglesey. Telford's road, A5 today, seems to run with unswerving straightness for kilometres on end across the island pointing towards the blue shape of Holyhead Mountain. At the crossing of the sea passages we find two of the major works of this pioneer among the great engineers of the Industrial Revolution, the Menai suspension bridge that was first opened to traffic in the wild winter of 1826 and the Stanley Embankment, thrown across the tidal sands to Holy Island. The road revolutionised the pattern of the settlement in central Anglesey. The post road that had been in use since Tudor times was neglected. Today you can follow it by taking the second road, B5109, westwards from Llangefni through Bodwrog and Bodedern. Telford's road encouraged the growth of a number of linear settlements devoted largely to the servicing of its traffic. On its route across the island the A5 cuts through a succession of widely dispersed townships lacking any kind of focus except a parish church, often a simple rectangular building from the late medieval centuries now difficult to find at the end of a deep lane. In the first half of the nineteenth century the road provided a new centre of attraction for settlement. For instance, Gaerwen, a roadside linear village stretches for almost 1.5 kilometres. It grew up in the widely scattered parish of Llanfihangel Esceifiog and dates from the opening of Telford's road. By 1847 a new church was built by the main road. Today the old parish church of Llanfihangel Esceifiog is a ruin, almost inaccessible in impenetrable undergrowth and overlooking the head of Malltraeth Marsh. Bryngwran again represents the concentration of settlement along the line of the main road in the dispersed parish of Llechylched. But the most dramatic transformation of the landscape was to take place at the terminals of Anglesey's section of the London to Holyhead road. Menai Bridge, a little Victorian red-brick town, is entirely the product of Telford's road; now in the high tourist season the long traffic jams at the approach to the bridge emphasise the role for which it was created. Holyhead has a much more complex urban history than Menai Bridge. First Telford's road and then, after 1845, the railway contributed to the growth of this Irish packet port; dark, gloomy and slate-built beside the bright sea. Several objects in the landscape of Holyhead commemorate its emergence as a port in the brief decades before the railway age. The Admiralty Pier, known as Salt Island Pier, with its lighthouse dates back to 1821. The Custom House and the Doric Memorial Arch, raised to commemorate the visit of George IV in 1821, belong to the same period—the first busy epoch of the road. But Holyhead is essentially a town of the railway age and the steamship. The breakwater, more than 1.5 kilometres in length, was built in the years about 1850 from hundreds of thousands of tons of rock quarried on the north-east face of Holyhead mountain. With Victorian grandiloquence a guide book of the time described Holyhead as 'one of the most splendid refuge harbours and packet stations in the universe'. Times have changed and *The Irish Mail* for many travellers to Ireland is now only a memory of the vanishing railway age. Holyhead, in turn, begins to return to its role as a port at the end of a road with the installation of a 'drive-on' ferry from the harbour that John Rennie built in 1801.

The evolution of settlement in nineteenth-century Anglesey was closely related to the axis of Telford's road. Only on the north-west coast, at Amlwch, do we find the emergence of another early nineteenth-century town out of the export of copper from Parys Mountain. Amlwch's heyday straddled the years about 1800 when its population touched upon 5,000 and it claimed to be the world's greatest exporter of copper. The exploitation of Parys Mountain's copper ores has been dead for nigh on a century and Amlwch is little more than a sleepy attraction on Anglesey's tourist coastline. Since the early 1930s the motor car has transformed the patterns of settlement development in Anglesey. The remotest of sandy bays and cliff encircled beaches are accessible to the throng of summer tourists. The winter quietness, clean air and mild Irish-Sea climate have made the island attractive to those who want to retire from the din and dirt of the conurbations of Manchester and Merseyside. Summer caravans and estates of retirement bungalows have been added to the coastline, especially in the post-war years. Much damage has been done to some of the most attractive coastal scenery in Wales, but one can be thankful that the stricter planning regulations of latter years and an instinct for conservation in some estate owners has left much to be enjoyed.

The Lleyn Peninsula

Although the broad promontory of the Lleyn thrusting out into the Irish Sea is a geological extension of the central part of Snowdonia, its character is completely different. For the most part it is lowland country carved out of various sedimentary beds of the Ordovician series with an overlay of glacial deposits in places. Rising out of it are steep-sided isolated hills, in nearly every case formed of igneous rocks which effectively resist erosion. At the neck of the peninsula there is the cluster of peaks of Yr Eifl (3664), fashioned out of a pale coloured microgranite. It has been extensively quarried on its northern slope where it overlooks the village of Trefor though the industry is now declining, the quays lying derelict and the whole area suffering from the effects of depopulation. A similar rock forms the flat-topped hill of Mynydd Tirycwmwd overlooking Llanbedrog (3331) from the south. Because of its resistance to marine erosion the microgranite stands out as a prominent headland with the sheltered bay of Llanbedrog, renowned for its fine sandy beach, in the lee. Much of the south coast of the Lleyn is of this character, with a succession of headlands formed of hard igneous rock acting as hinge points for smooth shoreline curves cut in soft Ordovician rocks or boulder clays. Even small rock outcrops like that of Carreg yr Imbill (3834) on the south side of Pwllheli Harbour or Pen y Chain farther east can have a profound influence on the shoreline plan. Occasionally as at Cricieth the coastal headland, in this case formed of felsite, was chosen for its defensive potential (Study 1).

Igneous rock outcrops of limited extent are also responsible for the hills which make up the backbone of the Lleyn Peninsula. Carn Fadron (SH 2835) rising to over 400m, is perhaps the most impressive because of its isolated position set in a plain of soft sedimentary and glacial deposits. It is formed of an intrusive granite porphyry, possibly representing the stump of an ancient volcano. If this is the case then the lavas which make up the lower hill to the east could represent the outpourings from this particular centre. On the whole, however, the extensive deposits of lava and tuff which dominate the geology of central Snowdonia are absent from the Lleyn Peninsula for either they were never deposited to the same extent or they have been subsequently removed by erosion. Here lies the key to the contrasting topography in the Lleyn and Snowdonia for without lavas and hard beds of tuff, stepped and craggy slopes cannot develop. Slopes remained steep on the igneous hills as they acquired their relief through the wearing away of the softer sediments all around them. They proved ideal natural defensive sites during the Iron Age and the succeeding Roman Period. Tre'r Ceiri (3744), on the southernmost hill of the group forming the Rivals, Boduan (3139), Fadron (2735), each have their fine hill forts commanding a wide view down the length of the peninsula as well as over both coasts.

As in Snowdonia the Ice Age made its own distinctive contribution to the scenery of the Lleyn Peninsula though here its effects were very different due to a lowland and more maritime setting. None of the Lleyn Hills was high enough to nurture effective corrie glaciers except perhaps on the eastern side of Yr Eifl and even here true corrie basins are not found. During the closing phases of the glacial period the central part of the peninsula was an ice-free zone hemmed in by the Irish Sea ice sheet to the north and a great glacier tongue which had moved out of Snowdonia down the Ffestiniog valley and progressed westwards along the south coast of the Lleyn. In the ice-free ground of the central part of the peninsula glacial lakes developed in suitable low-lying areas between the hills. The principal glacial lake was Bodfean whose site today is marked by the marshy hollow of Cors Geirch (3136). As the melting ice poured increasing amounts of water into the lake so its level rose and ultimately it overflowed at the lowest ice-free col which happened to lie at the head of Nant Bodlas (29 33). Here at a height of 84m there is still a well developed terrace feature by the side of the B4415 road marking the position of the overflow col (3035). The ice margins which contained Lake Bodfean fluctuated from time to time and ultimately uncovered an even lower col at a height of 69m in the south near Llanbedrog which then functioned as the main lake outlet. The existing route lay to the west of Mynydd Tirycwmwd (3230) and thence southwards where it cut the gap now used by the Afon Soch (3028), though the river is now flowing in the opposite direction to its glacial ancestor. With a continued retreat of the ice front along the south coast of the Lleyn yet another lower col was exposed, on this occasion near Penarwel north of Llandbedrog (3232). As waters poured through this new gap so the lake level fell once again, this time to 48m which was the height of the lake exit. The life of Lake Bodfean was limited for with the final withdrawal of the southern ice the impounded waters drained away completely. This was also true of many other smaller pro-glacial lakes which existed in the central parts of the peninsula during the late stages of the Ice Age. Each has left its mark as a boggy hollow and caused a complete disruption of the original drainage pattern as well as creating the fine gorge near Abersoch. Some gorge features, like that south of Dinas (2636) or near Sarn (2332), probably represent direct overflows from the melting Irish Sea ice which was pressing in along the north coast of the Lleyn. They, too, now form part of the newly created drainage system which is only slowly recovering from the effects of ice interference.

Nowhere else in Wales, except perhaps in the most westerly reaches of Pembrokeshire, is the long history of this Celtic land so clearly written on the present landscape. As a region the social individuality of Lleyn dates back almost 2,000 years, to the earliest surviving documentary reference in Ptolemy's *Geography*. There Lleyn is named as the *Ganganorum Promontorium,* the promontory of the Gangani who were one of the tribes of Iron Age Ireland. Contacts across the Irish Sea in late prehistoric times seem to have played a formative role in the development of the peninsula. In origin the name *Lleyn* is related to that of the Irish province of Leinster and other place names, Dinllaen, Nefyn and Abersoch for instance, seem to contain Irish roots. The Romans too perhaps recognised the individuality of the Lleyn peninsula in political and social terms. For long the absence of any substantial Roman remains in the form of roads, forts or striking archaeological finds led to the view that some kind of Celtic social order survived intact in the peninsula. The evidence of a community of non-Roman character living within the rampart of Tre'r Ceiri (3744) through the Roman centuries fortified this thesis. Lately the direct presence of Roman troops on the eastern margin of Lleyn has come to light with the discovery, in 1957, of a fort at Pen Llystyn (4845). Coins found there suggest that its enclosing bank and ditch were sketched out about AD 80 and that it was manned for no more than two decades. Further south and east, probably on a road that connected the Roman site at Tomen y Mur with the station of Segontium passing by the long lost site at Pen Llystyn, the remains of a Roman bath-house are known at Tremadog. Tremadog has been described as a posting house or inn, but lately C. E. Stevens in a highly original survey of the problems of rural settlement in Roman Britain has suggested that the bath-house at Tremadog may indicate 'a kind of centre—a locus—for an official group'. He has suggested that the lowland peninsula of Lleyn was recognised as a *pagus*, a regional unit distinguished by its landscape and its society. From the Roman use of *pagus* the word has been transmuted into the modern French of *pays*, a term that the founders of the classic school of French regional geography were to adopt to describe the basic unit of their studies—the region, a natural whole shaped to the purposes of man. Lleyn is such a unit among the landscapes of Wales, a *pays* whose character was already evident in the Iron Age.

The most striking feature of the prehistoric landscape of the Lleyn peninsula is the succession of hill forts that occupy the major isolated summits, scree-strewn, heathery viewpoints that look down to a tamer world of tiny fields and deep lanes and, beyond, the encircling pale blue rim of the sea. In the seaward end of the peninsula where the wild, cliffed northern coast and the deep-bayed southern coastline draw close together we find Garn Boduan (3139), Carn Fadryn (2835) and Castell Odo (1828). Garn Boduan rears steeply above the dull coastal plateau at Nefyn to some 280m above sea-level. Its ramparts enclosing most of the higher summit are built of rubble, 3.5m in thickness and still standing in places to heights of 1.5 or 2m. Within this massive Iron Age enclosure the sites of 170 huts have been located, now faint mounds and hollows deeply overgrown. On the lower slopes of the hill more foundations of huts suggest that Garn Boduan was an important settlement in Iron Age times and the post-Roman centuries. One can only speculate about the size of the population that occupied the clustered settlement of round huts on the summit and slopes of Garn Boduan. So far archaeology has uncovered little of the detail that provides the only sure foundations for the reconstruction of a settlement's history. After the excavation of 1954 A. H. A. Hogg was able to report that 'some inconclusive dating evidence' had been found; beads that might date to any period from the first to the seventh centuries AD and very coarse pottery resembling that from Dark Age sites in Anglesey. Such pottery from the neighbouring hill fort at Castell Odo has since been shown to belong to the opening centuries of the Iron Age. If the centuries of occupation still seem so ill-defined at Garn Boduan, the statistics of life and economy in that hill settlement lie even further from our grasp. Even so, it has been estimated that the population of this Iron Age settlement might have reached as many as 700—a figure comparable with that of one of the newly founded towns after the Edwardian conquest of Wales.

But Garn Boduan still bears evidence of a later stage in the history of its occupation. A wall, different in character from the large encircling rubble rampart, crowns the very summit of the hill. Hogg describes it as 'a small fort' of 'late or post Roman date'. Professor Glanville Jones has worked out a much more cogent interpretation of the late features at Garn Boduan. The ruined walled enclosure on the summit he describes as a 'fortified homestead', and he accepts the tradition that it was the home of Buan, a chieftain and nobleman who was living in the early years of the eighth century. The name Buan he finds commemorated in Boduan. The first element *bod*, as in the adjacent coastal site Bodeilias, means that the place was once the dwelling of a chief.

Scarcely five kilometres to the south-west of Garn Boduan another conical shaped mountain of granite, Carn Fadryn, rises to almost 400m above the subdued landscape of Lleyn's erosion surfaces. Here the use of the hill fort's site seems to reach forward in time to the threshold of recorded history, for Giraldus Cambrensis, journeying through Wales in the twelfth century and noting his impressions, mentions the recent building of a castle within the older earthwork. Westward again, where the land of Lleyn narrows towards Bardsey Sound, another embanked summit at less than 150m above the sea projects the history of the hill forts and their foundation backwards in time to the opening centuries of the Iron Age. Here the excavation of Castell Odo in 1958 and 1959 by Professor Leslie Alcock revealed for the first time the complexity and richness of an Iron Age site in the peninsula. An earlier investigation in the 1920s had dated the construction and occupation of Castell Odo to the decades between AD 400 and 700. It was considered to be one of the classic sites of the Dark Age in Wales. Professor Alcock's excavation revealed a place of much greater complexity in which he identified five main phases of occupation. The first, belonging to the early fourth century BC, predates the construction of the earth and rubble rampart. It sees the establishment of a village community living in wooden houses with turf roofs on the summit of Mynydd Ystum. Castell Odo is now recognised as one of the earliest Iron Age settlements in North Wales. Alcock believes it is part of the widespread migrations that brought the first Iron Age culture across the seas from Europe to Britain. Perhaps too it signals the appearance of one of the major themes of Welsh history, the coming of the Celts. As Professor Alcock has written 'Castell Odo pottery presents some of the earliest archaeological evidence for the settlement of Celtic communities in Wales'.

Castell Odo's earthworks, a double rampart in their final state, lack the design and building techniques of the crumbling ramparts of Garn Boduan or Tre'r Ceiri. The archaeological excavation of the late 'fifties produced evidence for three stages in the making of the enclosure before the appearance of Roman troops in Wales. The first was a timber stockade, a trench closely planted with wooden posts that encircled the hill-top village. In the second stage, possibly after a time of total desertion, the settlement was enclosed within a single bank of earth and rubble, scarcely more than 1.5m high. At a later time, the third stage in the evolution of Castell Odo was completed with the building of a second embankment and the facing of the original rampart with stone. Alcock has suggested that Castell Odo was not a fortification of Iron Age chieftains but only a farming village, the home of a pastoral community that threw up the earthworks to keep out wild animals and, in the wide space between the ramparts, to provide pens for domestic livestock.

The latest phases in Castell Odo's history have been equally revealing of the pattern of life in the Lleyn peninsula in the Roman centuries and after. The banks seem to have been deliberately reduced and, later still, huts were built over the ruined earthworks. From this period a rotary quern of a type that was introduced by the Romans has been found at Castell Odo. In a bold association of an archaeological site and a landscape feature with the known events of Roman history in Wales, Alcock has suggested that the systematic levelling of Castell Odo's earthworks was the work of Roman soldiers engaged on 'the forcible demilitarisation' of Lleyn. The date of these events may well have been AD 77 or 78 after the defeat of the Ordovices, the Celtic tribe that controlled North Wales. The latest feature in Castell Odo, a long, low mound of earth and stones, had earlier been described as the remains of a medieval house. Alcock explained it as a man-made rabbit warren of no determinable date.

Castell Odo has not only yielded a richness of detail that is still lacking from other Iron Age sites in the Lleyn peninsula, but it also seems to provide an important key to the settlement patterns of the region. Research has shown that this was clearly a settlement of farmers rather than a military strong-point. It is likely that the first settlers, as early as the fourth century BC made their way inland from landings on the beach at Aberdaron. Mynydd Ystum, the site of Castell Odo, lay scarcely a mile from the shore dominating the shallow converging valleys of the Afon Daron, Afon Cyllyfelin and the Afon Saint. Here was a natural, compact and comprehensible unit of settlement that survived down the centuries with its focal point first at Castell Odo and later adjacent to the shore at Aberdaron. Similar Iron Age enclosures on hills or bluffs upstanding above the coastal plateau seem to have composed primary nuclei in the prehistoric settlement structure as at Pen-y-Gaer (2928) above Abersoch, and Castell Caeron (3744) on the northern slope of Mynydd Rhiw.

Tre'r Ceiri is without doubt the most impressive and exciting of the prehistoric sites in the peninsula. The scale of Tre'r Ceiri becomes evident in the phrases that have been used to describe it—'a fortified hill-top town', 'a vast, fortified hill-top settlement'. But what is better than the literal meaning of this stone-walled enclosure that towers above the rocky screes of Yr Eifl's most easterly peak, 'the town of the giants'? The main rampart of Tre'r Ceiri was probably established before the Roman occupation of North Wales. The intrusive igneous rocks that form the mountain mass of Yr Eifl have provided an excellent building material that has been split into thin slabs in the construction of the rampart. Of the 150 huts that cluster the bleak summit of Tre'r Ceiri sixty have been excavated. The bulk of the finds are of Roman pottery and A. H. A. Hogg, in an attempt to work out a sequence of hill fort construction for Caernarvonshire, has concluded that the huts belong to two periods. The earliest were probably simple circular structures that have been lacking finds of pottery in the two excavations of the twentieth century. Other buildings with a central partition, rich in finds of pottery, probably date from the centuries of Roman occupation. Almost all the relics from Tre'r Ceiri belong to the years between AD 150 and 400.

Anyone who has climbed through the precipitous scree and heather into the crumbling ruins of Tre'r Ceiri is beseiged by questions to which the present state of archaeological knowledge can provide no certain answers. Beyond the fact that this desolate windy summit with its panoramic views into Lleyn was inhabited, perhaps continuously, through the Roman centuries little is known with any surety. For instance, were Tre'r Ceiri's chief purposes of a military or a civilian nature? Its carefully built stone ramparts and narrow inturned entrances with passages that were once closed by heavy wooden gates suggest a refuge, a place to be defended. Sir Mortimer Wheeler has claimed that the North Welsh hill forts were primarily designed as part of a defence system against raids from Ireland—a threat that gave way to extensive settlement from across the Irish Sea in the closing Roman decades. Alternatively this hill-top enclosure has been interpreted as a permanent settlement devoted to agricultural pursuits; its clustered hut circles have even suggested a community of the size of a small town. In this view Tre'r Ceiri might have originated as part of a deliberate colonisation of North Wales under the Romans. Even so, the character of life in such an exposed site eludes explanation. From the absence of querns in the excavation of scores of huts there emerges a hint that the inhabitants of the hill fort were not occupied with arable farming. If they were engaged only in stock rearing, the sensible suggestion arises that this place was at best occupied only in the summer months. Tre'r Ceiri was a summer settlement for those employed in the management of the upland pastures from the first weeks of summer until the autumn. An even more baffling problem follows in the train of this hypothesis. Where then lay the permanent quarters, the chief settlement of the hill fort's builders? It could be argued that even more substantial remains should survive from a site of presumably greater economic and social importance. The most likely solution to this problem emerges from Professor Glanville Jones' research into the social geography of Wales in the Dark Ages. He has suggested that links exist between the territorial units of the medieval Welsh countryside, known from information contained in surviving documents, and the social and administrative structures of the more ancient communities of the late Iron Age. Of this period the earthworks of the 'forts' form the chief tangible surviving evidence. Each hill fort seems to dominate a natural territorial unit 'bounded by marshy valleys and containing no other fort'. We may still discern the outlines of these prehistoric territorial units in the minor social units of later centuries, the *maenols*. Until the changes of the later Middle Ages the *maenol* was composed of numerous hamlets with their patchworks of tiny open fields and a dominating nucleus. The Dark Age Cantref of Arfon, substantially the coastal plain of Caernarvonshire and its adjacent foothills, was divided into nine *maenols*; each contains the site of a hill fort. Maenol Elernion encompassed the narrowing coastal plain to the north of Yr Eifl. Its focal settlement and a primary parish was Llanaelhaearn (3844), seated in the important pass that leads from Arfon into Lleyn. Here, perhaps, in this outwardly uninteresting village of grey chapels and cottages we must look for the home of the Iron Age community that raised the ramparts of Tre'r Ceiri. A few shreds of evidence survive in the landscape to show that Llanaelhaearn has been occupied for many centuries. At the parish church are two early Christian stones with inscriptions; they date back to the beginnings of the Celtic church in the years about AD 500. Here is evidence of a living community at a time not far removed from the Roman occupation and the years when we know that Tre'r Ceiri was inhabited.

The critical centuries in the establishment of the ground-plan of settlement—the sites of hamlets, the carving out of field systems, the making of a network of communications in footpaths and lanes—probably date back to the Iron Age in the Lleyn peninsula. But it is important to recall that the Iron Age invaders and settlers, bringing with them the techniques of hill-fort design and construction, were not pioneers of an unused land. Three thousand years earlier Lleyn, along with Anglesey, had provided a focus for Neolithic settlers of the lands around the Irish Sea. The sandy bays of the peninsula's southern coastline seem to have provided attractive landing places for Neolithic migrants, just as the earliest evidence of immigrant Iron Age farmers at Castell Odo indicates the bay at Aberdaron, as a point of arrival. In fact it is likely that the bays within sight of Mynydd Rhiw, a ridge that bounds the Aberdaron lowland on the east, acted as the chief landing place and trade centre of the Lleyn in Neolithic times. On the eastern slopes of Mynydd Rhiw we find the most important surviving burial chamber from Neolithic times in the whole of the peninsula. Tan-y-Muriau (2328) is a cairn of 36.5m in length. It probably had a complex building history beginning in early Neolithic times as a compact rectangular-shaped cromlech with a heavy capstone, a type of prehistoric burial place that is common in North Wales. The elongated cairn with a second and third chamber, the latter now erased from the landscape, was probably added at a later time. But Tan-y-Muriau seems to have been only one among several Neolithic sites located on the hills around the wide bay of Porth Neigwl. Nineteenth-century accounts speak of several tombs that have since been destroyed. Even today the remains of three ruined chambered tombs tell of the importance for Neolithic settlers of the little plains ringed around with low hills at the seaward end of the Lleyn peninsula. One lies scarcely three-quarters of a kilometre from Tan-y-Muriau at Plas-yn-Rhiw. Another burial chamber occupies the inner edge of the lowland defined by the valley of the Afon Soch on the northern slope of Mynydd Cefnamwlch and the third stands in what may be described as a classic type of site for the tombs of the Neolithic period, close to the sea at Cilan Uchaf on the rocky headland that forms the eastern flank of Porth Neigwl.

If the pattern of chambered tombs points to the nodes of population in Neolithic times, then the southern tip of Lleyn must have been of considerable importance. This hint contained in the distribution pattern of a relict feature of prehistory surviving in the present landscape was reinforced by the discovery in 1956 of the site of a Neolithic axe factory on the north-eastern shoulder of Mynydd Rhiw (2329). The burning of gorse on common land revealed a succession of hollows surrounded by low banks that were composed of flakes of a fine-grained rock. Two summers later a programme of excavation revealed the silted-up remains of a quarry in which the local rock, a hornfelsised shale capable of producing sharp cutting edges, had been worked for the making of scrapers, knives, choppers, adzes and axes—tools that Neolithic and Bronze Age peoples had used in cutting timber, shaping wood, boat building and the flensing of whales. A further exploration by archaeologists of the site in 1959 revealed a continuous opencast working 30m in length and, in places, 3m in depth. The beginning of the 'axe factory' at Mynydd Rhiw has been dated to about 2000 BC, but a radio-carbon date of material found at one of the hearths on the site indicates a time about 1150–1100 BC. The stone there seems to have been worked, perhaps discontinuously, over a time span of more than a thousand years from the Neolithic period deep into the Bronze Age.

The bays within easy reach of Mynydd Rhiw must have formed a focus of trade in prehistoric Wales. It is likely too that another centre of human activity occupied the narrowing coastal plain, between mountains and sea at Clynnog-fawr (4149). Two megalithic tombs, at Penarth (4351) and Bachwen (4049) still survive in this distinctive tract between the Afon Llyfni and the gloomy precipitous northern slopes of Yr Eifl. Bachwen's cromlech with its four widely spaced upright stones supporting a wedge-shaped capstone, inscribed on one side with mysterious ring-like markings, stands in a field within a few hundred metres of the cliff's edge. It has been suggested that the chief lines of communication in prehistoric Lleyn lay across the peninsula between units of settlement located close to the northern and southern coastlines. One such trans-peninsula route may have joined the mouth of the Afon Erch near Pwllheli with the coastal plain at Clynnog-fawr, using the important pass to the east of Yr Eifl beneath the summit that later was to be crowned with the extensive ramparts of Tre'r Ceiri. The role of Lleyn has changed over the centuries. What was once the major link in the prehistoric communications of the Irish Sea basin has for long been an isolated backwater. Its remoteness from the main currents of Welsh history has long been evident. Those who planned the strategic geography of North Wales after the Edwardian Conquest found no need to establish castle-towns west of Caernarvon and Cricieth. The railways too only brushed the approaches to Lleyn. This peninsula, a refuge for monks and pirates, has only truly felt the impact of the world outside with the coming of the car-age when the citizens of the Merseyside, Manchester and West Midland conurbations have discovered bays and beaches and an interior landscape of shapely volcanic hills far more enticing than that of Cornwall.

The Harlech Dome

Few parts of North Wales are as wild and rugged as the country which extends inland from the shores of Tremadog Bay at Harlech. Although the area is not exceptionally high a combination of rock type and erosional process has left a firm and distinctive imprint on the landscape, quite distinct from the mountain heart of Snowdonia. The basic cause is an upfold of the rock strata which brings old Cambrian beds to the surface. These are dominated by thick beds of grit, about 800m in all, which effectively resist attack by the agents of erosion. The result is a summit ridge, dominated by Rhinog Fawr (6529) and Rhinog Fach (6627), both of which rise to over 700m. Between these two highest points of the range there is one of the few real breaks, the pass of Bwlch Drws Ardudwy, with only a track through it, perhaps little altered since it was first used in prehistoric time. Another col, Bwlch Tyddiad lies a few kilometres to the north below the slope of Rhinog Fawr. This is the better known of the two for along its approach from the west hundreds of large slabs of gritstone have been laid to make a well-defined track climbing the slope to the summit of the col. Although picturesquely named 'The Roman Steps', the paved way is most likely of early medieval date being built towards the end of the thirteenth century when Edward I assumed control and rebuilt the nearby Harlech Castle. This inland route through the Rhinogs and then across moorland country to the Dee trench at Bala offered a possible supply route for the castle when the more normal access by sea was threatened. Later, in more settled times, the Roman Steps were probably used as part of a packhorse trail.

The country through which the route passes is one of rugged splendour, with boggy hollows, huge boulders partly buried in peat and heather, bare rock precipices and knobbly ridge crests, all contributing to a wild terrain which is quite different from the more mountainous tracts of Snowdonia farther north. Inland from the main ridge of the Rhinogs and closer to the axis of the upfold, where Cambrian beds even older than the grits are brought to the surface, the scenery suddenly becomes much tamer as shales offer much less resistance to the forces of erosion. This is the open country well seen from the main Dolgellau to Ffestiniog road (A470) with the uneven skyline of the Rhinogs providing a contrasting backcloth. Much of it is now under conifer plantations, an outlier of the extensive Coed y Brennin forest. The name Rhinog probably means threshold, an apt description for the ridge which separates the inland plateaus of central Wales from the rich coastal lands of Dyffryn Ardudwy. From prehistoric times onwards this coastal fringe has always proved attractive to settlement. A steadily dropping sea level throughout the Late Tertiary time has left a succession of coastal platforms which climb, like a gigantic stairway, from sea level up to the high summit ridge. The treads form relatively flat areas where farms, with their patchwork of hedged fields, give the landscape an ordered, man-made appearance. The risers of the stairway, marking the old cliff lines which were cut during temporary halts in the gradual lowering of sea level, are usually too steep to cultivate and have been left either as rough grazing ground or woodland. This countryside of narrow coastal platforms has a wealth of remains dating back to the Bronze Age and even to the earlier Neolithic period. Continuity of occupation is very apparent in the area between the coastal road at Egryn Abbey (5920) and the long summit ridge of Llawlech. From the track leading past the Abbey two cairns, the Carneddau Hengwm (6120), can be seen across the moor. On approaching closer the southernmost of the two carneddau is seen to consist of a number of burial chambers of considerable size, dating from about 2500 BC. To the north across the valley the Iron Age hill fort of Pen y Dinas stands out prominently on a bluff. It has an inner circular rampart of earth whose sides have been strengthened with masonry. Outside this there is a second rampart on the north and west sides with a deep ditch in between. The whole layout of the defences of the hill fort suggests that it was originally built about the third century BC, possibly the work of a new wave of immigrants who came to settle here at that time. Away to the north towards Dyffryn Ardudwy there is another group of burial chambers. Close to the one at Cors y Gedol (6022), with its fallen capstone, there are extensive remains of hut circles and terraced fields. Part of the area has been excavated and suggests that there was occupation of the huts early in the second century AD so that even in Roman times the old way of life went on very much as before in this isolated corner, well away from the mainstream of activity.

There is little evidence to show that the Romans were ever

interested in the coastal lands of Dyffryn Ardudwy. Away to the north-east, on the other side of the Rhinogs they established a major camp at Tomen y Mur (7038). The first fort on this prominent site dates from the time of Agricola's defeat of the local tribe of the Ordovices in AD 78. It was subsequently rebuilt early in the second century when the earlier clay and turf ramparts were replaced. Outside the walls of the camp a small hollow by the side of the modern lane has long been looked upon as an amphitheatre and is named as such on the current Ordnance Survey map. In view of its small size it most likely functioned more as a cockpit where the soldiers whiled away the hours in this lonely and desolate countryside. The most prominent feature of Tomen y Mur today is not the Roman remains but the motte of a much later Norman castle which was built within the ramparts of the old fort. Even in this isolated corner the theme of continuity in the settlement of the landscape occurs time and time again.

Along the coastal fringe natural changes over the past few thousand years have completely altered the original setting. The old cliff line now runs several kilometres inland at places like Llanbedr (5826) and Lasynys (5932). On its seaward side great areas of sand dunes and marshland have developed to form Morfa Harlech and Morfa Dyffryn.

4   *Sarn Cynfelin north of Aberystwyth where a huge ridge of cobbles runs out at right angles to the coast*

The sand to build up the dunes probably came from offshore, having been dumped here as the outwash debris from great ice lobes which occupied Tremadog Bay during the later stages of the Ice Age, perhaps less than 20,000 years ago. The dunes are still highly mobile and great hollows or blowouts can develop especially where the cover of marram grass is patchy. At Llandanwg (5628), the old church by the sea, the mother church of Harlech, has been almost overwhelmed by the advancing sand dunes. At the southern end of the former island of Mochras (Shell Island) the advancing sands effectively closed the southern entrance to Llandanwg Harbour in the middle of the nineteenth century.

Mochras Island, unlike similar emininces which rise out of the marshland of Morfa Harlech, is not composed of solid rock but consists of a 15m ridge of boulder clay. Great boulders can be seen where the sea has gradually eaten into the soft cliffs of clay on its seaward side. They litter the beach over a wide area and extend as a narrow ridge of stones and boulders for a considerable distance off-shore. Sarn Badrig (St Patrick's Causeway) is a remarkable feature which because of its unusual form has attracted many theories of origin. The most fanciful regard it as an artificial feature created by man when sea level rose and inundated the low lying acres of Cantref y Gwaelod, now beneath the waters of Tremadog Bay but once a rich land with twelve cities. Once it was shown that the sarn could not possibly be man-made various suggestions were put forward to explain its natural origin. All theories had to take account of the fact that Sarn Badrig is not unique but one of three similar features which run out from the coast into Cardigan Bay. The other two, Sarn y Bwlch, lying off Tonfanau and Sarn Cynfelin, just north of Aberyst-wyth, are shorter but in other respects are closely similar to Sarn Badrig. The fact that all three boulder ridges tend to lie between the major west coast estuaries led to the suggestion that they are the reduced remains of a former watershed area composed of glacial debris. As sea level rose in the last 10,000 years the soft, unconsoli-dated glacial clay deposits were gradually removed by the sea with only the huge boulders left behind to form the sarn. One particular boulder at the seaward end of Sarn Badrig was noted as early as 1737 to be 'four yards across'. The remarkable linear form of the sarn makes it unlikely that the mere reduction of a former boulder clay watershed provides an adequate explanation. It now seems more probable that all the sarns arose as side moraines thrown up where parallel ice lobes met as they pushed out into Cardigan Bay. Only at the extreme seaward end did ice associated with the main sheet occupying the Irish Sea make any impression on the feature, trimming it and creating a broad spatula-shaped shoal in contrast to the extreme linear form of the greater part of the sarn.

The gradual rise of sea level which followed the final melting of the ice in the Irish Sea Basin, whatever its role in the formation of the sarns, certainly led to the drowning of the major river valleys of the Mawddach, Glaslyn and Dyfi. Even today, although a certain amount of infilling has occurred, the West Coast estuaries provide major breaks in the continuity of the coastline. They have led to difficulties of communication throughout the centuries. The great prehistoric north-south route, Sarn Helen, took a course well inland to avoid the detours of a coastal track and the Romans adopted a similar strategy for their main line of communication. It was only with the building of the Cambrian Coast Railway that the Mawddach was bridged near its mouth. In the case of the Dyfi, however, there is still the long detour inland to cross the estuary head near Machynlleth.

On its eastern fringes the Harlech Dome is surrounded by a 'Fiery Girdle' of igneous rocks which are found associated with the overlying Ordovician sediments. As in Snowdonia it is the volcanic rocks, lavas and tuffs in particular, which have responded most dramatically to the forces of erosion. In the Arenig Mountains, with their twin peaks separated by the valley of the Tryweryn (8239), the ashes of past vulcanism, very much compressed and hardened through aeons of time, are responsible for much of the scenery. Arenig Fawr (8236) is the more impressive of the twin peaks, being more rugged and higher than its counterpart farther north. It has a tableland top with only a slight rise to its highest point at 854m. Away to the south-west there is the tame, rounded lump of Moel Lyfnant, again formed of volcanic ash. Only where glaciation has sharpened up the topography, as in the corrie basins cut into the eastern sides of both Arenig Fawr and Fach, is there some semblance to the Snowdonian type of landscape. Much of the impact of the short Arenig range is due to the fact that it rises out of a dull plateau formed mainly of Ordovician sedimentary rocks. Large areas of the headwater basin of the Tryweryn, especially in the region known as Migneint (7742), is exceptionally boggy and therefore trackless. Here is a wild landscape of open moorland with its rushes, cotton sedge and occasional tarns that has been left virtually untouched throughout history. With adequate drainage the Migneint could benefit from forestry, a change which would meet with universal approval. Already a small forest enclosure has been created

53

5 *The Dyfi Estuary with its broad expanse of drying sand flats at low water forming a major barrier to coastal communications*

on the better drained land to the west of the highest summit of Migneint, Carnedd Iago (the cairn of James).

The Southern Mountains

Across the Mawddach the ring of Ordovician volcanic rocks which surrounds the Harlech Dome makes its most impressive appearance in the Cadair Idris range. For over thirty kilometres this great backbone between the deep inlets of the Mawddach and Dyfi forms a battlemented barrier which is difficult to cross save near its seaward end. Though not as high as the peaks of Snowdonia, the Cadair Idris ridge has always attracted attention because of the scale of erosion which has etched great corrie basins on both sides of the crest. It is from one corrie basin (supposedly the chair of Idris a mythical giant) that the range takes its name. In its work of gouging out the corries the ice has shown little respect for the various types of rock which are present. In the case of the amphitheatre containing Llyn Cau (7112) the presence of relatively soft mudstones has undoubtedly helped to fashion this deeply set recess into the southern slopes of the ridge. The more open but equally impressive corrie containing Llyn y Gadair (7013) just across the ridge crest is cut for the most part in much tougher granophyre, a fine-grained granite with intergrown crystals of quartz and felspar. This igneous rock was intruded into the mudstones and lava flows as they accumulated on the sea bed of the time forming a sill of hard rock which has given rise to the impressive north-west facing scarp. With its columnar jointing well displayed in the sheer wall of rock it forms one of the finest precipices in the country, rivalling those of the volcanic districts of Western Scotland. The granophyre is succeeded near the scarp top by a bed of sedimentary mudstones and then along the crest itself by a capping of volcanic lavas and ashes. Although the steady cutting back of opposing corrie basins has left a very narrow crest ridge in places like the highest part at Penygadair (7113), the top broadens considerably towards the east as it drops slightly and then climbs once again to the rounded summit of Mynydd Moel, literally the bare topped mountain (7213). From here to the north east the rocky face of the ridge has now moved to the south-eastern side where ice fretting during the closing phases of the Ice Age has left an imposing splintered precipice overlooking the upper part of the Tal y Llyn valley.

The most popular approach to the Cadair top is from Dolgellau by way of the road past Llyn Gwernan (7015) before striking south following the stream bed up to Llyn y Gafr (7114) and then up the steeply inclined loose screes used by the Fox's Path. The foothill country around Llyn Gwernan has been carved out of Ordovician strata with its succession of igneous rocks. One of these, the Crogenau granophyre, makes only er impression on the landscape which is perhaps surprising when it is recalled that it is another granophyre sill which is responsible for the steep face of Cadair Idris. The difference in topographic expression results from the fact that the Crogenau granophyre has a closely-spaced system of joints which help degradation and erosion by ice. Llyn Gwernan itself is a rock hollow formed as ice exploited the shattered rock associated with a major fault running across the foothill zone.

The attraction which the Cadair Idris country has long held for the English tourist is understandable in view of its fine mountain prospects which rock type and erosional processes have combined to produce. It is more than a century since the Cambrian Railway reached Barmouth and opened up the area to both the ardent Victorian hill walker and day excursionist alike. The adjacent Aran range, however, never achieved the same popularity for it is scenically tame in comparison and rather isolated from the main routes. Even today when pressure on the better known areas is forcing many to seek solitude in the lesser known parts the Arans are little visited. The highest part of the north-south ridge, Aran Fawddwy (8622) is actually slightly higher than the peak of Cadair Idris so that height alone is no guarantee of grandeur. Nor is the presence of igneous rocks which occur in the Arans necessarily the architect of impressive scenery. In part the lack of appeal of the Arans lies in the fact that the side of the ridge most commonly seen from the main Bala to Dolgellau road (A494) is one of smooth slopes which rise steadily to the ridge crest. Once over the crest, however, the Arans have a completely different appearance for here erosion has bitten deeply into the volcanic rocks and created crags almost the equal of those of the Cadair range. Corrie lakes also add to the diversity of this fine eastern edge of the Arans. Although no great distance from the main roads this is country which is seldom visited and still retains the isolation and air of mystery which it has always held.

The line of the Aran crest, a fine promenade with its unrivalled views to all points of the compass, is more than simply a major topographic divide. Historically, this was the boundary of the kingdom of Gwynedd, where North Wales ended and a new cultural region began. The marcher characteristic of the Aran range is shown in the naming of its two principal peaks after the two districts of Penllwyd and Mawddwy which came together here. Here was a linguistic frontier for to the east of the Aran crest the inhabitants spoke with a softer tongue more akin to South Wales and had a different vocabulary. Even place names like Llaethnant (the milk valley) reflect this difference for in Gwynedd the equivalent form would be llefrith. The frontier zone of the Aran divide, far from the main centres which controlled the region, was almost an independent kingdom in the late Middle Ages. For a time it was under the control of the so-called Red Brigands of Mawddwy. This band of independent hill folk had no respect for the law and order which the English sought to impose and in 1554 Sir John Wynn of Gwyddir (near Llanrwst) was commissioned to rid the area of the insurgents. But even in 1860 when George Borrow came to Dinas Mawddwy he still sensed the independence of the region. Today the car and tourism have broken down the traditions of the past. Dinas Mawddwy, once a borough of Merioneth along with Dolgellau and Bala, is little more than a single street of cottages now by-passed by the main road.

The isolation of the Cantref of Mawddwy well into the present century stands out in marked contrast to the country around Bala to the north. This area of Penllyn was always on a major through route to the west, the Bala fault giving rise to a marked topographic break through the mountains of central Wales. It was a natural avenue of communication from prehistoric time onwards and later became part of the Roman road system. At Caer Gai (8731) overlooking the south-western end of Bala Lake, the Romans established a fort in the early part of the second century. The extent of Saxon influence here was probably not great, as elsewhere in North Wales though it is perhaps significant that they gave their own name to the lake, Pimbermere.

After the Conquest it was part of Powys though very much a fringe region under the control of the local Welsh Prince. Bala was his capital and he built a castle here, the mount of which survives behind the main street. Ultimately the Cantref of Penllyn came under the control of Llewelyn the Great in 1202 who included it in his kingdom of Gwynedd. With the Edwardian conquests in Wales at the end of the thirteenth century both Penllyn and the neighbouring cantref of Mawddwy were annexed to form the new shire of Merioneth. Bala itself became a royal demesne with Edward I here for a time in 1284. As elsewhere in North Wales Edward ultimately created a new town in Bala in order to provide an element of stability in an area notorious for raiding brigands from the surrounding hill country. The laying out of the town on a regular grid-iron plan began about 1310 with Roger of Mortimer in control. Fifty-three burgage plots were set out, most of them on land of the royal demesne of Penllyn. The old Welsh castle was probably rebuilt at the same time but there is no suggestion that the town was ever surrounded by a wall. The town was given its borough charter in 1324 when it was allowed to hold a weekly market and two annual fairs. As Bala grew in importance so the earlier settlement of Llanfor (8336) nearby declined, particularly when it lost its market and fairs to the new town. The area set aside for the borough was of limited extent, less than a square mile being carved out of the old parish of Llanycil (9034) for the purpose. Bala never grew outside these early boundaries though in later centuries it became a considerable centre for Welsh flannels and woollens. Today, with its railway closed, it is very much dependent on tourist traffic passing through en route to the resorts of the west coast though it still retains the air of a small market town serving the area around. The pattern of its streets and the burgage plots laid out along the main axis of the town still recall the period of frontier rule almost 600 years ago when Edward I attempted to bring stability to the new area through artificial settlement and trade.

Throughout the Middle Ages Bala shared the role of county town of Merioneth with Dolgellau. Today it has lost ground in comparison with its near neighbour, 30 kilometres away down the Bala trench. No two small county towns so close together provide a more striking contrast in layout for whereas Bala has a street plan of geometric· simplicity, Dolgellau lacks any defined pattern. Its narrow, twisting and curving streets focusing on the open space of a small central market place, suggest an early foundation. The houses, in their dark hues of the local building stone, cast deep shadows over the narrow streets and give a sense of urbanity and shelter in defiance of the bleak hill country around. Like Bala it is very much a local meeting place for the surrounding farming community as well as functioning as an administrative centre. Much of the present town dates from the period of re-building in the eighteenth century when the English influence—so apparent in the metropolitan street names—was so strong. There is, however, a sense of history in its streets and houses which reflect Welsh aspirations and a desire to preserve a cultural tradition.

Barmouth, the English derivative of Abermaw, succumbed readily to the established pattern of a typical English seaside town of the nineteenth century. Until that time it was a small port exporting the produce of a local cottage woollen industry. At first there was no road along the north side of the Mawddach estuary and its contact with the country inland was limited. Groups of terraced cottages hung precariously on the steep slopes overlooking the foreshore leading to the harbour. The whole atmosphere was to change when the cult of sea bathing gradually spread into these remoter parts and led to building on the flat terrain of the backshore. The arrival of the railway in 1866 speeded up the process of development and separate three-storey blocks of apartments were built very close to the shore. The hopes expressed at that time have remained partly unfulfilled and even the blocks of boarding houses were never completed to form a continuous promenade as at Llandudno. The church, dating only from 1889, found some space for itself on the steep backslope to the town and perhaps, symbolic of the influence of the railway age, was built not of local stone but of red sandstone brought in from Chester.

If Barmouth has succumbed to English influences then Machynlleth, the principal town of the Dyfi valley, has clung to its Welsh traditions. The town, with its charter dating back to 1291, has a simple T-shaped plan with the stem, Maengwyn Street, wide and tree-lined and still carrying on the centuries-old tradition of a Wednesday market. Machynlleth has intimate associations with Owen Glyndwr who established his Welsh Parliament here in 1410, the site though not the original building being occupied by the present Institute. The medieval flavour is preserved by a number of houses in this street but the dominant feature of the town is the Victorian clock tower dating from 1873, an almost immediate response to the arrival of the Cambrian Railway. This line is still open, being the only railway link between the west coast and the English network at Shrewsbury. It still gives a distinctive air to the town, though more and more Machynlleth is at the mercy of the motor car, lying as it does at the lowest bridging point of the Dyfi valley. The Dyfi was not navigable as far as the town and Derwenlas (7299) grew up as its port. When the lead mining flourished in the hill country to the west great quantities of ore were loaded here (Study 12) and in the nineteenth century there was a considerable export of slate from the Corris quarries (7507). Today Derwenlas has little to show for its past activity, a few cottages by the side of the main road and overgrown basins running in from the Dyfi being the sole survivors of a brief but intensive phase of prosperity.

The Denbighshire Moors and Clwydian Hills

The great tract of country lying to the north of Telford's Holyhead road—the present A5—is composed mainly of Silurian and Carboniferous rocks which give rise to a succession of plateaus. Inevitably the region suffers in comparison with the more majestic mountain scenery further west. Because of its lower height and lack of volcanic beds the Denbighshire Moors form a series of summit levels which rise to just over 500m in the countryside of Mynydd Hiraethog in the south-west. Anyone using the A5 between Cerrigydrudion (9548) and Pentrefoelas (8741) is aware of its dull landscape with wide, open marshy valleys rising gradually to flat-topped ridges. Only harder grit bands within the shales and mudstones which dominate the Silurian formation provide any variation to the general monotony of the scene, giving rise to minor scarplets of bare rock. Towards the north and east, where rejuvenation of the valleys draining to the north coast or the Vale of Clwyd has occurred, the landscape comes to life. The presence of a narrow strip of Carboniferous Limestone also helps to diversify this peripheral zone. Near Bont-newydd (0170) the river Elwy enters a fine wooded gorge cut in the limestone. The steep sides are a mass of penetrating caves and there is also a rare feature of the British landscape—a natural arch—as an added attraction.

Where the narrow outcrop of limestone reaches the north coast it provides a much needed diversity to what is a dull low shoreline with its rash of caravan sites, especially in the east around Prestatyn and Rhyl. But even the limestone headlands have not escaped human interference. The rock itself and its coastal location have led to extensive quarrying at Llanddulas (8978) which has marred the natural setting. Only at the Little Ormes Head, one of the two enclosing limestone headlands which make the bay of Llandudno so attractive, has this stretch of the North Wales coastline escaped from human interference and despoilation. The Chester to Holyhead Railway built in the 1840s must take the major responsibility for the present sad state of the coastline for not only did it encourage industry to develop but it led to a mass invasion of holiday makers from the Lancashire industrial towns. Little attempt was made to control development except at the superior resorts of Llandudno and Colwyn Bay (Study 7) so that today large areas have been abandoned to caravan camps, holiday chalets and great bungalow estates for the retired. The concentration of people in the narrow coastal strip stands out in marked contrast to the markedly dispersed settlement of much of the Denbighshire Moors. It is a countryside of small villages, mainly with valley sites like Llangernyw (8767), Llanfair Talhaiarn (9270) and Llandsannan (9365). Towards the south even villages are absent and only hamlets with an inn, farmhouse and one or two cottages like Gwytherin (8761) are able to retain a footing amidst the untenanted hectares of moorland around. Large areas are without any human habitation so that recent planting of many square kilometres of country to form Clocaenog Forest and the creation of reservoirs like the Alwen (9553) seem to be the most sensible use of land which in many places defeats even the hardy hill farmer. The area undoubtedly suffers from poor drainage which stems from the lack of a truly integrated river system. The disruptive effect of glaciation, which masked the lower parts with an extensive cover of boulder clay and led to the development of marshy hollows where thick beds of peat have accumulated, has not helped farming though it is noticeable that alongside the A5 many fields have been recovered from the moorland waste and crops of oats are even grown at heights well above 300m. One area which has benefited from the effects of glaciation is the Eglwysbach basin (8070), lying high up on a side valley of the Conwy. A small temporary lake existed here for a time in the Ice Age and when it finally drained it left behind a fertile basin which proved attractive to early settlement.

Both to the east and west the Denbighshire Moors are bounded by major valleys of the Clwyd and Conwy respectively. Although both have a common origin in the sense that their original alignment coincided with fault zones, their appearance is very different. The Conwy is a narrow straight but deep trough set between abrupt valley sides. Its flat floor and shorn off valley spurs carry the hallmarks of a typical glacial trough. The Afon Conwy which meanders across the whole width of the floor is prone to flooding so that the principal settlements of the valley tend to seek the slightly higher ground of the margins. Llanrwst, with its attractive bridge-church setting dominating the town, is one of the primary settlements of the valley and today retains the air of a small busy market town. Trefriw, on the opposite side of the valley, is more industrialised with a fine, restored woollen mill occupying an old site which utilised water power. Two kilometres to the north there is a chalybeate spring which has been

6   *The ordered landscape of the Denbigh Moors with its pattern of hedged fields and isolated farms forming a typical 'Tyddyn' effect*

known since Roman times. In the mid-nineteenth century an attempt was made to create a spa with a bath house erected in 1863. Although Trefriw Spa had its devotees it never succeeded in blossoming into a notable centre and today is seldom used, though the distinctive architecture of its bath house still recalls the hopes of the past. Farther north, along this western side of the Conwy Valley, Dolgarrog (7767) is of a completely different character. With an extensive aluminium works on the valley floor and depressing pre-fabricated council housing alongside, it seems out of place in the essentially rural setting of the valley. Water power from the mountain lakes above was instrumental in bringing the industry here although in the 1930s it led to disaster as the retaining wall of one of the reservoirs collapsed and brought a great torrent flood onto the industrial hamlet. Great boulders wrought considerable destruction and can still be seen in the now dry torrent bed.

The Vale of Clwyd has a different character from the Conwy Valley. It forms a lowland embayment set within the hills of North Wales as a result of faulting in the form of a rift valley structure. The collapse of the rock strata has preserved younger Triassic sandstone beds which recall the landscape of the West Midlands. Soils here are deeper and more fertile than on the open moors, more adequately drained, and with a less harsh climate and notably less rainfall, the Vale has extensive arable farming. The Vale is not flat for various harder sandstone beds make their presence felt topographically. The small compact towns of the vale like Ruthin, Denbigh and St Asaph tend to make use of low hills rising out of the flatter land around, though here, unlike in the Conwy, the reason was largely defensive rather than to avoid the risk of flooding (Study 8). Everywhere in the Vale there is an acute consciousness of the dominating eastern wall. This fault-line scarp probably dates from Mid-Tertiary times and runs almost unbroken for over thirty kilometres from Rhyd y Meudwy (1251) in the south to the steep bluffs behind Prestatyn near the North Wales coast. The western boundary to the Vale is much less distinct and although the margin is faulted, the land rises in a series of low foothills rather than making the dramatic feature which characterises the abrupt scarp face of the Clwydian Range.

The main effect of faulting of the Vale of Clwyd has been to lead to a repetition of strata so that in the Clwydian Range we have Silurian beds once again. Here, however, they make a much more impressive contribution to the landscape than where they outcrop on the Denbighshire Moors, largely as the result of rejuvenation caused by faulting. There are few major breaks in the fault scarp. Only in the north near Bodfari (0970) where the River Wheeler, a westward flowing tributary of the Clwyd, has succeeded in cutting back right through the scarp crest were conditions suitable for the breach to be exploited by glacial waters in the Ice Age. Here the former watershed near Nannerch (1669) has been worn down and waters clearly flowed across into the opposing drainage basin, cutting the fine Hendre gorge (1967) as they did so. The through valley of the Wheeler-Hendre system has proved of great value in crossing the Clwydian Range. It is used by the present A541 road while the former railway connecting Mold with Denbigh also took advantage of the gap with its easier gradients. Farther south, although short valleys and coombes have cut into the scarp face, there is no comparable breach like the Wheeler-Hendre system. The high level pass of Bwlch Pen Barras (1660), lying under the shelter of the fine hill fort of Foel Fennli, has formed through the gradual headward recession of aligned scarp and dip-slope valleys; the same is true of the Bwlch y Parc, a little to the south. The partially completed dissection of the Clwydian Range, as evidenced by these high level 'wind' gaps, has meant that the scarp top consists of a number of isolated moels which dominate the topography throughout its entire length. Hill tops like Moel Fammau (1662) and Moel y Parc (1170) are sufficiently isolated to provide good vantage points overlooking the Vale, a natural advantage not lost on the builders of the string of Iron Age hill forts which dominate the highest points of the Range. Today the Clwydian crest makes fine walking country though here, as elsewhere, the conifer plantations are shutting out the view and there is the inevitable conflict between the interests of the hill farmer, forester and hill walker. That the area has a great attraction for those seeking unspoiled country within easy reach of both the Flintshire industrial towns as well as the overcrowded summer resorts along the coast, is undisputed and hopefully this will be taken into account in any decision of future land use. Not only are the higher tops fine viewpoints but the lower country in the upper Alyn valley has its own attraction. Here, at places like Loggerheads (1962), the Carboniferous Limestone makes its appearance once again through the repetition brought about by faulting. Even more striking is the gorge section of the Alyn river as it makes its way eastwards through the limestone outcrop, scenery which recalls the similar setting of the Elwy on the other side of the Vale of Clwyd.

The Berwyns and·the Foothill Country

The Berwyns are the last of the great hill ranges of North Wales. In the past they have attracted little attention because their most accessible parts are rather tame. Much of the area consists of a great flat-topped tableland which inevitably lacks the dramatic qualities of the more mountainous tracts to the west. Its summit ridge in the west, however, cannot be lightly dismissed for not only does it rise to 827m both at Cadair Berwyn (0732) and Moel Sych (0631), its eastern edge has been scalloped by a number of cwms where ice would have lingered at the end of the Ice Age. Only one of the cwms contains a true corrie lake, Llyn Lluncaws (0731), where overdeepening by ice has left its mark. The other more open cwms act as feeders for the headstreams which ultimately swell the waters of both the rivers Tanat and Ceiriog draining away through the foothill country to the east. It is here that a ridge and valley landscape has developed on rocks which are relatively easily eroded and which seldom protrude to give bare escarpments. The igneous rocks, which play such a dominant creative role in the landscape around the Harlech Dome and in Snowdonia itself, are everywhere absent. The outcropping Ordovician and Silurian rocks are predominantly mudstones and shales and this accounts for the rather muted character of the Berwyns and the eastern foothill zone. If the strata lacks the harder rock types which would be immediately reflected in a more expressive topography, it has not escaped the folding which past earth movements have brought about. The whole area consists of a succession of anticlines and synclines, each with a south-west or north-east trend. This is not, however, reflected in the relief for the main valley systems are mainly aligned to the east or south-east. Only near Llanfyllin (1419) and Meifod (1513) is there any apparent semblance of structural control over the topography. Even here its effects have been masked by the influence of glaciation. Ice was still occupying much of this area even as recently as 24,000 years ago so that the drainage must post-date this time. As the main ice sheet melted, pockets of dead ice lingered in places and caused the developing drainage to find alternative routes around it. This seems to have happened in the case of the Afon Vyrnwy downstream from Dolanog (0612). Up to this point the river has behaved normally by pursuing a course towards the south-east in a fairly broad and open valley. Below Dolanog the river forsakes its direct route to join the Tanat and instead takes a course to the north-east, cutting through a number of ridges to give rise to a steep gorge section in the valley profile. The more obvious route is not difficult and even in the present topography it is represented as a wide and open valley, now drained only by a small stream. This apparent choice of a more difficult route must have arisen through ice blocking the original lower section of the valley and forcing the Vyrnwy to take a more circuitous course to the north. A similar river diversion by ice probably took place in the valley of the Banwy east of Llanerfyl (0309) forcing the river to head around the northern end of Moel Bentyrch (0509) instead of using a more direct route. The old course remains as a dry gap sufficiently wide and open for it to be used by the present B4385 road. Not every gap or through valley is the result of ice interference. The route which runs in a north-easterly direction from the lower end of Lake Vyrnwy across to the Tanat Valley—for long a packhorse trail but now without a metalled road—coincides with a zone of structural weakness in the rocks which erosion has been able to exploit.

Lake Vyrnwy is an artificial reservoir built in 1890 by damming and flooding the upper part of the biggest headwater valley of this drainage system. The creation of the man-made lake meant that the original village of Llanwyddyn, with its church and cluster of cottages, had to be submerged. A new settlement was established just below the dam taking the name of the original village. Although the passage of time has allowed the lake to merge gracefully into the landscape, especially since the planted conifers have grown to full stature, Lake Vyrnwy still retains an air of artificiality. The major effect of glaciation in this foothill country, apart from the diversion of drainage discussed above, has been one of depositing debris rather than erosive scouring, so typical of the mountainous regions farther west. Lake Vyrnwy would fit more neatly into such a setting where the great erosive power of the valley glaciers is matched by the bare and rugged mountain sides which tower above natural lakes like Ogwen and Cwellyn. Each element of lake and mountain contributes to the whole whereas Lake Vyrnwy must always remain a man-made intrusion ill at ease with its surroundings.

The foothill country to the east of Lake Vyrnwy, a stepping stone to the higher plateaus and mountains of the west, has a settlement history which also distinguishes it from the heartlands of North Wales. It is a region of small villages and hamlets set, for the most part, in the valleys, with a scatter of hill farms occupying the land in between. The dispersed nature of the settlement has resulted in a maze of lanes without any semblance of a regular pattern. In this it recalls the Celtic landscape of the South West Peninsula. Except perhaps in the Bronze Age, settlement has favoured the lower country to the east. The penetrating valleys of the Banwy, Vyrnwy and Tanat have always provided routes into the interior and it is here that the settlement is mainly concentrated. Even in the Iron Age, when the higher slopes were preferred for the fortified camp sites, it is noticeable that there is a concentration of remains on the foothill tops in the east and on the valley side slopes farther inland. One of the best sites lies on the top of Craig Rhiwarth above Llangynog (0527), where there is a large collection of hut circles. The settlement has a natural wall of crags on three sides while on the fourth there is an impressive wall of stones over a kilometre in length. Altogether there are more than sixty huts, mainly concentrated on the south-east corner of the defensive enclosure and this alone gives a true indication of the size and importance of the site. From this single camp nearly all the nearby hill forts of the Tanat Valley edge country can be seen. The Vyrnwy valley also has its sequence of hill forts, each located on a prominent hill top or spur overlooking the valley. Around Mathrafal (1211) where the river joins the Banwy, there is a cluster of no fewer than six within an area of a few square kilometres. All are fairly small and probably accommodated less than a hundred people when in use but their density points to a considerable population during the Iron Age in this favoured foothill zone. In contrast in the west, where the plateau rises to over 500m there are no forts apart from that on Craig Rhiwarth which seems to be the limit of penetration of Iron Age culture from the east.

In historic times this area continued to be a frontier region with an emphasis on defence as shown by the building styles adopted. The Romans were content to hold the area with a few defensive strongholds like that of Y Gaer near Llanfair Caereinion. A recent excavation here proved inconclusive for no archaeological evidence came to light to substantiate the long held view that this was a Roman fort. The rectangular shape, rounded corners and the form of the entrance are, nevertheless, strongly suggestive of Roman workmanship. If the tangible evidence in this foothill country suggests that the Romans made little impact, it seems likely that the way of life must have continued uninterrupted in the hill forts. Craig Rhiwarth (0527), with its cluster of hut circles, continued to be occupied throughout the period. The present landscape is at best an imperfect record of past settlement history, a palimpsest where later centuries have all but erased the evidence of former occupance. This is particularly true of the lower country where farming and the establishment of villages and hamlets have, in many cases, destroyed the only visible evidence.

The south-east foothill country was the only part of North Wales which did not come under the control of the Welsh Princes of Gwynedd. Instead this was part of the territory of Powys, an administrative division re-born in recent years. Local Welsh princes were in control for many centuries and usually exerted their authority over a small tract of country centred on a fortified castle centre. The motte or mound is, in nearly every case, the only survival of this phase though occasionally the plan included a fortified enclosure or bailey alongside, recalling the pattern of the Norman castle on which it could have been based. Many of these Welsh castles date from the eleventh and twelfth centuries and acted as the 'caput' or controlling nucleus for a limited territory around. They were mainly sited in the valleys or on the lower slopes. In the Banwy, for example, motte fortifications have survived at Castle Caereinion, close to the church (1605), at Llanerfyl opposite the present village (0310) and at Llangadfan where the hotel has been sited on the edge of the former motte and bailey (0110). Each castle site in the Banwy valley is thus closely associated with the only nucleated villages in the area today. This is not the case in the Tanat valley where the mottes of Cefn Coch (1026) and Castell Moch (1124) are too far removed from the nucleated settlement of Llanrhaeadr ym Mochnant (1226) to have influenced its growth. The relationship between the 'church' settlements and the castle sites is not necessarily a close one. Some of the motte castles, like those of Moel Froehas (1122) and Domen yr Allt (1221), have no close ties with any subsequent settlement and must have been sited to exercise control over the col leading from the Tanat into the neighbouring Cain Valley. It was here on the valley floor that the newly planned settlement of Llanfyllin (1419) was established towards the end of the thirteenth century. It was granted a market charter and fair in 1293 and a decade later there is a record of thirty burgages having been established. It was probably not an original settlement on a virgin site for the church was already in existence in 1291. Instead the newly laid-out borough, with its long wide market street and burgage plots arranged on either side, was grafted on to the church hamlet. The foundation of Llanfyllin as a planned town in this border region marks a phase of settlement history which is repeated time and time again in the areas under English control where Edward I, in particular, tried to bring stability through trade. In the case of Llanfyllin the creation of the new 'town' was the work of a Welsh Prince of Powys, no doubt motivated and strongly influenced by the English examples taking place nearby at Old and New Montgomery. In this area, however, the experiment was not repeated elsewhere and today only Llanfyllin, still a sizeable village and clearly distinguishable from other settlements by its planned layout, stands out as the sole example of this interesting phase of colonisation.

Large parts of this foothill country to the south-east of the Berwyn range were little affected either by the development of castle villages based on a dominant motte and bailey earthwork or by the attempts at planned growth taking place at Llanfyllin. The Vyrnwy valley, draining the intervening country between the Banwy and Tanat, has no medieval castle sites or 'llan' villages, still less a planned borough on the pattern of Llanfyllin. Settlements, like Dolanog (0612) and Pontrobert (1012), were little more than hamlets with a mill using the power supplied by the adjacent river. Even a source of power did not bring them within the fold of the Montgomeryshire flannel industry centred on Llanidloes, even though at Meifod (1513) the industrial revolution took hold after the foundation of the first woollen mill in 1789. Instead the foothill country on either side of the Vyrnwy valley remained untouched and continued to practise a pastoral economy based on the scattered farm or tyddyn. This 'tyddyn' landscape still dominates the present day setting of the area, with the isolated farmhouse at the centre of a patchwork of hedged fields, some of which are used for arable crops like oats but mostly under grass. The long established practice of sub-dividing the landholding between various sons—a form of gavelkind—led to enormous pressures on the available good quality land. It often necessitated taking into cultivation poorer quality land and the full use being made of summer pastures on the higher plateau tops to the west. The summer migration of animals to these pastures (transhumance) was once a common feature of this area and sometimes the early established summer dwelling or 'hafod' became a permanent farm, thus pushing the frontiers of cultivation to higher levels. Sometimes the transhumance involved movement of animals over long distances although occasionally, as at Llangynog (0526), the nearby plateau top of Craig Rhiwarth, was used. The cattle would be allowed to roam over the pastures, returning each evening to be milked at the hafod which would function as a dairy for the making of butter and cheese. Occasionally the name 'lluest' or dairy house is used for these temporary upland quarters and like hafod the designation has survived in a number of places as on Pen Coed (9708). In this same area is Hafod beudy (9807) as well as the permanent home farm at Pant yr hendre (0107). Transhumance in its original form has long ceased and it is only in place names that we have a hint of the former way of life which characterised not only this corner of North Wales but was once common throughout the entire region.

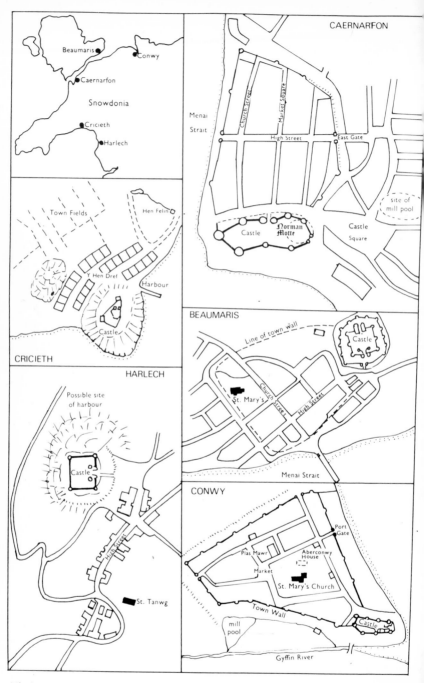

The layout of the castle towns around Snowdonia

1. The Edwardian Castle Towns of Snowdonia

The Norman hold on North Wales and in particular the mountain fastness of Snowdonia was always a precarious one. Only at places like Caernarfon and Deganwy, overlooking the Conwy Estuary, where they built their motte and bailey castles, did they gain a foothold in what remained a predominantly hostile region. From time to time, especially in the reign of Henry II (1154–89), attempts were made to conquer the country but after an initial success, the strength of the Welsh Princes proved too great and an alliance rather than conquest was sought. This allowed the Welsh to become masters in their own land and they immediately began to strengthen their hold by building castles themselves. The usual plan adopted was a variant of the English style to suit the local terrain. Dolwyddelan (5272), in the upper valley of the Lledr and in the heart of Snowdonia, was probably built some time in the latter part of the twelfth century. Its most striking feature is the rectangular keep, very much in the style of contemporary English castles. Llewelyn the Great is reputed to have been born here and it was he, more than any other Welsh Prince, who achieved virtual independence of the Principality. He cleverly exploited the weakened kingship of both John and Henry III but after his death in 1240 there was a period of disorder and disarray. Ultimately in 1255 his grandson, Llewelyn ap Gruffyd assumed control and restored full independence. He was even recognised by Henry III as Prince of Wales when the Treaty of Montgomery was signed in 1267.

The accession of Edward I completely transformed the balance of power in North Wales. Llewelyn suffered defeat in the war of 1277 and had his power reduced. His death at Builth five years later brought to an end any real hopes of a true Welsh state. Edward I was anxious to exploit this change of fortune and immediately made plans for the complete subjugation of Wales. In mountainous Snowdonia this took the form of creating bastide towns, the emphasis on defence being matched by a desire to encourage permanent settlement and generate trade. Settlers from England were invited to move into the towns and by this process of anglicisation in a few selected areas, it was hoped that the whole country could be held. For this purpose he established castle towns of Dinbych (Denbigh), Flint, Rhuddlan, Conwy, Caernarfon, Harlech, Cricieth and Beaumaris. The sites chosen allowed supplies to be brought in by sea, an important consideration in a hostile region with poor land communications. No attempt was made to control directly the mountainous heart of Snowdonia, Edward being content to ring it with coastal castles. These also had the effect of cutting off the important granary of Anglesey. It is a measure of Edward's astuteness in choosing his sites, that nearly all have survived to this day as sizeable towns. Only at Castell y Bere (6648), under the shadow of Cadair Idris and some distance inland, did the attempt to create a castle town fail.

Denbigh was one of the earliest of Edward's towns in North Wales. The hill which overlooked the town on its southern side had long been a Welsh stronghold and it was therefore essential, if the English plan of conquest was to succeed, for this to be reduced. With this accomplished, Henry de Lacy was given the task of erecting a new castle and town in October 1292. Although there was a Welsh uprising in 1294, this did not stand in the way of Edward pushing forward his plans for subjugating the more mountainous country to the west. In the short span of a few years at the end of the thirteenth century, Edward founded Caernarfon, Conwy, Harlech, Cricieth and Beaumaris.

Caernarfon

Caernarfon's history goes back much further than the castle town founded by Edward I. Some distance away to the east on the crest of a bluff, the Romans under Agricola established their fortress of Segontium in AD 77–78. Even after their withdrawal the site seems to have been used and it is perhaps significant that the parish church of St Peblig—a Celtic saint of the sixth century—was founded here. It was a Norman earl, Hugh d'Arranches, who really determined the situation of the present town when he built his motte and bailey castle. The site he chose was a low peninsula formed of Ordovician shales between the rivers Seiont and Cadnant. This early Norman castle was incorporated in the much larger castle when Edward turned his attention to the area in June 1283. Alongside the massive walls of the castle, built largely of limestone brought down the Menai Strait, the town was laid out in a broadly grid-iron plan (Fig. 2). The main High Street ran from the East or Exchequer Gate to a Port Gate overlooking the waters of the Menai Strait. It was crossed at right angles by a succession of north-south streets whose names—like Church Street or Market Street—were determined by the main buildings they contained. The blocks resulting from this street pattern were then subdivided into standard burgage plots, each measuring 24m by 18m. These became the holdings of the English settlers who were encouraged to come to the new town. By 1298 it was recorded that there were fifty-six whole and one half plot occupied. At a later date the whole urban area was enclosed within a substantial wall. Outside this lay the mill pool, formed by blocking the lower part of the River Cadnant. Today this has disappeared as the town has outgrown its medieval site but its former existence is commemorated in the names of Pool Hill and Pool Street. Rather surprisingly, only a town chapel was built into the north-west corner of the walls and St Peblig retained its status as the parish church. Although heavily restored in the nineteenth century so that little now remains of its early fourteenth century foundation, the chapel of St Mary's still provides a link with the original new town.

The founding of a new town proved a costly enterprise for Edward I. Not only materials for building the castle, walls and town had to be purchased, but also masons, smiths and carpenters had to be brought in from England. Limestone from quarries at Penmon in Anglesey was the most widely used building material and proved ideal for shaping into large blocks. Some Carboniferous Sandstone from Aberpwll was used for cornices and the occasional use of the local grit from the town quarries in Twrt Hill (482530) is also recorded. Perhaps the most unusual building stone is the red sandstone often used for door lintels. With no outcrop nearer than Chester it seems likely that the sandstone largely came from the Roman fort of Segontium which suffered almost complete reduction at this time. The cost of building must have been an enormous drain on the royal treasury, bearing in mind that the castle, walls and town were all started within a few years. From accounts which have survived, it has been estimated that it cost the Royal Exchequer about £19,000 to carry out the works at Caernarfon. Of the other castle towns, only Conwy cost more. The building of the castle went on steadily between 1283 and 1327 and it is possible to distinguish the various phases of construction. The whole of the southern and eastern walls, for example, were raised to a great height during the first decade.

To the English, Caernarfon, perhaps more than any other of the bastide towns of North Wales, was symbolic of the achievement of the conqueror. The castle, in particular, was an edifice of stupendous power, majesty and strength, a description used by Dr Johnson when he came here in 1774. The Denbighshire traveller, Pennant, took a different view and looked upon it 'as a magnificent badge of our subjection'. In a historical context it is the castle rather than the town which has given Caernarfon a distinctive role to play. From 1301 onwards successive Princes of Wales have been crowned here and for long the Royal Borough could claim to be capital of Wales. Even today when thousands of visitors throng the castle green and crowd the narrow streets, its distinctiveness among Welsh towns is still very much apparent.

Cricieth

This castle town in the Lleyn Peninsula stands out in complete contrast to Caernarfon for the intimate relationship between the needs of defence and the necessity of attracting permanent settlers from England is much less apparent. Edward I was fortunate that he was able to use an existing Welsh castle as a defensive core. This was built about 1230 and consisted of a simple polygon of walls, now the Inner Ward, with a massive gatehouse facing inland. It was sited on the top of one of two hills which dominate the coastline at this point. The hills owe their existence to an outcrop of the orange-coloured felsite, a resistant rock which is much tougher than the surrounding shales. It was perhaps fortunate for Edward that the original castle builder chose the more seaward of the two hills as it allowed his supplies to come in from the sea. A small harbour lay just below the eastern walls in the lee of the headland formed by the igneous rock. The name Cricieth for the settlement is apt in that the element 'crug' means mount or hillock, an undoubted reference to the Castle Rock.

Following the defeat of Llewelyn in 1282, Edward I made immediate plans for re-shaping and extending the original Welsh castle. The amount of money spent, however, was not great, certainly when compared with that lavished on Caernarfon and Conwy. Nevertheless the castle fitted in well with the grand design of containing the mountainous Snowdonia. Only a town where the English might settle was missing, for apart from a few cottages under Castle Hill, there was nothing resembling real urban development. Accordingly a township was created, Tre Ferthyr—the Martyr's Township—and

7 *Cricieth Castle set on a felsite hill with the old planned town nestling at its foot*

possibly the church, about a kilometre away inland. Although it may have been Edward's intention to build his bastide town between castle and church, the first allocation of burgage plots was restricted to the land immediately inland from the castle. A charter was granted in November 1284 as an aid to urban development. We know from later records that the size of the burgage plots was 24m by 18m, that is, the same size as for Caernarfon. In addition each burgess was entitled to other land in the vicinity and in this way the king hoped to attract settlers who would give loyal support to the garrison.

Even after 700 years it is still possible to seek out the original burgage plots of Edward's borough. They occur near the castle in the area known as Yr Hen Dref—the old town. The original cottages have become modified over the centuries and in many cases pulled down to make way for Victorian houses. But even where this has occurred, the layout and size of the original burgage plots are still discernible. Many of the frontages of the cottages measure 18m, the original width as laid out in the late thirteenth century. On the other side of the castle, in the lane now known as Rock Terrace but originally called Lon Bach, other cottages sited on the burgage plots still survive. Beyond the second hill of Dinas, the arable plots granted to the burgesses are situated in the area now occupied by the recreation ground, bowling green and recent bungalow estate. In spite of this later development it is still possible to make out the relict field system. On either side of the path which leads across to the railway station were two fields with names Y Llath and Y Ddwy Llathern. The name *llathern* here refers to the old square measure of land holding, sometimes translated by English surveys as a virgate. Here, then, lay the town fields where the early burgesses grew their subsistence crops.

The other feature of the medieval town was the mill. This has not survived as a building but only in the name of a cottage, Hen Felin, occupying its original site near the present lifeboat station. The mill pond lay immediately above, close to the old cottages·of Glan'rafon. Adjacent to these was the old common, Yr Maes Glas—the green field—the upper part of which still forms the present green north of the main coastal road. Development in this quarter of the town, apart from the church, is almost entirely nineteenth century and followed the building of the coastal road in 1807. The effect of the road was to create a new centre to the town and, as a result, the original core of the bastide town around the castle became something of a backwater. Even the growth of the resort in the last hundred years has had only a minimal effect on Yr Hen Dref.

Beaumaris

In contrast to the bold site enjoyed by Cricieth, Edward's only bastide town in Anglesey, built to command the northern entrance to the Menai Strait, was sited on a low marshland—the beau marais—which became the adopted name of the place. Development came late and the castle, begun in 1295 following·a revolt by the Welsh Prince Madog, was the final expression of Edward's attempt to subdue Snowdonia. Perhaps because of this and also the lack of restriction of the open marshland site, Beaumaris castle has the most perfect of designs. It consists of an inner ward contained by a high wall with turrets, then an outer concentric wall and finally a deep moat. It was built of local limestone and sandstone. Building went on quickly with over 3,000 men employed in the summer of 1295. The cost was enormous and by 1330 it has been estimated that £14,400 had been spent, a prodigious sum for the early fourteenth century. Like all Edwardian castles, it was supplied from the sea. A dock was built close to the southern entrance and this was connected by a short canal with the Menai Strait. No trace of the canal remains following the laying out of the greensward, one of the most pleasing features of the present town.

The town laid out alongside the castle was traditional in plan, with a grid network of streets on its western side. Although a few medieval buildings remain, having survived the Georgian re-building which gave the town the Bulkeley Arms, it is the street plan which betrays the planted character of Beaumaris. Burgage plots, again measuring 24m by 18m, were allocated to would-be settlers from England and as an encouragement they were granted rent free for the first ten years. As early as 1296, 140 were occupied so that a sizeable town had already grown up within a few years of foundation. The town wall, which only survives in fragments, came later. Several burgage plots were allocated for the building of the town church of St Mary on a raised site close to the centre.

Although both town and castle appear to have been built on virgin territory they were sited very close to an existing, flourishing Welsh settlement in the township of Llanfaes. Its parish church of St Katherine lies about a kilometre away (6077) but this is all that

8   *The squat form of Beaumaris Castle with its succession of formidable towers overlooking the moat*

remains of the former Welsh town. Perhaps it posed a threat to the new English town and for this reason Edward decided to move its inhabitants to the other side of the island. Thus Newborough (4265) came into being and was granted its charter in 1303. The site chosen was unfavourable for commerce and it is therefore not surprising that Newborough has remained a street village on the edge of the great expanse of sand dunes forming Newborough Warren. Beaumaris, in contrast, has retained its urban appearance. A large number of well-to-do merchants came to live in the town and local tokens were in use in the seventeenth century. The main trade was in leather and several old tan pits formerly existed in the vicinity. In the nineteenth century, Beaumaris flourished as an exclusive watering place, a position which to some extent it has retained to the present time.

Conwy

This town, so sited as to control the important crossing of the Conwy estuary, is perhaps the finest surviving example of Edward's policy of containing the Welsh by planting a number of strategically placed bastides around the mountainous heart of Snowdonia. Its foundation, as at Beaumaris, led to the moving of existing occupants, this time the monks of Aberconwy Abbey. They were given a new site higher up the valley at Maenen (7865) and Edward himself contributed £427 by way of compensation. The only other building on the site that was to become the new Conwy was the Hall of Llewelyn named after the Welsh Prince who was buried in the nearby Cistercian abbey. Both groups of buildings were useful to Edward in that they provided ready accommodation while the new town was being built. The abbey ultimately became the parish church of St Mary which still dominates the centre of the town.

What attracted Edward most was the great potential of the site as a castle town. The environs of the abbey provided reasonably flat ground for laying out a town without much difficulty. Along the eastern side lay the estuary of the Conwy which provided a sheltered anchorage and easy access to the sea. To the south, a tributary of the Conwy, the Gyffin, effectively demarcated the town on this side and because of its steep fall, it could be harnessed for power. Already an abbey mill was sited there. The dominant feature, however, was the long spine formed of a hard grit which ran out into the estuary, an obvious choice for the castle as it had both height and natural water defences on at least two sides.

After overcoming the inland Welsh stronghold of Dolwyddelan the English advance into North Wales reached this area during March 1283, and immediately plans were put in hand for the building of both castle and town. Some idea of the speed of construction can be gathered from the fact that by November 1284 almost £6,000 had already been spent. Two hundred woodcutters and a hundred diggers were brought in from Chester, masons and quarry hands were recruited from over a wide area of the kingdom and supplies of iron, nails and tin purchased in Newcastle-under-Lyme. In a space of five short building seasons, between 1283 and 1287, the basic elements of the new town had taken shape. Although the site was almost ideal, the topography did impose some restrictions on the form the town walls could take. A triangular area rather than the more normal rectangle emerged, with the castle situated at one apex overlooking the Conwy estuary. This in turn led to difficulty in laying out a truly grid-iron pattern of streets (Fig. 2). A further limitation was imposed by the abbey church which was allowed to remain on its existing site.

The building materials used were, for the most part, of local origin. The walls of the castle were constructed in part of the hard Silurian grit on which it stands, though most of it was brought from quarries a short distance away on the south-west side of the town. Part of the town wall was built of a similar rock. The quay wall, however, is largely built of a lava rhyolite which forms the headland on the north side of the town. This could have acted as a quarry although one opinion favours the ruins of Deganwy Castle (7879) across the river as the most likely source. As both these rocks are difficult to shape it was necessary to import the red sandstone of the Chester area for use in window casings and mouldings, as well as for the springers of arches. It is possible that some of the sandstone was obtained from pulling down the existing abbey buildings where these were not needed for use in the new town.

The fact that Edward's town of Conwy has weathered the storms of succeeding centuries and still exists as a flourishing centre to this day, has meant that little, apart from the castle and town walls, has survived intact. The building known as the Hall of Llewelyn, which was already in existence prior to 1283 and provided the king with much needed accommodation at the outset, was an early casualty. There is a record in the early years of the fourteenth century of it being carefully dismantled and the timberwork shipped to Caernarfon to be used in a storehouse for victuals in the castle there. It is doubtful whether any of the buildings in the present town date from the fourteenth century although it has been suggested that the stone basement of the house known as Aberconwy (now under the care of the National Trust) may be original. The large house known as Plas Mawr in High Street dates from about 1585 although it may occupy the site of Otto's Hall, a building on an original burgage plot of the new town. In Upper Gate Street the old house, known as The College, may have been the successor of the medieval hospital. Apart from these buildings and the Black Bull inn, which is said to date from the sixteenth century, there is little apart from the street plan to take us back to the first planted town. The church, which incorporates parts of the pre-town monastic buildings of Aberconwy Abbey, can claim undisputed continuity of site over seven centuries. The present building is basically fourteenth century, though this, too, has seen many changes through repeated restoration. By the eighteenth century Conwy's declining importance led to Pennant commenting that 'a more ragged town is scarcely to be seen, within,' though he did add, 'or a more beautiful, without'. Even this is no longer true in the sense that the bastide character has suffered from successive bridgings of the Conwy Estuary, by Telford in 1825, Stephenson in 1848 and finally Fitzsimon's span bridge in 1958. Although not distasteful in themselves, the three closely spaced bridges have completely altered the setting of the town when viewed from the opposite shore.

Harlech

The castle of Harlech is broadly contemporaneous in date with those of Caernarfon, Cricieth and Conwy. In its setting it is the rival of Cricieth whose walls can be seen across the waters of Tremadog Bay. Like Cricieth there was probably a Welsh castle on this coastal promontory but it is not clear whether Edward's army of masons, carpenters, woodcutters and smiths made any use of it when they arrived to begin work in June 1283. The castle site lay on one of the few areas of flat ground on top of a headland, 60m high. Inland the flanks of the Harlech Dome rose quite steeply so that the castle was overlooked from this direction. This was obviously a weak link in defence which had to be remedied by digging a deep ditch on the landward side of the castle. The seaward side presented no problem for there was a sheer drop to what was, in the late thirteenth century, a great sandflat. Whether Harlech possessed a useful harbour is doubtful, and it is more likely that use was made of the inlet of Llandanwg, some distance to the south (5628).

Harlech never attracted a large population and there was probably no more than a handful of cottages around the castle. The site was a difficult one for immediately to the south lay a deep coombe. Some settlement may have taken place here but any houses would have to cling precariously to its steep slopes. There was certainly no development of a grid-iron plan nor does there appear to have been a wall. In its scale of development Harlech is closely comparable with Cricieth. In 1294–5 the population numbered only eighty-six, almost equally divided between the townspeople and the garrison. Only about thirty burgage plots were set out for those who could be encouraged to come to this isolated spot overlooking Cardigan Bay, a figure which compares with 154 at Beaumaris. Such limited urban development did not justify a church of its own and use was made of the church at Llandanwg, in whose parish the new town was situated. The present church, dedicated to St. Tanwg and by the side of the coast road which runs right through the town is of later date. It is, however, on the same site as the church shown on John Speed's plan of Harlech, dated 1610. In spite of its fine defensive site the castle was not invincible and was taken by Owain Glyndwr when he rebelled against Henry IV in 1404. The town also suffered from burning in later centuries so that any early cottages have long since disappeared. Apart from the majesty of its castle there is little to suggest in the present town that it once enjoyed the rights and privileges of a bastide, or that it was an important link in the chain of defensive strongpoints on which Edward relied to maintain a tenuous hold on this inhospitable region.

SUGGESTED ITINERARY

The only way to appreciate the site, layout, historic buildings, present day functions of each of the bastides is to walk around the streets with a town plan. Each is different but a common starting point would be the castle. At Caernarfon the quay and old harbour area adjacent to the castle should be visited before walking through the walled town. Beyond lies the modern harbour on the site of the tidal inlet of the River Cadnant. By making a circuit outside the town walls in the direction of the East Gate, the site of the former mill pool and bridge is reached. The whole layout of Caernarfon is best appreciated from the top of Twrt Hill (482630) to the north east, the site of one of the medieval town quarries. From here a return can be made to the quay (now a car park) but formerly used for exporting slate from the Llanberis quarries.

The layout of Cricieth is on a much smaller scale. Begin at the Castle and then walk through the lanes of the original town centred on Yr Hen Dref. Passing around the other hill, the site of the town fields, now the recreation ground, can be reached. Continue across the railway near the station to the nineteenth-century town which grew up following the building of the coastal road. To the north of this, and in an isolated position, is the parish church with its dedication to St Catherine. From here return to the castle by way of the harbour.

Beaumaris Castle, the most regular of all in plan, occupies a site at the western end of the town. Only fragments of the town wall remain, especially near the north-west corner. In the centre of the roughly grid pattern of streets lies the parish church which occupies a whole chequerboard square. The tour of the town can be completed along the waterfront with its fine early nineteenth-century buildings.

Conwy Castle, because of its elevated site, provides a good view-point overlooking the town. The walls are almost complete and parts of the rampart can be walked. Within the roughly gridded pattern of streets, the most noteworthy buildings are the parish church, on the original Cistercian abbey site, the late sixteenth-century Plas Mawr and Aberconwy House, with its stone base forming a foundation for the upper wattle and daub structure. The quay, overlooking the Conwy estuary, still retains something of the bustle of past centuries and is free from the traffic which dominates the main part of the town.

Harlech Castle is best seen from the road below. The road leads up through the coombe onto the shelf where the main part of the town is situated. Because of the difficulties of topography, there is no regular pattern of streets. The modern church is a replacement for the original St Tanwg, now abandoned close to the inlet which probably functioned as the port for the town (568282).

2. The glaciated landscape of Nant Ffrancon

The upper part of the Ogwen Valley, known as the Nant Ffrancon, portrays in expressive simplicity many of the landforms which we associate with a mountainous area which has recently undergone glaciation. Together with the neighbouring Glyder and Carneddau ranges, which line each side of the valley, the area contains within a small compass some of the most majestic scenery in the whole of Snowdonia. In recent years its ice- shorn slopes, particularly those of Tryfan and the Idwal Slabs, have become increasingly popular for the variety of climbing routes which they can offer, both for the beginner and the expert. Long before the full significance of the scenery was appreciated the area had been visited by the geologist Adam Sedgwick and his naturalist friend Charles Darwin. They came to Llyn Idwal in 1831 in search of fossils which might help them to unravel the complex rock succession. So intent were they on their search that they failed to notice the distinctive character of the scenery around them. A decade later when, through the efforts of Agassiz and Buckland, the glacial theory was beginning to be more widely accepted, Charles Darwin revisited the area. On this occasion he was not blind to the effects of ice and was greatly struck by the appearance of the hillocks of morainic drift around the shores of Llyn Idwal. What had previously passed unnoticed was now tantalisingly clear for here was evidence that glacier ice had not long vacated this very area. Darwin was the first to admit his own shortcomings and wrote 'these phenomena are so conspicuous that a house burnt down by fire did not tell its story more plainly than did this valley'.

After Darwin's visit in 1842 the Nant Ffrancon and Llyn Idwal area became classic ground for the glaciologist and was much visited by the scientists who began the task of understanding the complexities of landform evolution now that the basic premises were firmly established. Foremost amongst these was the geologist Andrew Ramsay who, year after year, came to Snowdonia and painstakingly unravelled the geology of the mountainous area, often having to wait weeks for suitable weather when working on the peaks. Ramsay became increasingly aware of the role of ice both as an eroding and depositional agency and his views were summarised in a slim volume with the title *Ancient glaciers of Switzerland and North Wales* which was published in 1860. This had a profound effect on the rapidly developing science of landform analysis and undoubtedly influenced the American geomorphologist William Morris Davis who came to North Wales and from the nearby Llanberis area made a detailed study of the effects of glacial erosion which he subsequently published in 1909.

Nant Ffrancon, strictly defined, relates to that part of the Ogwen Valley between the Penrhyn Slate quarry close to Bethesda and the great rock step below Llyn Ogwen (6460). It is a typical glacial trough with ice-shorn sides of bare rock in its upper parts but with a

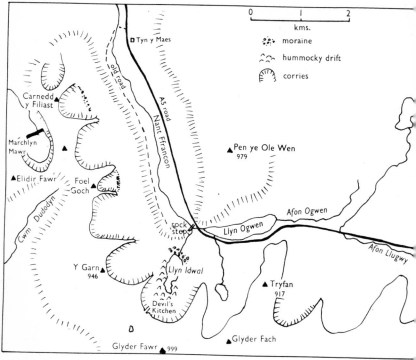

Nant Ffrancon and its associated glacial features

more gently sloping mantle of debris at the foot where the slope grades into the extremely flat valley floor. Considerable quantities of rock and other unconsolidated debris have accumulated on the floor of the Nant Ffrancon since the ice finally left the valley so that its present cross section is not that of the original U-shaped trough hewn out of solid rock. The rock base lies a considerable depth below the floor with the infill providing a complicated record of the sequence of events which have occurred over the past 20,000 years. Borings taken through the valley floor show that after the valley glacier had melted a stiff blue clay was laid down. This material was probably derived from the surrounding slopes which would still be subject to frost shattering and mass movement of surficial layers of debris under the extremely cold conditions which then prevailed. Above this layer there is a significant horizon of fine stoneless clay which could only have been laid down on the bed of a lake. This clay shows distinct layers or varves representing different types of deposits, fine and coarse, deposited at different seasons of the year. A double layer of material represents the accumulation of sediment on the lake bed in a single year and so by counting the varves it is possible to work out a time scale for the period when the lake covered the floor of the Nant Ffrancon in Late Glacial time. For the lake to exist at all, the lower end of the valley must have been blocked, most likely by ice pushing into this foothill zone of Snowdonia from the Irish Sea. The exact depth of the temporary lake is not known but it is perhaps significant that the former lake delta above Pentre Farm (6361) hangs well above the present valley floor, suggesting that at the time of its formation it was graded to a lake perhaps 30m deep. Throughout its life the Nant Ffrancon lake would be dependent on the lower end of the valley being impounded by the Irish Sea ice. In the absence of a rock threshold or morainic barrier here the retreat of the ice front would immediately lead to the draining of the lake. Time has not erased the valley features which are associated with the former lake basin so that it is still easy to visualise the Nant Ffrancon submerged under water just like many of the other Snowdonian valleys. Green pastures and darker patches of brown where rushes flourish on the waterlogged soils now dominate the scenery of the valley. Nevertheless it forms a tamed salient running into the barren mountainous topography of the heartland.

Much of the distinctive character of the Nant Ffrancon arises from its abrupt trough end formed by the great glacial rock step below Llyn Ogwen (6460). The step, about 70m high, with smoothed rock surfaces on its shoulder and plucked craggy slopes below, represents the finest glacial feature of the area. It is best seen from below near Blaen y Nant Farm (643608) especially after heavy rain when the Ogwen forms a sequence of cascading waterfalls. The rock step coincides with an outcrop of hard grit beds strengthened with a lava flow suggesting that the ice which once passed over it found difficulty in eroding these tough tenacious beds. In pre-glacial times the site of the present rock step might well have been a watershed col marking the then head of the Ogwen Valley (Fig. 3). On the other side of this watershed the drainage ran away to the east by the Llugwy Valley and ultimately linked up with the Conwy drainage system. Dury has suggested that these two valleys of the Ogwen and Llugwy nurtured their own separate glaciers which flowed in opposing directions. The glaciers would be fed continuously by snowfields in the corrie basins lining the flanks of both valleys. The Idwal corrie, lying to the east of the original watershed, would tend to feed the eastward flowing Llugwy glacier. This glacier would be plenteously supplied with additional flows from the main Glyder and Carneddau ridges and at

9 *The glacial trough of Nant Ffrancon with its abrupt trough end of the rock step and the steep slopes rising to Glyder Fawr above*

Capel Curig (7258) a particularly strong ice stream entered from the Snowdon area. At times this would be dominant over the Llugwy glacier and tend to prevent its eastward advance. When this happened the headwater corries like Idwal would accumulate snow and ice and it has been suggested that when this occurred there was a spilling over of the ice into the adjacent Ogwen Basin. This watershed breaching by ice only affected the uppermost layers and is termed glacial diffluence. The lower layers of the Idwal ice probably continued to flow eastwards using the Llugwy valley. Erosion of the pre-glacial col at the head of the Ogwen would proceed rapidly due to intense ice pressure although the hard grit beds would resist complete reduction. By the time the ice began to wane the pronounced rock step still remained and subsequent river erosion has been even less effective than ice in attacking the hard grit beds. Since the end of the Ice Age the Ogwen waterfalls have made little impression in cutting back into the rock step.

Another common occurrence associated with the process of glacial diffluence is the migration of the pre-glacial watershed to a new position. This has happened in the case of the opposing Ogwen and Llugwy drainage basins. As we have seen, it has been suggested that the original watershed lay approximately along the site of the Ogwen rock step where it formed a col between the adjacent peaks of Y Garn (6359) and Pen yr Ole Wen (6561). Today the watershed lies about 3 kilometres farther east so that Llyn Ogwen, a shallow rock basin only 3m deep, is now drained to the north whereas previously this section of the valley formed part of the headwater section of the Llugwy. The actual watershed at Pont Rhyd Goch is rather indeterminate so giving rise to a prominent through valley which Thomas Telford was able to use when he was seeking a route for his Holyhead road. Even since the end of the Ice Age there has been some re-adjustment of drainage in this area for the upper section of the Afon Llugwy, issuing from the corrie lake cut into the slopes below Carnedd Llewelyn (6962), starts its journey to the sea by heading for the upper Ogwen but then, close to the A5 road, makes an abrupt turn to the east. This pronounced elbow suggests river capture at a fairly recent date, probably shortly after the end of the Ice Age when masses of dead ice were still occupying the valley and providing temporary obstacles which later disappeared when climatic conditions became less severe. In such a continually changing situation small scale changes of drainage would be likely to occur and even today the drainage of the whole area is immature for, as yet, no properly integrated system has developed.

Anyone using the main road through the Nant Ffrancon as it makes its graded ascent from Bethesda to Ogwen cannot fail to be impressed by the succession of corries which lie high up on the western side of the valley. Each consists of a dark, cup-shaped hollow cut into the slopes of the Glyder range. Their presence is all the more striking since the opposing valley side is completely lacking in this distinctive glacial landform. Here bare crags and boulders perch precariously on the steep slopes so that it is clear that this side of the Nant Ffrancon also felt the full effects of glaciation but the fashioning stopped short of creating a suite of gigantic armchair hollows. The reason for the dissimilarity between the two valley sides is not hard to find. The north-east facing slopes, in the lee of the main Glyder ridge, would be more likely to retain snow for longer periods due to minimum insolation compared with their sunnier counterparts across the valley. If the prevailing winds during the Ice Age were from the south-westerly quarter as they are today (there is no firm evidence to the contrary) then snow would be carried up the exposed slopes on the western side of the ridge and then tend to accumulate in the shelter of high peaks like Foel Goch (6162), Mynedd Perfedd (623619) and

Carnedd y Filiast (621628), which all exceed 800m and are therefore likely to attract high precipitation. The snow on the lee of the slopes would first accumulate as patches in the small hollows but as it became thicker and compacted into ice it would become a potent eroding force, gradually enlarging the hollows into distinct basins. The exact mechanism for corrie formation is not precisely known though it is believed that the corrie ice tends to undergo a rotatory movement, grinding and gouging out the floor of the hollow as it does so. Eroded debris, from both the backwall and sides, acts as a powerful tool as the sole of the glacier bites even deeper into the rock. When the ice finally melts the overdeepening which has taken place is often reflected in the presence of a rock basin lake, like Llyn Idwal. Rock debris, once pushed by the snout of the glacier, now forms a terminal moraine or a spread of jumbled boulders. Individual corries, such as those which flank the Nant Ffrancon, all have a similar basic form but there are variations of shape, size and the extent to which their moraines have developed. All, however, have a common orientation facing north-east, perhaps the clearest indication of the important role of insolation in their origin and development.

Of the corries of the Glyder range only Marchlyn Mawr (6161) appears to be anomalous with its backwall facing north-north-west. There is no structural or other form of rock weakness which might account for the development of this corrie and we are therefore forced to seek an explanation involving the potency of erosive forces in this particular situation. In recent years it has become increasingly recognised that corrie growth, in some measure, reflects the form of the original landscape. Pre-existing hollows, particularly those with a continuous supply of snow, make ideal sites for corrie development as is shown by the armchair hollows bordering the Nant Ffrancon, as described above. In the case of Marchlyn Mawr, a pre-existing valley head lay along this northern flank of the Glyder Range and was gradually eating back in a southerly direction towards the head of another valley, the Cwm Dudodyn (6160). This latter valley, completely open to the south-west, acted as a funnel for snow to be carried up towards the crest ridge of the Glyders. While some of the snow would spill over onto the lee slope and accumulate in Cwm Perfedd, considerable quantities would tend to surmount the col lying between the prominent peaks of Elidir Fawr (6161) and Mynydd Perfedd (6261). Here, at the head of the Marchlyn valley, it would gradually etch out another great corrie basin, with its steep craggy backwall and sidewalls draped with morainic debris such as we see today.

The best known and most accessible of the corries of the area is that containing Llyn Idwal (6459). Not only is it easy to reach by the old pack-horse trail which makes a gradual, graded ascent from Ogwen Cottage but it is also possible to study the details of the corrie basin by walking around the lake shore. The lake level is at a height of only 374m making Cwm Idwal one of the lowest of the corrie basins of the area. In Late Glacial times it must have nurtured a considerable glacier which bit deeply into the predominately slate and shale beds at the entrance of the basin. Towards the backwall the slate beds give way to much tougher volcanic tuffs forming the well-known Idwal Slabs. The whole rock sequence has been gently folded and the backwall of the corrie displays this synclinal structure with great clarity. In the centre of the downfold is the great cleft of Twll Du or Devil's Kitchen through which it is possible to gain access to the ridge crest of the Glyder Range. From the top there is an impressive view over the whole corrie with the great bastion of Pen yr Ole Wen forming a backcloth. At the lower end of the lake the great morainic ridge of jumbled boulders stands out prominently while the hummocky drift forms prominent hillocks, particularly along the western edge of the lake. This same morainic debris also occurs on the floor of the lake and gives it a very irregular bottom form. The lake is not very

10   *Cwm Idwal, a corrie etched out of a downfold in the volcanic rocks of the Glyder Range*

deep, only 12.5m being recorded towards the western shore. The narrowing head towards the south is very shallow and this reflects the steady accumulation of sediment brought down by streams since the ice finally retreated from the area.

In the topography of the Llyn Idwal basin we have evidence of two stages of development. The main corrie basin was fashioned in Late Glacial times when an active and well-sustained corrie glacier occupied this north-east facing depression below one of the major cols of the Glyder range. It was at this time the basic elements were etched out, the glacier carving a rock basin at the lower end and then laying down a rim of morainic debris which has helped to impound the present lake. A gradual amelioration in the climate caused the melting of the glacier but a return to cold conditions about 8800 BC led to the small glaciers forming once again in the old corrie basins. This mini-glaciation only lasted about 500 years but in that short time the Idwal corrie glacier had succeeded in freshening the whole landscape through increased frost shattering on the rock slopes above and the deposition of hillocks of morainic debris at a lower level. When the ice finally melted the rock hollow was sufficiently deep for Llyn Idwal to develop and as it did so it partially submerged the hummocky drift laid down shortly before. Because of the relatively recent date of this mini-glaciation the morainic debris left behind and the craggy slopes cut in the volcanic beds still retain their fresh appearance. Until weathering and the general smoothing hand of erosion through landscape reduction have had sufficient time to obliterate the effects of the Ice Age the terrain will still retain the sharpness of form which characterises all recently glaciated regions, not the least this small area on the northern flanks of Snowdonia.

SUGGESTED ITINERARY

The slate quarrying settlement of Bethesda, founded in the early nineteenth century around the chapel from which it took its biblical name, makes a suitable starting point from which to explore the Nant Ffrancon valley and its neighbouring peaks. The first part of the excursion involves a walk southwards along the main A5 road as it climbs alongside the gorge of the Ogwen River with the towering spoil tips of the Penrhyn Slate Quarry dominating the opposite side of the valley. Just before Ty'n y Maes Motel is reached, take the turn to the right and follow the old road which hugs the west side of the Nant Ffrancon. Almost immediately the road crosses the Ogwen by a fine bridge constructed in 1790 by Lord Penrhyn. Below the bridge the river is entering its gorge section, threading its way through the great rock outcrops once smoothed by ice. The view upstream into the Nant Ffrancon is one of complete contrast for the flat glacial trough with steeply dipping sides immediately suggests a former lake basin. Until the recent dredging of the river and the building of embankments, the valley floor was subject to flooding so that the farms and road keep to the lower slopes and avoid the valley bottom. Three working farms now exist in the valley, taking hay from the bottom pastures and using the adjacent slopes of the Glyders for mountain sheep pasture. At Blaen y Nant Farm (6360) the road begins to climb the valley side in order to gain height to surmount the great rock step at the trough end of the Nant Ffrancon, ultimately reaching the main A5 road once again near Ogwen Cottage.

From Ogwen Cottage a well marked track leads up to the moraine lying across the lower end of Llyn Idwal. Skirting the western shore of the lake the fine hummocky drift forms associated with the mini-glaciation about 10,000 years ago can be seen. Also prominent is the downfold of the volcanic beds in the back wall of the Idwal corrie. By ascending this backwall through the gully of the Devil's Kitchen access can be gained to the main Glyder ridge in the vicinity of Llyn Cwm (6458). From this small lake the main track along the Glyder crest leads northwards over the successive peaks of Y Garn, Foel Goch, Mynedd Perfedd. The ridge top route gives fine views down into the succession of corrie basins with their steep drop to the flat floor of the Nant Ffrancon trough. At the end of the ridge, near Carnedd y Filiast, (6262) the route leads down the steep side wall of Marchlyn Mawr corrie and then on by an easy route back to Bethesda through the crofting settlement of Mynedd Llandegai (6065) where workers in the Penrhyn quarry were once given smallholdings to supplement their income.

3. Tremadog and Portmadog

EARLY NINETEENTH-CENTURY TOWN PLANNING

Man's role as a creative force in landscape design is clearly seen in the development of towns. Even in a rather inhospitable region such as Snowdonia new towns, planted in a virgin countryside, are by no means uncommon. The need for defence, for example, led to the founding of the Roman fortress town of Segontium near present-day Caernarfon and in later centuries the ring of Edwardian castle towns. Tremadog is unique in that it represents the fulfilment of a life-long ambition of one man, William Madocks, Member of Parliament for Boston, but of a Denbighshire family. From an early age he had a vision of improving this corner of South Caernarfonshire. Tremadog and, to a lesser extent, Portmadog were the result of his grandiose plan, a plan which involved land reclamation, road building, harbour works, the introduction of rural industry as well as providing the means by which the Ffestiniog slate quarries could expand and export their products to all parts of the world. He himself wrote 'I employ my mind incessantly in thinking how to compass those important objects necessary to complete the system of improvement in Snowdonia. If I can only give birth, shape and substance before I die, they will work their own way to posterity'. The present landscape with its surviving forms provides adequate proof of the extent of his success.

The natural setting of the area was by no means helpful to Madocks' ambitions. Two shallow arms of the sea, Traeth Mawr and Traeth Bach, penetrated deeply into the mountainous fringes of Snowdonia. Before Madocks set to work, the approach route into the Lleyn Peninsula involved a long and circuitous journey round the head of the estuary through Aberglaslyn (5946), the original mouth of the fast-flowing Glaslyn river. The idea of reclaiming the Glaslyn sand flats by building an embankment to exclude the ebb and flow of the tide had been raised on numerous occasions but all the early schemes foundered on the question of cost. Piecemeal reclamation around the margins of the Traeth had been attempted by landowners whose holdings ran down to the shores of the estuary. They were all on a small scale and never formed part of an overall plan. From the outset, Madocks thought big and planned accordingly and even though this ultimately brought him to the verge of bankruptcy, he largely succeeded where others had failed.

His interest in the area took root in the closing years of the eighteenth century in an age when it was still fashionable for the country gentleman to attempt to improve the natural landscape. From his small house near Dolgellau he often visited the Glaslyn area and mused on its possibilities. His opportunity came in 1798 when he was able to buy some small farms near Penmorfa (5440), a hamlet close to the head of the western arm of the Glaslyn estuary. One of the holdings he acquired was Ynys Fadog, an islet set in the sands of the estuary and traditionally the point from where the Welsh Prince Madog set sail for the New World. It was here that William Madocks attempted his first reclamation. He brought in an engineer, James Creassy, who had considerable experience of similar works in the Fens of Lincolnshire. In 1800 an earth embankment was thrown across the inlet, 200 men being brought in to carry out the work. Altogether about 500 hectares of marsh and tidal sands were reclaimed and converted into good grazing ground. Pig rearing was started, a rope walk laid out and paving stones exported from a nearby quarry.

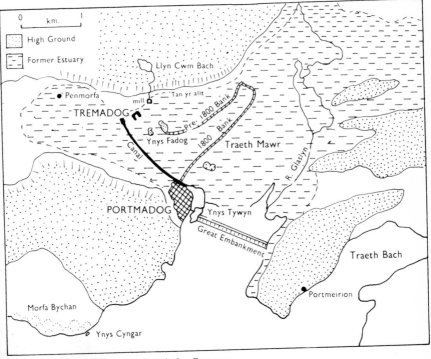

Madocks' scheme for reclaiming the Glaslyn Estuary

It was at this time that Madocks began to alter one of the cottages he had acquired when he bought his holding. It lay high above the newly reclaimed land under a steep cliff so that the name he gave it, Tan-yr-allt (under a wooded cliff) was singularly appropriate. This became his principal residence where he subsequently entertained his guests and distinguished visitors who came to see his schemes of improvement. A new gently pitched roof of slate, brought from the Penrhyn quarries on the other side of Snowdonia, gave Tan-yr-allt a very distinctive appearance and initiated a style of architecture that was to be followed in many of the other buildings of the neighbourhood. Woodland was cleared and a garden laid out to give an unimpeded view to the south, an open aspect which the house still retains. It was from Tan-yr-allt that Madocks engineered his more ambitious scheme for closing off the whole of the Glaslyn Estuary. Before attempting this, however, he began the second stage of his grand design, the laying out of the town of Tremadog on land which he had already reclaimed.

The site chosen lay a little distance from Tan-yr-allt and was dominated by the towering crags of a sheer rock face to the north. Along the foot of this cliff the main road ran westwards into the Lleyn Peninsula and so a new town here was strategically placed as a staging post of a main route to Ireland using Port Dinllaen (2741). (In the early years of the nineteenth century this was a distinct possibility, for Telford had yet to build his finely graded road through the mountains of Snowdonia—the present A5—which in time led to the choice of Holyhead as the Irish packet station and not Port Dinllaen). If the Glaslyn estuary was reclaimed this would considerably strengthen the claims of a route from London, through Worcester, Welshpool, Bala, Tremadog and thence on to Port Dinllaen. Madocks was so convinced that this would become the main route to Ireland that he named one of the main thoroughfares of his town, Dublin Street. A T-shaped plan was adopted with the top of the T forming part of the Dinllaen turnpike road. It was here that Madocks built his coaching inn, town hall and market house. These looked out onto a square which formed the market place. Around this open plan, Madocks arranged houses, shops and some smaller inns. Running southwards lay London Street, the present main road to Portmadog, which at that time did not exist. It was here that provision was made both for a church and a chapel. The church was sited on a low rocky knoll while the chapel lay on the opposite side of the road. The whole layout was extremely simple and, apart from a new housing development, it has survived almost

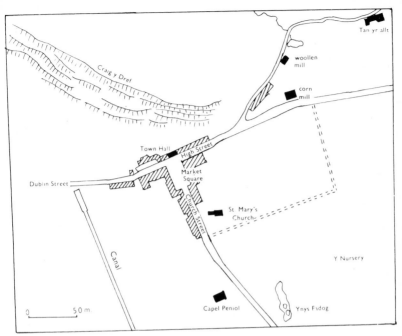

Plan of Madocks' new town of Tremadog

untouched to the present day. It is thus an outstanding example of early nineteenth-century town planning, the initiative of one man who was able to give substance to his ideas. Although Madocks had many friends in London, few were willing to invest capital in such a remote region and so the bulk of the money for building the town came from Madock's own pocket.

Building began in 1805 with a group of houses known as Pentre Gwaelod along the road which ran under the steep cliff face. The centre-piece of the town, the Town Hall and Market Hall forming a single unit, came later in 1807. Its classical design, with pillars dominating the ground floor market area, was very much in keeping with the renaissance style that was fashionable at that time. Above the open arcade lay a long room, variously known as the Town Hall or Dining Room. At first the only access was from the Madocks Arms Hotel next door so that it was kept entirely separate from the market below. The whole building was meant to symbolise the dual function of the town, with commerce and trade on the one hand and social life in congenial surroundings on the other. Within a year of the building of the Town Hall plays were being presented here under the auspices of the *Theatre Tre-Madoc*. Together with the church and chapel it played a major part in establishing a closely knit urban community. The church was begun in 1806, Madocks once again providing the money for what a contemporary observer called 'a handsome small church, in the later style of English architecture, with a lofty spire which forms an interesting object to be seen from the coast'. The dedication was to St Mary and the fact that the services were in English is an indication of the anglicized nature of the new town. As a building, the Nonconformist Chapel, built between 1807 and 1810 in the classical style with a portico, adopted a more imposing and ambitious design.

If the town was to have any real meaning other than as a showpiece or practical expression of Madocks' idealised views on the improvement of the landscape, industry and commerce had to be generated to give employment. Madocks was keenly aware that the town could not hope to exist in an economic vacuum and therefore one of his first tasks was to build a woollen mill. It was sited just outside the town on the lane up to Tan-yr-allt. Being built on sloping ground, the entrance was placed at the back and ran into the middle of the five floors. It was perhaps the earliest woollen mill in Wales to be based on a factory system rather than a cottage industry principle. Another outstanding feature was the use of water to drive the machinery. For this purpose water was diverted from Llyn Cwm Bach, high up on the

11   The Town Hall, theatre and hotel forming one side of the Market Place at Tremadog

crags above, and led to a small reservoir 50m above the factory. The head of water was sufficient to power two engines which Madocks had brought in from England. The woollen mill was completed by July 1805 and so that it would merge with the bare rocky crags behind, it was painted a dull olive colour. This attention to detail was typical of the care which Madocks lavished on his town. Local wool was available in abundance from the sheep farms of Snowdonia and it was not long before the mill was exporting considerable quantities of cloth to London. Use was made of ships which were already carrying slate to the metropolis from the quarries around Ffestiniog. Although Madocks was forced to sell his factory as a going concern in 1810 to raise capital for building his great embankment, he could at least take credit for establishing an enterprise based on local resources. As well as the woollen manufactory, there was also an ancillary fulling mill and rather surprisingly, a corn mill. Today the mill stands idle, a monument in stone lying beside the laundry. With its typical flat roof outline it is a building ripe for preservation.

The other commercial enterprise built to promote trade was the canal. This ran in two straight lines from a point on the Glaslyn estuary just north of the present bridge in Portmadog. It was already partly in being as a drainage ditch so that it was only necessary to deepen and widen it to establish a water link which Madocks thought essential for trade in this inland town. At the head of the canal, behind the houses on the west side of the Market Place, a basin was dug to allow ships to load or unload their cargoes. This has now disappeared under the new housing estate but the canal still exists in part. Madocks thought of both the canal and its basin in the town as a thing of beauty and his friends were always taken to see his boat which he had permanently moored within sight of the town.

The creation of a nursery was yet another example of Madocks' role as an improver. This lay on the east side of the town beyond the church. Apart from the dominant oak and beech this was stocked with Scots pine, larch and other conifers. The young trees were later planted in various parts of his estate, especially crowning rocky knolls or as shelter belts around farmsteads and other buildings out on the exposed marsh. Like so many of Madocks' schemes the nursery survives as a glade with pleasant walks, the whole area dominated by the rock knoll of Ynys Fadog, the name of which Madocks adopted for his new town.

The building of the great embankment to seal off the Glaslyn estuary undoubtedly represents the most difficult and biggest undertaking of Madocks. Although his earthen bank of 1800 was looked upon as a trial in reclamation techniques, the proposed new bank was in a much more vulnerable position and therefore meant a much stronger and more costly structure. The line chosen was from the islet of Ynys Tywyn—near the present terminus of the Ffestiniog Railway—across the estuary mouth to the rocky bluff on the opposite shore, a distance of just over a kilometre. Work began early in 1808 with rock obtained from local quarries and it was built out simultaneously from the two opposing shores. Considerable quantities of stone were needed for the embankment which was 4m wide on top and raised 6m above the sands of the estuary. Before the two arms could be finally joined it was necessary to divert the Glaslyn River from its mid-estuary course. The diversion took the form of an artificial cut through the solid rock of Ynys Tywyn, with sluice gates to control the river flow. After three years of effort the gap was finally sealed in July 1811 and the embankment completed. Six months later, in February 1812, a combination of high spring tides and an onshore gale breached the bank. Although the gap was sealed by the summer, the extra expense involved ate into Madocks' meagre financial reserves and left him virtually bankrupt. He was, thereafter, never really in a position to exploit fully the results of his labours.

The diversion of the Glaslyn to an exit at the western end of the embankment led to the scouring out of a good harbour alongside the rocky isle of Ynys Tywyn. Thus began Portmadog, for which a harbour act was obtained in 1824. A new quay was built and rented to Samuel Holland who owned one of the slate quarries high up in the mountains near Ffestiniog. The development of the slate trade through Portmadog represents the final phase of the Madocks enterprise. Various schemes were tried to bring the slate to the port before it was finally decided to build a narrow gauge tramway, the present Ffestiniog Railway, in 1836. By this time Madocks was dead and therefore was not able to see the slate trains crossing his embankment to unload their cargoes into the holds of waiting vessels at Portmadog. Transport costs were reduced from 15 shillings to 5 shillings a ton and this enabled the Ffestiniog slate to compete effectively with that obtained from the quarries on the other side of Snowdonia, at places like Llanberis and Bethesda. A measure of the success of the new railway is provided by production figures for slate which rose from 18,113 tons in 1835 to 89,294 tons in 1865.

It was largely as a result of the slate trade that Portmadog grew steadily in the middle decades of the nineteenth century. Its population rose from 885 in 1821 to 3,059 in 1861. Although Madocks could not claim to have founded the port in the same way as he created Tremadog, it is clear that without his embankment Portmadog could hardly have grown up on its present site. Unfortunately without his controlling influence the port lacked the planning and architectural unity of Tremadog. Streets of terraced houses were quickly built running back from the axial High Street, a type of development which was so common in the industrial towns of northern England at that time. The key to the commercial success of the port lay in the harbour which Madocks had built in 1825 at an estimated cost of £1,200. In a single year it was estimated that over a thousand vessels used the harbour, vessels mainly engaged in the export of slate. In the peak year of 1873 over 116,000 tons of slate left the port for all parts of the world. By this time a new factor had begun to enter into the fortunes of the slate trade for in October 1867 the Cambrian Railway had reached Portmadog. This offered an alternative means of exporting the slate to the growing industrial towns of England and by 1900 approximately equal quantities of slate left the area by rail and sea. In the present century the railway gradually assumed dominance so that today the former slate quays have disappeared. The leisure industry has already taken over part of the harbour area, with the South Snowdon Development Company having built holiday flatlets on the site of one of the former slate quays.

The recent harbour development stands out in great contrast to the appearance of the old town where much remains dating from the heyday of the slate trade. Substantial chapels were quickly built like the Congregational Salem dating from 1827, the Wesleyan Ebeneezer from 1840, the Baptist Seion and the Methodist Moriah in 1845. Perhaps it is a commentary on the social history of the town in its early formative years that it was not until 1875 that the established church built St John's. Although the standard of architecture varied considerably, the chapels of Portmadog form the only buildings of note in the town. The most pleasing quarter is undoubtedly the square known as Cornhill, close to the west side of the harbour. Here four-storyed warehouses stand cheek by jowl with low terrace houses and have achieved an effect which perhaps more careful planning might have ruined. In some ways the open aspect of the site overlooking the harbour recalls the Market Place of Tremadog.

For the most part Tremadog and Portmadog are very distinct urban entities. But as Portmadog grew, so Madocks' inland town became more fossilised. When the Cambrian Railway entered the area in

1867 it chose Portmadog rather than Tremadog for its route towards Pwllheli. This undoubtedly conferred considerable advantages on the port and gradually the difference between the two towns became more accentuated. It is easy to appreciate these differences at the present time for while Portmadog is a thriving and bustling town, especially in summer when it is crowded with visitors, Tremadog retains its quiet charm and sober appearance, more of an early nineteenth-century showpiece than a centre of commerce. Whether this would have pleased William Madocks, visionary and entrepreneur, is difficult to tell. It remains, however, a fitting and lasting monument to this early nineteenth-century 'improver'. Perhaps in some small way its mere presence in this isolated corner of North Wales impressed Clough Williams Ellis when he conceived his Italianate cliff village of Portmeirion, only a few kilometres away across the reclaimed land of the Glaslyn Estuary.

SUGGESTED ITINERARY

The achievements of William Madocks as a landscape improver can best be appreciated by studying both Tremadog and Portmadog and the countryside around. A walk through Tremadog can begin in the area of the Market Place where it is possible to appreciate the whole layout of the town. From there the road to the east leads towards Tan-yr-allt and it was on the lane to the house that Madocks established his woollen mill. The building survives, as well as the water power supply. From Tremadog the road southwards towards Portmadog runs alongside the nursery and then across the now defunct canal. Portmadog is entered at one end of the High Street, the commercial centre of the town and housing some of the mid-nineteenth-century chapels. At the eastern end lies the harbour as well as the spacious square of Cornhill. Crossing the bridge onto the islet of Ynys Tywyn, the famous embankment stretches across the Glaslyn Estuary. Much of the island beyond the Ffestiniog Railway terminus is developed with holiday flats which occupy the site of one of the former slate quays. Across the road a track leads around the rocky outcrop of Ynys Tywyn and then onto the secondary embankment of Llyn Bach. A walk along here brings one into the small industrial quarter of Portmadog with its slate works and former corn mill, now a craft centre. The circuit of Portmadog can be completed by passing down one of the many streets of terraced houses back to the High Street.

4. The sand dunes of Aberffraw, Anglesey

The coast of south-west Anglesey, between the entrance to the Menai Strait and the coastal resorts of Rhosneigr and Trearddur Bay, is made up of a succession of sandy bays set between low but prominent headlands. The promontories are made of rocks which resist the full onslaught of waves driven onto this coast by the prevailing south-westerly winds. These hard rocks include conglomerates and grits, such as are found at Rhosneigr and a tough, micaceous gneiss which outcrops along the coastline near Porth Nobla (3371). In contrast, the intervening embayments have been fashioned out of softer rock. The Malltraeth estuary, for example, coincides with a coarse, though relatively soft, sandstone of the Millstone Grit formation. Originally the coastline must have been much more irregular than it is at present but the steady infilling of the bays with sand and the subsequent growth of the extensive dune belts behind the beach, have led to a gradual smoothing of the shoreline plan.

The orientation of this section of the Anglesey coastline, lying as it does almost at right angles to the prevailing south-westerly winds, has been a major factor in determining its characteristic features. Waves approaching directly onshore have etched out the bays in softer rocks and then brought in the sediment to partially fill them. As a result of this twofold process, wide bay-head beaches of sand are characteristic of this shoreline. Each is gently shelving, the width at Aberffraw (3568) approaching half a kilometre at low water. The sandy foreshore ends when the enclosing headlands are reached and in its place there are rock girt cliffs and off-lying reefs. It is this variation of wide sandy beaches, bold cliffs, rugged inter-tidal rocks and pools and jagged reefs offshore which makes the coastline so scenically attractive. With the backing of extensive dune belts at Newborough and Aberffraw and the occasional and unsuspected lakes like Llyn Coron (3870), the varied coastal setting is complete.

At Aberffraw the extensive dune complex still remains in its natural state and forms part of the Bodorgan Estate. It is crossed by the main coastal road (A4080) and also by the minor road from Aberffraw to Bodorgan. Though fully accessible and very much used for recreation, it is basically in its natural state, though sand pits have been dug in one or two places near the road. The dune area extends inland for about three kilometres and averages about one kilometre in width. At the time of the last major rise of sea level, about 4000–3500 BC the coast here must have been dominated by the penetrating estuary of the Afon Ffraw. The sand dune complex which we see today, began to develop shortly after this. One of the first changes to occur was an adjustment to the original drainage. Partial blockage by sand dune belts has confined the Afon Ffraw to the extreme western edge of its former wide estuary, while its tributary, the Afon Frechwen, has undergone a complete reversal of drainage. Although rising within a short distance from the coast the Frechwen stream now flows inland to join the main river.

The nearby Llyn Coron also owes its existence to the blocking of the former estuary by sand dunes. It has a maximum depth of just over 4m and is therefore only a shallow depression in the former valley floor. The ponding back of a lake here and in similar situations elsewhere, for example Llyn Maelog (3272) and Llyn Traffwll (3276), is a pointer to the antiquity of the dune system along this part of the Anglesey coast.

The sand complex at Aberffraw is dominated by four irregular belts of parabolic dunes. The oldest lies furthest inland and forms a set of broken, eroded hillocks which no longer receive sufficient supplies of sand to maintain their distinct parabolic shape. The dunes lie mainly to the north of the main coastal road (A4080). The second belt of dunes has the form of three major parabolic structures although in detail there are many minor indentations. Within the main dune parabolae, damp dune slacks are common. There is much bare sand exposed on their windward sides where the effects of sand blast are most severe. As individual dune crests exceed 10m in places this second dune belt forms a distinctive topographic feature. Sand is highly mobile where unprotected by vegetation and tends to be carried over the dune crest; in time this leads to a steady advance of the dune front inland. The greatest degree of change occurs in the next dune belt lying about a kilometre inland from the coast. It lies entirely on the seaward side of the minor road which runs from Aberffraw to the Bodorgan Estate. There are no fewer than six well developed dune parabolae in this compact ridge. Their short tails are very exposed to erosion as they face an open stretch of links which make them subject to the full force of the south-westerly winds. Great convex masses of sand are slowly advancing inland as material is carried over the top of the ridge or through low cols. On its eastern side this dune belt merges with a complex area of parabolic dunes,

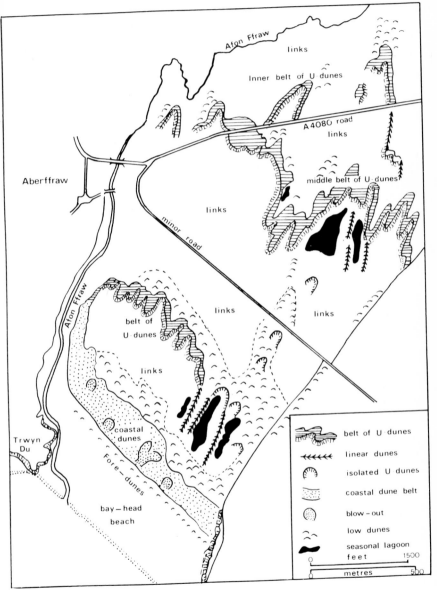

The Aberffraw dune complex

linear ridges, damp slacks and even occasional rock outcrops.

The Aberffraw dune complex is completed by a series of irregular dune forms lying immediately behind the beach. Their crests top 10m in places but in between there are great hollows as blow-outs have developed, often extending down to the level of the water table. This is particularly true of the central section where changes are noticeable from season to season. High seas associated with winter storm conditions often pare back the face of this outer dune belt. In more quiescent periods a low belt of fore-dunes can form, often as a result of the previous deposition of masses of seaweed which act as an obstruction for the blowing sand. Although colonized by sand-loving vegetation, the fore-dunes can only be looked upon as an ephemeral feature as they seldom survive the succeeding winter's storms.

Between the various dune belts, the Aberffraw Warren is characterised by flat, rather featureless areas for which the name *links* seems most appropriate. Small patches of dunes occur at intervals but they only form low mounds when set against the height of the main dune ridges. Occasionally the links are crossed by long linear ridges which represent the tails of the dune parabolae, left behind as the main part of the nose moves inland. Their slopes are steep, as much as 30° in places and they have very narrow crests. Bare sand is quite common, especially on the side facing the dominant winds. The other remaining features of the Aberffraw Warren are the slacks which occur between the dune lines. During the winter months they often contain water so that they appear as miniature lagoons. In the succeeding summer they dry out, although the dampish hollow is still characterised by distinctive vegetation.

Any dune area, unless completely covered by vegetation, will be liable to change. Aberffraw Warren is no exception and it is therefore possible to study the effect of sand movement and developing dune structures. As has been noted above, the greatest advance in recent years has been along the line of the first of the inland dune belts. Great bulbous spreads of loose sand are steadily moving inland across open links in the direction of the minor Aberffraw-Bodorgan road. In the past three years movements of up to 6m a year have been recorded. The other dune belts are also active, though not to the same extent. From time to time the main road (A4080) is covered by blown sand, although the bare faces of the sand pits are often partly responsible. Here, as elsewhere throughout the Aberffraw dunes, the considerable influx of summer visitors has led to some erosion, particularly along tracks which lead to the beach. Man's influence must not be overemphasised, however, for great changes take place even where his effect is minimal.

The orientation and shape of an individual dune parabola is in direct response to the dominant direction of the wind. Measurements made with a prismatic compass show that the long axis of the sand dunes lies between 25° and 35° True North. For the linear ridge dunes their direction only varied within narrow limits of 28° to 30° True North. These measurements can be compared with wind data based on observations at Valley airfield, only a few kilometres away to the west. Calculations based on wind speed and direction show that the main approach of the wind on this part of the Anglesey coast over a thirty-year period is from a point 30° west of south. This is so close to the measured value of the axis of the parabolic dunes and the line of the linear dunes that it suggests that wind is the sole process involved in creating their distinctive form. There is also evidence that the two dune forms are directly related, one being the sequential development from the other. It is now generally recognised that the parabolic or U-shaped dune develops first, at a time when there is a plentiful supply of sand and when the vegetation cover is incomplete. The part of the parabola most likely to change is its nose which can push steadily forward. As the flanking ridges of the parabola become more stable through colonisation, the supply of sand to the nose falls off and in time it can become completely breached. Two convergent ridges of sand are thus formed and these can develop into a system of parallel ridges which follow the direction of the dominant wind. At Aberffraw the sequence of change is not complete so that the U-shape dunes still co-exist with the linear dune forms.

Contrary to what is generally believed, the greatest changes in the dune landscape often take place in the spring and autumn rather than in the winter months. Sand movement is most marked at these seasons, largely because the surface layers are relatively dry and easily disturbed by winds with speeds in excess of 20 knots. While gales are more likely to occur during the winter, the surface sand is usually damp and therefore less easily disturbed. The fact that most of the dune vegetation is perennial also means that there is little difference in the plant cover at the various seasons. As most of the gale force winds on this exposed coast of Anglesey are from the south-west and are usually associated with the passage of a frontal system, this means that they are often preceded or accompanied with a period of heavy rain. These have the effect of wetting the exposed sand surface and thus making them much more stable than otherwise would be the case. In spring and autumn the degree of drying out of the superficial sand layers is much greater and therefore the rate of sand movement is correspondingly higher.

Vegetation of the dunes

Over the greater part of Aberffraw Warren there is an almost complete plant cover. It is dominated by marram grass which covers all the dune forms except those which develop from time to time on the upper part of the beach. As marram grass can only tolerate about 2 per cent salt, it cannot survive periodic inundation here on the upper beach. The marram flourishes best under conditions of sand mobility when fresh supplies are continually available. It can withstand burial to depths of half a metre because of its strong rhizomes which allow it to grow through new sand with considerable vigour. Under these conditions it has lush green leaves which stand out in contrast to the withered brown of the marram on the old fixed dunes. In part this change in appearance of the marram is due to the leaching which takes place in the surface sand unless minerals are constantly being replenished. The main function of the marram is dune fixation which it does with varying degrees of success. However, the steep slopes of blow-outs or exposed wind-blasted faces of parabolic dunes are usually too hostile a habitat for even marram to succeed.

The other dune plants also reflect the very dry sandy habitat and many are true xerophytes. The sea spurge, with its light green fleshy leaves and erect stature, is very common at Aberffraw. Like marram it can survive and flourish on mobile sand by means of its deep roots. The equally distinctive sea holly, though not as common, does occur in a number of patches landward on the coastal dunes. It has a characteristic blue-green foliage with stiff leathery leaves covered with a waxy cuticle to reduce transpiration to a minimum. Another common dune plant and one of the earliest colonisers of bare sand is the sand sedge. With its long creeping root system it often gives rise to straight lines of young plants on the virgin sand of a recently formed blow-out.

The belt of low fore-dunes of the upper beach has a restricted variety of plants. Only those which can withstand periodic immersion in salt water, the true halophytes, can hope to survive here. At Aberffraw the dominant halophytes are the prickly saltwort and the sea rocket. They are the first colonisers of the low sandy hummocks which tend to accumulate around piles of seaweed brought in during the winter storms. Being annuals they cannot hope to survive the winter months and therefore play no real part in the establishment of a permanent dune ridge.

The rather flat and featureless links, between the major dune ridges, contain the greatest variety of plants. Throughout the summer months the area is covered with a colourful carpet dominated by the purple of thyme and the yellow of bedstraw. Other common plants are heartsease, dog violet, hare's foot clover and the occasional group of pyramidal orchid, sea centaury and ragwort. Associated with the scented thyme is the semi-parasite, eyebright. Throughout the links the water table is never far below the surface and therefore in this west coast environment there are a large number of different varieties of mosses. In recent years a few shrubs of sea buckthorn, much more typical of the East Coast of England dune belts, have established themselves in front of the first parabolic dune ridge.

The other distinctive habitat on the Aberffraw Warren is the wet slack. In winter months these are often occupied by long shallow lakes but by April these have dried out. The dominant plant here is the creeping willow which can survive total immersion during the winter months. As the water disappears during the summer the willow, with its semi-prostrate stem, covers almost the entire floor. In spring the plant is covered with numerous cylindrical catkins which appear at the same time as the leaf burst but as the year advances these are replaced by the equally distinctive silky grey fruits. Although the creeping willow is most characteristic of the damp slacks it can extend onto the lower margins of the neighbouring dunes. Associated plants include silverweed, pyramidal orchid, centaury, thistle and eyebright which appear on the floors of the dried-out slacks in the summer. If blown sand from the neighbouring dunes invades the slack the damp-loving vegetation is replaced by the ubiquitous marram and sand sedge. Such a development is part of a continuous cycle of change which is always taking place in this dynamic environment.

SUGGESTED ITINERARY

A traverse of the dune belt can be made starting from the shore of Aberffraw Bay and then proceeding inland across the successive dune belts until the impounded Llyn Coron is reached. Each part of the dune system has its distinctive features, both in the form of the individual dunes, and the associated vegetation which reflects the varied habitats of the whole complex. The nearby village of Aberffraw is interesting, for although only of a small size it has the layout of a town, but perhaps this is not surprising when it is recalled that it once was the 'capital' of the Princes of Gwynedd.

5. The copper mines of Parys Mountain

From a distance Parys Mountain has a similar appearance to many other hills which rise so abruptly out of the lowlands of Anglesey. A closer view, however, suggests otherwise for the hill is covered with vast spoil heaps and its interior is honeycombed with former mine workings. Virtually the whole of its centre has been removed in one large open excavation which presents a multitude of coloured rocks to the sky. A walk over Parys Mountain gives convincing proof that in its heyday, here was the site of the largest and richest copper mine in Europe. As early as the eighteenth century it excited the curiosity of visitors like Richard Pennant and the Reverend William Bingley who came here when mining was in full swing. Bingley, in particular, has left a vivid account of the mining activities which he saw in the summer of 1798. Admittedly his account contains the exaggerated style which characterised the writings of that period when, for the first time, the delights of the wilder and more remote parts of the country were being discovered.

On the morning of my arrival, I walked up to this celebrated place. Having ascended to the top, I found myself standing on the verge of a vast and tremendous cavern. I stepped on one of the stages suspended over the edge of the steep, and the prospect was dreadful. The number of caverns at different heights along the sides; the broken and irregular masses of rock which everywhere presented themselves; the multitudes of men at work in different parts, and apparently in the most perilous situations; the motion of the whimsies and the raising and lowering of the buckets to draw out the ore and the rubbish; the noise of picking the ore from the rock with at intervals, the roar of the blasts in the distant parts of the mine, altogether excited the most sublime ideas, intermixed however, with sensations of terror. The shagged arches, and the overhanging rocks which seemed to threaten annihilation to anyone daring enough to approach them, fixed me almost motionless to the spot.

Half a century earlier Parys Mountain had been a deserted hill top covered with stunted trees and low scrub. The immense wealth under its surface was, as yet, hidden even though the presence of some copper had been known for some considerable time. There is even the intriguing possibility that prehistoric man actually used some of the copper ore for his hammer stones and querns, features of Celtic mining, have been found on the northern slopes. Evidence of Roman mining is more convincing, in that copper cakes, with a distinctive marking, have been found in various parts of Anglesey. Two large cakes, for example, have turned up near Trysglwyn Farm (439896) at the western end of Parys Mountain. After this initial interest in the copper deposits, activity largely ceased until the middle of the eighteenth century when the Macclesfield firm of Roe and Company began prospecting in 1764. Three trenches were dug across the mountain in a north to south line and the result was the discovery of good quality ore close to the surface. This was part of the Great Lode on which the future prosperity of copper mining was to be based during the next hundred years.

12   *Parys Mountain copper mine where the whole interior of the hill was gouged out in the search for the rich ores*

The geology of Parys Mountain is complex in that both sedimentary and igneous rocks outcrop at the surface. In general they follow a west-south-west to east-north-east axis. Shale beds, sometimes green in colour, occur on both the north and south flanks while in between there is a dividing dyke or sill of a much altered rock called felsite. Mineralisation has been most marked in this rock and extends over an area measuring approximately 1500m by 500m. In addition to the copper veins found in the felsite, there is another black, cherty rock called 'bluestone' which contains deposits of lead, zinc and copper. Some of the richest copper, however, has come from the main quartz vein of Carreg y doll.

The excitement which followed the discovery of rich copper deposits in 1768 was the signal for large scale mining operations to begin. By the standards of the time it was a massive industrial enterprise. Inevitably there was some initial wrangling over the ownership of land which overnight had become so valuable but when this was resolved two mining companies were left to exploit the vast copper deposits. The western part of the hill was under the control of the Parys Mine Company founded in 1778. After the lease of Roe and Company ran out in 1785 the Earl of Uxbridge formed his own company, the Old Mona Mine Company and this concentrated mainly on the eastern side of the hill. Both underground and opencast mining were practised by each of the companies so that the maximum

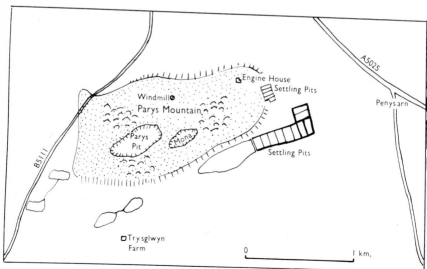

Parys Mountain copper mines, with surviving features

output could be achieved in the minimum of time. Due to the heavy demand for copper as a sheath on the hulls of British warships as well as a host of domestic uses, even lean copper ores, with a metal content of less than 5 per cent, were worked.

Contemporary accounts give a clear picture of mining methods in use at the time and even paintings portray the dangers facing the miners in the great opencast pits. The men were let down into the pit on a rope and set charges into the vertical face of the rock to blast it away. The rock was then loaded into buckets (kibbles) and hauled to the top by means of a windlass or whimsy. Two men or horses turned the whimsy which was so arranged that it raised and lowered a bucket simultaneously. From time to time great falls of rock occurred like the one in 1790, when, after heavy rain a large part of the pit collapsed. As the better ores became exhausted many of the supporting pillars of the underground galleries were removed and this too, brought about a collapse of great areas. In time the massive pit which we see today on the western side of the hill was excavated.

After the ore was brought to the surface it was broken up by teams of women and boys—the copper ladies—into pieces the size of a walnut. It was then bagged and carried in farm carts to the smelting works built on the coast at Amlwch (4493). Local farmers were engaged initially, receiving a handsome payment of 3d a bag but as they tended to be missing at harvest time the transporting of the ore was later regularised and passed into the hands of William Hughes.

Another method of producing copper was by precipitation from the waters which drained out of the mine workings and collected in the bottom of the opencast pits. Settling tanks were built here and at many other places around the hill to collect the rich waters whose value was assessed at 1½d a quart. Iron was placed in the bottom of the settling tanks and this led to the precipitation of the copper. In time the residue contained 20 –30 per cent copper and in this state it was dug out, dried and then carted to the smelter. The precipitation tanks are one of the features which have survived to the present day, both in the Great Opencast Pit as well as along the south-eastern fringes of the hill.

Full records of production during the first decades of mining were not kept and it is only from the size of the profits that it is possible to gain some idea of the prosperity of the great mining undertaking which had taken over the whole of Parys Mountain. Mona Mine, for example, is estimated to have produced copper ore worth £24,000 a year while Parys Mine had an output which probably approached

£50,000 in value. From 1773 to 1785 the annual production of copper ore was of the order of 3,000 tons. Output and profitability rose steadily at the Mona Mine in the years before 1785 but when the lease of Roe and Company ran out, there was a considerable drop in production until the new company could establish itself. By 1793, with new capital investment at last beginning to show dividends, the profits reached as much as £16,905. This achievement was largely the result of the efforts of one man, Thomas Williams, the son of an Anglesey farmer who in 1778 had taken over the Parys Mining Company and after 1785 was virtually running the Mona Mining Company as well. Williams was the sort of industrial entrepreneur who arrived on the scene at a crucial phase in the mining development and who, with resourcefulness, foresight and a measure of good luck, succeeded where lesser men would have failed. It was during the last decade of the eighteenth century that, under his guidance, the copper mines and pits of Parys Mountain achieved their greatest production. Thereafter, as the more accessible ores were worked out, the industry entered a phase of decline. Well over a thousand men were employed in 1798 but ten years later this had dropped to a mere 122.

In 1811 an attempt was made to revive the industry by bringing in the Cornishman, James Treweek, as manager. The move was a bold one in that Treweek was able to bring his expertise on deep mining techniques to the flagging Anglesey industry. Cornish engines, in their distinctive housings, now began to appear on all sides of the hill, a scene quite reminiscent of the tin mining landscapes of the Penwith Peninsula. Output of ore from the Mona Mine rose from 383 tons in 1812 to over 9,000 tons a year between 1822 and 1826. The Company was now making a profit of 12 shillings on every ton of ore raised but this high water mark of prosperity was not to last long for, with a fall in copper prices, the profitability decreased. Although there was some recovery subsequently the previous level was never again reached. By the time that the Reverend Bingley produced a new edition of his *Tour through North Wales* in 1839 he could only observe that 'the mines are but a wreck of what they formerly were, the veins of ore being so exhausted that not more than 300 persons are employed. The receipts now scarcely do more than cover expenses'. Output of copper ore dropped to as low as 1,480 tons by 1847 and a few years later many of the workings had been abandoned. Closure came gradually however, and as late as 1904 a horizontal level was driven between the old Parys and Mona Mines in an attempt to boost production. By this time the competition of foreign ores (with a copper content of up to 60 per cent) was proving too great for the lean 3 per cent Anglesey ores. Although from time to time the precipitation of copper was revived, to all intents and purposes the Parys copper mines died at the beginning of this century.

The impact of mining was felt all over the surrounding area. The nearby coastal village of Amlwch underwent a complete transformation from the middle of the eighteenth century. It became the main port for the export of the copper, smelters were located close by and the village itself housed the greater proportion of the miners. Between the original village core and the port there were no fewer than thirty-one furnaces in operation as early as 1786. Coal was brought into the port from Lancashire after the local coal from the Malltraeth area had proved unsuitable. Much of the copper which had been partially refined to contain about 50 per cent metal left Amlwch Port *en route* to Swansea or St Helens. In some way the establishment of local refineries was a mixed blessing. It certainly brought employment to the area but on the debit side it caused considerable pollution. The combination of sulphurous fumes at the mines themselves together with the noxious gases at the Amlwch smelter led to devastation over a wide area. The Reverend Bingley, following his visit in 1789 remarked:

> Of the town itself, I observed nothing remarkable except that it was in general a most bleak and dismal place, from the scoria of the metal, of which the roads are all formed. On the exterior of the town there seems to be the utmost desolation. The sulphurous fumes from the mine have entirely destroyed the vegetation for a considerable space around, and little else than earth and rock are to be seen even within a short distance of Amlwch. On the Paris (sic) mountain, there is not even a single moss or lichen to be found.

Most of the damage was caused, in the early days at least, by the burning of the ore in open kilns on the top of the hill to remove the sulphur. Later the smelterworks themselves added to the misery of the polluted environment so that even the Vicar of Amlwch could claim a 'smoke trespass' of £15 a year for the discomfort he suffered at his vicarage in the town.

Once large scale mining got under way on Parys Mountain the need for a port became an urgent necessity. The north coast of Anglesey is not particularly well endowed with natural harbours and therefore use had to be made of a narrow cleft in the cliff line a little to the east of Amlwch village. When Lewis Morris made his famous survey of the coast of Wales in 1737–44, he dismissed it as 'no more than a cove between two steep rocks, where a vessel hath not room to wind even at high water'. In spite of the narrowness of the inlet there was no real alternative within a reasonable distance of the mines. In 1782 the Parys Mine Company built a wharf for vessels to load the ore, but it was another decade before powers were sought to enlarge and deepen the harbour. Following an Act of Parliament of 1793 work began in earnest so that the traveller Aiken in 1797 was able to note that the port 'is entirely artificial, being cut out of the rock with much labour and expense and is capable of containing thirty vessels of 200 tons burthen each'. He was probably over-estimating the size of vessel for it is known that the copper exporting trade was carried on largely by a fleet of small coasters of less than a 100 tons burden. In spite of the valiant attempts at improvement Amlwch Harbour suffered from being directly open to the north and a gale of 1824 caused considerable damage to the harbour and the vessels sheltering there. To lessen the danger the Cornish practice of blocking the harbour mouth with timber beams was adopted when northerly gales threatened. In spite of its natural limitations Amlwch Port served the mining industry well. Perhaps it was fortunate in not having to accommodate really large vessels for by the time they became common in the coastal trade, the mines themselves had become largely unproductive. The port then ceased to have any practical value and gradually assumed the fossilised appearance it has today. The early harbour engineers did their work so well that much remains in a reasonable state today when an increasing interest is being shown by the owners of small craft.

The nearby village of Amlwch also responded to the changing fortunes of the copper industry. It was the main settlement which housed both the miners of Parys Mountain and the smelters of Amlwch Port. In addition there were those who served the mining community in other ways. At one time, for example, there were no fewer than sixty alehouses in the town ready to take advantage of any rich strike in the mines. A new church was built in 1800, partly from money contributed by the mining companies. A school followed in 1820, again with their help, to cope with the rapid rise of population in the first part of the nineteenth century. By 1831 no fewer than 6,000 people lived in Amlwch and the immediate area around. This was later to fall as the mines became worked out one by one. With the closure of the Parys Mine in 1871 and the Mona Mine in 1883 the influence of copper mining on this quiet corner of north Anglesey came to an end after about a century of activity.

Although it is now many years since mining on any real scale has taken place on Parys mountain the present landscape still conveys a vivid impression of the size and scope of the original enterprise. A walk to the top of the hill, past spoil tips, old mine shafts and ruined buildings, is to take a journey back in time. Vegetation is still sparse, with only the occasional patch of heather struggling to survive amidst the bare rocks and piles of stones. An acrid sulphurous smell is apparent in places but it is nothing compared with the choking atmosphere which must have once pervaded the hill top when the roasting of the copper ores was in full swing. The most memorable feature, however, is the multi-coloured, lunar landscape left by the former open workings. Rock faces and spoil heaps present an ever-changing scale of reds, russets, browns, greens, yellows and orange tints, especially on the sides of the Great Opencast Pit of the former Parys Mine. Spires of unwanted rock, particularly quartzite, project at intervals and settling pits, with their tumbled loose stone walls, cover the bottom of the former mine workings. Buildings are few although the derelict former mine manager's office remains by the side of the Great Opencast Pit. The base of the former windmill which used to provide power for the underground mine workings, still dominates the skyline. On the lower slopes an old Cornish engine house remains. With the enormous expense which any scheme of reclamation would entail, Parys Mountain is likely to remain in its present untidy, haphazard and derelict shape for many years to come. The chances of a mining revival do not appear to be great, even though various mining companies have expressed an interest and a number of trial boreholes have been made at points around the hill. Parys Mountain seems destined to remain a relic of a relatively short period of intense mining activity without any real parallel elsewhere in North Wales.

SUGGESTED ITINERARY

The best starting point for a traverse of Parys Mountain is the crest of the main Amlwch to Llanderchymedd road (B5111). From here a track leads in an easterly direction to the edge of the pit known as the Great Opencast (440903). Skirting around the edge the route passes several derelict buildings including the offices, storehouses and work-shops associated with the mine in its heyday. The track now climbs to the summit of the hill towards the prominent stump of the old windmill, with its numerous abandoned and dangerous mine shafts around. After passing the summit the route then continues in a north-easterly direction. To the right lie some of the workings of the Mona Mine Company and a prominent group of settling pits in the valley bottom. On the extreme edge near Cerrig y Bleiddiau (408909) lie the remains of the ivy-covered engine house which was used to drain the Marquis shaft of the Mona Mine higher up the hillside. From this point a rough track leads northwards to Amlwch. The port lies about a kilometre to the east, and although little remains to indicate its former bustling activity, the harbour is still of interest although its character is changing rapidly.

6. The Lleyn Peninsula

THE MAKING OF A MEDIEVAL LANDSCAPE

As one travels south-westward beyond Caernarfon one becomes conscious of a landscape with subtly different qualities from the rest of the scenery of North Wales. There are no towns or crowded trunk roads—features that characterise the north Welsh coastal belt all the way from the outskirts of Chester to the shores of the Menai Strait. Equally there are no dominating mountain masses that, as in the Snowdon range, can become oppressive elements in the landscape out of their sheer size. Lonely isolated hills and mountains rise sharply from the extensive undulating platforms that make up the dominant feature of the landscape of Lleyn and all around there is a glow of light close to the horizon that on sunlit days speaks of the presence of the sea. In this remotest part of North Wales we are conscious of the survival of many ancient elements in the present landscape. Already in the introductory pages to these more detailed studies, the prehistoric foundations of Lleyn have been discussed; an equally important survival from the past is the medieval contribution to the making of the peninsula's landscape.

The tempo of Welsh history and especially that of the heartland, the princedom of Gwynedd, is very different from that of the other major cultural units of the British Isles. The Anglo-Saxon settlements and the Norman Conquest have no part in the design of the local history of Lleyn. The time of revolutionary changes in the medieval history of North Wales comes at the close of the thirteenth century with the Edwardian Conquest. The native kingdoms were extinguished and new features began to appear on the man-made landscape. New towns were established, each dominated by vast military works, and changes in the social structure were to gather momentum in the closing centuries of the Middle Ages that were to be reflected in the size and shape of settlements and the field patterns of the countryside. By the beginning of the nineteenth century, except in a handful of archaic locations; all traces of open-field farming had vanished. The pattern of settlement too had become more scattered so that the nucleated village, or the hamlet with its farmsteads gathered along the rim of a patchwork of open-field strips was then a rarity in the Welsh landscape.

The earliest elements of the medieval landscape of the Lleyn peninsula date back to centuries that followed the Roman abandonment of Britain. In the church sites founded by the Celtic saints one senses a continuity with the prehistoric geography of the region. For instance, at Llanfaglan (4760), scarcely three kilometres from the

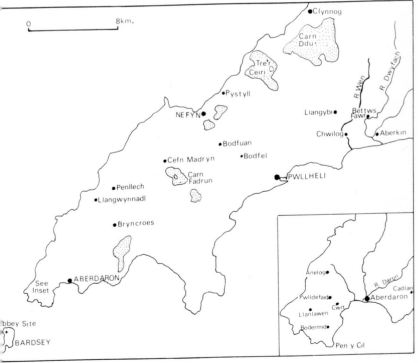

Lleyn Peninsula with locations of places discussed in the text

busy market streets of Caernarfon, we enter a different world—a surviving element of medieval Wales. Its parish church, a simple rectangular chapel, stands in a rough, wide, windy pasture close to the southern entrance of the Menai Strait. It occupies a walled enclosure, screened by a clump of bent trees stunted by the Irish Sea's winter gales. Llanfaglan is still a medieval church untouched by the pious restorers of the nineteenth century, but the lintel on the inside of the door recalls a much more remote moment of the region's history because it consists of a Roman tombstone. Further south, where the plain of Arfon narrows towards the pass that leads into Lleyn, another church site speaks of the long continuity of the settlement elements in Welsh history. Clynnog-fawr (4149) is linked with St Beuno who ranked among the most famous names of the Celtic church. His cult and the holy well, a few hundred metres to the west of the church, established Clynnog-fawr as a stopping place on the Pilgrims' Road to Bardsey. Out of the gifts of pilgrims one of the finest of Welsh medieval churches was built in the closing decades before the Reformation at Clynnog-fawr. Its massive square tower, the spaciousness of its nave and the light that streams through the wide Perpendicular windows proclaim a building from the turn of the sixteenth century and a church that seems out of proportion to the needs and resources of its local countryside. St Beuno's church is unique also in that it has a detached chapel, reached through a narrow stone-roofed passage. Here, outlined in stones inset in the floor, we see the shape of what was probably the earliest church at Clynnog-fawr—the church of St Beuno that was founded in the year 616.

Further south in the Lleyn peninsula another close link with the remotest medieval centuries may still be seen in the landscape at Llangybi (4241). The name commemorates the sixth-century Cornish saint, Cybi. Within the graveyard the outline of a circular vallum carries the mind back to the Dark Ages and beyond. So often in Wales and the Marches a circular churchyard or ring of gnarled yew trees crowning a faint grassy bank within the graveyard may mark the site of some prehistoric earthwork that was chosen by the first Christians of the fifth and sixth centuries. Llangybi also possesses an inscribed stone of this early Christian period. But the most striking feature that survives from the remote past at Llangybi is the holy well, a spring and pool lying a few hundred metres to the north of the church at the foot of the steep slope of Garn Pentyrch. The pool is found in a small rectangular building composed of huge rough stones, megaliths. Today it is roofless, but formerly it seems to have been covered with a beehive-shaped vault. It seems likely that this building enclosing Ffynnon Gybi may date back to the sixth century, to the beginnings of Christianity at this place.

Aberdaron and the monastic lands of Bardsey

At the remote south-western limits of the Lleyn peninsula, the Land's End of North Wales, it is possible to discern a medieval structure beneath the topography of the present day. For almost a thousand years, until the Reformation brought an end to the monasteries in the second quarter of the sixteenth century, the greater part of the district around Aberdaron (1726) had been under monastic control. The abbey whose ruins crouch beneath the steep upland spine of Bardsey Island was founded about the year 1200. But this monastery, belonging to the Augustinian order, was only the successor to a far older religious foundation—a monastic community of the Celtic church whose centre was on the mainland at Aberdaron and which was founded early in the sixth century. The religious community at Aberdaron, known as a *clas* in the Celtic Church, was responsible for the spiritual life of the neighbouring countryside. The property of the *clas* consisted of estates scattered through the south-western part of the peninsula. Their members, named in later medieval documents, were hamlets associated with patches of open field. Today we recognise their names as belonging to single consolidated farms in the countryside around Aberdaron. For instance on the wild exposed peninsula that one crosses to the cliff-bound coast above Bardsey Sound one comes across such names as Anelog (1527), Llanllawen (1425) and Bodermid (1525). All of these places, now lonely undistinguished Welsh farms, were hamlets—little farming communities—within the complex estate structure of the Celtic monastery at Aberdaron.

The fragments of evidence that survive in inscribed stones, place-names and late medieval documents suggest a long and complex history for the monastic community at Aberdaron. The earliest forerunner of the *clas* at Aberdaron, probably in the late fifth or early sixth century, was located about 1.5 kilometres to the west where the springs that feed the headwaters of the little Afon Saint break out at the foot of Mynydd Anelog. Nothing remains of this Dark Age monastery that was probably a simple collection of beehive-shaped huts within an enclosure, but its presence is known through the discovery of two stones with inscriptions in Latin. The Anelog stones rank among the earliest of the inscribed stones of Wales, probably from the years about AD 500. Their Latin inscriptions follow the Roman tradition and are written horizontally, naming Veracius and one Senacus who is described as a presbyter. The phrase *cum multitudinem fratrum,* with many brothers, suggests that Veracius and Senacus were to be remembered along with other nameless members of a religious community. Here at Anelog the Dark Age missionaries from Gaul must have founded a community of monks in the first years of the sixth century or perhaps earlier. At some unknown date the community or *clas* at Anelog was to transfer its centre to Aberdaron where the Afon Daron empties into the wide bay. One can only speculate about the motives for such a change. There is little doubt that Aberdaron's gently shelving beach of grey sand had provided a comparatively safe landing place for the prehistoric coastal trade of Cardigan Bay. Perhaps the monastery was moved from the hidden and secure site at the headsprings of the Afon Saint down to the exposed coast in order to participate in trade. There is little doubt too that the location on Aberdaron's beach provided much easier communications with the site of the hermitage on Bardsey, a place that in later centuries was famous for the sanctity of its monks. Giraldus Cambrensis, the Archdeacon of Brecon who made his historic tour of Wales in 1188, refers to the celibates, 'the very religious monks', on Bardsey. It might also be argued that the site of the first monastery at Anelog, screened to the south and west by a rocky ridge and the fierce cliffs of Mynydd Mawr (1425), provided greater security from the raids of Irish Sea pirates than an exposed location close to the beach at Aberdaron. The removal of the *clas* might suggest a more settled epoch in the Irish Sea basin, perhaps in the seventh and eighth centuries before the destructive onslaught of the Vikings.

By the time that Giraldus Cambrensis paid his visit to Aberdaron it is evident that two monastic communities were in existence—the *clas* that included the church site above the beach, and a remote hermitage on Bardsey Island. When the latter came into being is not known. The earliest archaeological proof of a religious community on the island is the foot of a cross shaft that probably dates from the time of the Viking raids in the ninth and tenth centuries. Tradition would place the establishment of the hermitage hundreds of years earlier in the age of the Celtic saints. Two sixth-century saints and bishops of the Celtic church, Dubricius and Deiniol, were buried on Bardsey Island. Their relics became objects of veneration and were transposed to Llandaff in South Wales in the year 1120. It seems evident that the religious associations of Bardsey date back to the sixth century. St Deiniol is reputed to have been buried there in 584 and it is likely that the clergy of the earliest mainland community at Anelog used the island as a spiritual retreat.

In the later part of the twelfth century a revolutionary change affected the monastic life of Aberdaron. The Welsh princes, the rulers of Gwynedd, encouraged the great Norman monastic orders to acquire properties in Wales. They received gifts of land at Nefyn (3040) and towards the close of the twelfth century Llywelyn Fawr established the Cistercians at Aberconwy, a monastic site of high strategic importance that a century later was to be confiscated for the building of the most important of the Edwardian castles. Several of the Celtic monasteries were reorganised in the closing years of the twelfth century at Beddgelert, Penmon and Bardsey. The island hermitage passed under the rule of the Augustinians. The first documentary evidence of the new order on Bardsey appears in the *Record of Caernarfon* that contains an Agreement between 'the secular canons' of Aberdaron and the new community of St Mary's Enlli (i.e. Bardsey). An earlier reference to the 'the Prior of the Isle of Saints' suggests that Bardsey was already under Augustinian rule at the beginning of the century, and this date must lie very close to the time when Bardsey and the adjacent properties on the mainland around Aberdaron were absorbed by this great medieval religious empire whose territories were widespread in Western Europe.

St Mary's on Bardsey ranked among the most famous monasteries of Wales. The buildings that have long lain in ruins were raised in the early years of the thirteenth century. The island's associations with the founders of the Celtic Church made Bardsey a place of pilgrimage. There were the graves of twenty thousand saints, and the Saints Road led through the length of the Lleyn peninsula with its favourite resting places for pilgrims at Clynnog-fawr (4149) and Pistyll (3242). A medieval story of Elgar the Hermit reveals the importance of Bardsey before the Reformation—'Among the Welsh it is called the Welsh Rome because of the long and risky journey to the very end of the kingdom, and because of the holiness and purity of the place'.

The remoteness of Bardsey and the limited resources of the island meant that a great monastic community could not survive without its properties and economic interests on the mainland. A survey of 1538, taken at the time of the dissolution of the monasteries, shows that the later inmates of St Mary's Abbey had made little attempt to cultivate the lower coastal platform in the western part of the island. There is no trace of 'habitations' except the abandoned buildings of the monastery. The record mentions only 'a few small assarts'—clearings among the rocks and heather for the pasturing of sheep. As the survey says 'no land had ever been cultivated because of the ravages of rabbits with which this land is plentifully supplied'. It seems that in the thirteenth century the Augustinian canons of St Mary's had acquired a nice income from the sale of rabbit skins. But the chief resources of the abbey lay on the mainland in the vicinity of Aberdaron where several features of the landscape today may be traced in surviving documents that relate to the last days of the monastery. Apart from the flocks and herds pastured on Bardsey Island, another common grazing in which the monks had their share was Rhoshirwaun (1929)—an extensive tract of heath and rough grazing at the head-springs of the Afon Daron whose enclosure did not take place until the nineteenth century. Even so, among its patchwork of tiny fields you can still see tracts of unfenced land with gorse and bracken that call to mind the vanished medieval commons of the Lleyn peninsula.

Apart from rights to graze livestock on the commons, another mainland interest of the monastery was in the 'granges'—farms that were owned and managed by the abbey. Cadlan (1926), a lonely farm at the head of a narrow valley that opens out above the sudden boulder-clay cliffs of Porth Cadlan, was the site of a monastic grange. St Mary's Abbey had another grange farm at Llangwnnadl (2033), a place where the parish church was rebuilt in the early years of the sixteenth century, scarcely a decade before the destruction of the monasteries. Another grange was at Bryncroes (2231), and there the landscape still bears some witness to the presence of the monks before the sixteenth century. A holy well in the hamlet, Ffynnon Fair or St Mary's Well, records the presence of the Bardsey Abbey as a land-owner. Again, on the slopes that rise steadily to the south of the hamlet towards Mynydd Rhiw, we find Ty Fair or St Mary's Chapel. Was this also the site of the grange that belonged to St Mary's Abbey? Bryncroes lay in the heart of lands that were in secular ownership. It was surrounded by bond hamlets, settlements with patches of open-field, that belonged to the lordship of Cymydmaen. The grange at Bryncroes was probably granted at an early date to the *clas* at Aberdaron before the foundation of the Augustinian monastery on Bardsey island.

Another mark of its medieval monastic history that is still borne by the landscape of Aberdaron occurs in the place-name Pen y Cil (1524), the headland that guards the western approach to Aberdaron Bay.

Y Cil was the name given to the rocky south-western tip of the Lleyn peninsula, the broad blunt headland that obstructs the view of Bardsey Island from Aberdaron. On the eastern side of this headland, just above Aberdaron Bay, stood Llys-y-Cil, the site of the court through which the monastery administered its mainland properties. A survey of the Abbey's estates in 1547 describes the place where the courts were held:

> a house within walls nigh the said isle called the Court of Bardsey with orchards and garden rooms and courts containing by estimation two acres . . . in the neighbourhood of the court were also 157 acres of demesne comprising arable, pasture and meadow, including furzy land, partly arable measuring six acres called *Tredom*.

We still know the place where the monastery's Exchequer Courts gathered from the name of a weather-beaten farm, Cwrt, standing beside the lane from Aberdaron that finally loses itself in deep hedged tracks above the headland of Pen y Cil.

The economic base of the monastic properties of St Mary's consisted of a number of hamlets that were gathered into four townships occupying the extreme end of the Lleyn peninsula, to the west and north of Rhiw Mountain. Embedded within the compact area of monastic lands were three townships—Penllech, Bodfferin and Bodrhydd—that formed free clan communities. Professor T. Jones Pierce, whose research has thrown a fresh light on the hard problems of Welsh settlement history, has used two Tudor surveys to identify the components of Bardsey Abbey's monastic territory. The later survey, a rental of 1592, provides a detailed picture of the hamlets that were still surviving in the four townships more than half a century after the destruction of the monastery. We still know the names of these settlements from the maps and the signposts in the lanes around Aberdaron, but now most of them point to isolated farms. The social and economic unit in all four townships, as in all the settled and cultivated tracts of Lleyn in the Middle Ages, was the hamlet whose homesteads were laid out in 'girdle-like clusters' along the margin of the shared arable land, an open field that was cultivated in strips. In the most westerly township of Uwchsely that occupied the peninsula between the Afon Saint and Bardsey Sound we can still recognise through their names the former hamlets of Anelog (1527), Llanllawen, Bodermid, Ystohelig and Pwlldefaid. Similarly between the Afon Saint and the Afon Daron another group of compact settlements formed the economic and social structure of the monastic estate

123

in Lleyn. Today the hamlets and their open fields have long since vanished and we know them as consolidated farms at Dwyros, Anheg-raig, Bodernabwy, and Cyll-y-felin. The nodes of settlement in the landscape of Aberdaron were obviously already clearly defined in the later Middle Ages when the documentary record is able to hand down their names to the local historian working in the twentieth century. What remains a problem for settlement studies in this region is the dating of the creation of this settlement pattern. It is clear when the monastery was re-established as an Augustinian abbey about AD 1200 that the supporting estate of four townships with their several hamlets had already been in existence for several centuries. It seems likely that some of these places had an existence in a remoter prehistoric past, and that the founders of the earliest monastery at Anelog, possibly in the closing years of the fifth century, perhaps went to serve the spiritual needs of an existing community of farmers—people who may have carried a knowledge of Christianity from the late Roman decades.

The dissolution of a medieval landscape

The patterns of the man-made landscape reflect social structures and are influenced by the laws that define the lineaments of a society. The transformation that was to dissolve the pattern of the medieval Welsh landscape is the result of a complex historic process extending over 400 years from the thirteenth to the seventeenth century. The most striking result of these changes was the disappearance of the hamlet, a nucleus of a dozen or so farmsteads, and its shared strips of arable in an open field. Wales became a country of isolated farms, of irregular small hedged fields and extensively enclosed hill-pastures. The out-standing events in the political history of this slow transformation of Welsh society and its environment are the Edwardian Conquest at the end of the thirteenth century, the failure of Glyndwr's rising at the opening of the fifteenth century and the Act of Union together with the destruction of the monasteries that took place in the 1530s. But these events only mark stages in a process of social change that is much more complex. It is particularly concerned with the break-up of a communal medieval society and the acts of individuals who were acquiring compact farms and estates, shaping their holdings by gathering together strips in the common fields or enclosing fields out of the common pastures and hill grazings. These economic and social changes began under the Welsh princes before the Edwardian Con-quest with the grant of land to prominent freemen; important among them were officials who had power and influence in the government of medieval Gwynedd. The conquest of North Wales by Edward I, completed in 1284, encouraged the trend towards the individual ownership of land and the making of estates. Estates of the Welsh royal household passed to the English Crown and alien English families moved into Wales in the wake of the conquering army and under the shelter of the fortress towns began the accumulation of landed wealth. The activities of the Bulkeley family on the outskirts of Conwy and Beaumaris and the Salusburys around Denbigh illustrate this theme in Welsh history. A century later, after the failure of Glyndwr's revolt further clan holdings were confiscated to become ripe for development as individual, freehold estates. By the time of Henry VII several freehold estates of considerable size had emerged and the nuclei of many small estates were apparent. They formed the geographical, economic and social base for a new class in Welsh society, the squirearchy.

The disintegration of a medieval society with its clan structure was hastened in the sixteenth century. The Act of Union in 1536 was followed by the extension of English Common Law to Wales. Of great importance was the abolition of the custom of gavelkind, a system of inheritance in Celtic societies that divided a property between the heirs of the deceased. Under the laws of gavelkind an inheritance of land could descend in small shares among as many as forty or sixty co-inheritors. The introduction of English law and with it the system of primogeniture that passed an estate intact to the eldest son of the deceased was to confirm the revolution in land-holding that had gathered momentum over two centuries. At the same time the dissolution of the monasteries was to place much fresh land in the hands of individual speculators.

The revolution in land holding and settlement patterns that marks the close of the Middle Ages proceeded at different speeds and in varying ways in the regions of North Wales. We have already noticed the early activity of estate-building families in the neighbourhood of the Edwardian castle towns. The seaward end of the Lleyn peninsula was affected only late in time by the influx of the new ways of land organisation. The powerful hold of Bardsey Abbey over the affairs of the region was no doubt a factor in the perpetuation of the hamlets, their patches of open field and the extensive commons that were broken from time to time for an arable crop. Even half a century after the dissolution of the Augustinian Order on the island the Rental of 1592 reveals the survival of a medieval organisation of the land with a large number of small homesteads gathered in hamlets. For instance, at Bryncroes (2231) there was a nucleated settlement of considerable size near the present church with a number of outlying tributary hamlets such as Brynhunog or Eglwys Cadell. Elsewhere estate-making started earlier and was more successful than in the vicinity of Aberdaron. For example by the beginning of the seventeenth century the borough of Nefyn was surrounded by properties that had been pieced together out of scattered units in the bond townships and enlarged by enclosures from the wastes of the commons. Such were Cefnamwlch (2335), Boduan (3237), Madryn (2736) and Bodfel (3437). Each in time was to become more distinctive as spacious mansions were erected and the enfolding ground subjected to the fashionable English ideas of landscape management. But the estates of Lleyn reflect the modest wealth of the Welsh squirearchy, a wealth to which the earnings of the cattle trade and the illicit proceeds of piracy made their contribution. The landscaped areas are never great; the plantations only colour and soften the austere windswept scenery of the peninsula.

The changes that the social and economic revolution of the late Middle Ages worked in the Lleyn peninsula are clearly illustrated in the parish of Llanystumdwy (4738). Colin Gresham in an excellent piece of analysis, has traced the history of the eight townships that made up the parish of Llanystumdwy, a parish that is crossed by three rivers, the Afon Wen, the Afon Dwyfor and the Afon Dwyfach, making their way to Cardigan Bay. The present landscape contains scarcely any hint of the original pattern of hamlets and their associated open fields. Only through the persistence of place-names and the information that survives in documents is it possible to reconstruct the details of the vanished landscape of the Middle Ages.

The most westerly of the townships that made up the parish of Llanystumdwy lay in the shallow valley of the Afon Wen. The site of the hamlet and medieval fields of the place named in the documents as Chwilog is not known with certainty. The village that now bears that name, a street settlement on the road from Cricieth to Nefyn, came into existence in the early nineteenth century with the building of the turnpike road to Porth Dinllaen. Later the opening of the railway from Caernarfon to Afon Wen Junction was to reinforce the growing road-side village. It is likely that the site of the medieval hamlet lay on the flat-topped hill three-quarters of a kilometre to the east of the present village, close to the farm called Chwilog Fawr (4438). Another medieval hamlet, Abercain, occupied the last great bend of the Afon Dwyfawr before it empties into the sea. Now it is represented by a single farm, Aberkin (4738). This is an old estate that was already well established by the end of the fifteenth century. Another lost township within Llanystumdwy was known as Betws. The hamlet and its common field with shared strips must have been located close to the modern farms of Betws Fawr and Betws Fach (4639). There is a reference to Betws in a survey of the lands of the Bishop of Bangor that was drawn up in 1306. It shows that one carucate of arable was here rented to seventeen tenants. By the eighteenth century the process of estate-building had gathered the whole of the township of Betws in the hands of one owner, the Vaughans of Corsygedol. Their property, a single block of land, stretched for six kilometres along the west bank of the Afon Dwyfach.

A comparison of the history of the township of Betws with that of Chwilog suggests the important part played by individuals in the shaping of the landscape. Chwilog was not the scene of any major estate building; by the mid-nineteenth century the common lands of the township had been divided up amongst several small owners. Chwilog had evolved a landscape typical of so many parts of lowland Wales with small hedged fields, an absence of woodland, scattered farms and cottages that are reached along deep, winding, dead-end lanes. The life of the township has been reorientated and refocused on the nineteenth-century roadside settlement with its now defunct railway station, school, chapels, shops and garage. At Betws the influence of a single owner in shaping and managing the development of an estate has been indelibly written on the landscape. In 1791, when the last of the Vaughans died without children, Betws passed to the Mostyn family. Sir Thomas Mostyn, Sixth Baronet, employed John Maughan, a Northumbrian, as his agent in the management of the estate between 1817 and 1833. Under his guidance drainage works, road-making and tree-planting were carried out. Perhaps the most striking feature of this period was the cutting of a road to serve the lands of the Mostyn estate. The Ffordd Maughan, as it has become known, ran from the estuary of the Afon Wen at Pont Ffriddlwyd (4337) for almost eight kilometres to the foot of the Mynydd Cennin. For its whole length it was ditched and planted with trees on both sides. The aim of this major piece of road-making was to provide access to all farms, particularly for the importing of coal and lime by ship into the mouth of the Afon Wen.

The medieval landscapes of the Lleyn peninsula have been slowly erased by innumerable local acts—by humble peasants enclosing their strips in former open fields or adding fresh patches of improved land through assarts from the commons as well as by rich landowners shaping their properties with an eye to aesthetics as well as economics. Today the medieval past is known largely through place-names and the resistant skeleton of the settlement plan. It is astonishing how much of the past landscape has vanished without trace. Only here and there can one find a hint of some ancient feature in the present scene. The field pattern of long narrow enclosures between Anelog and Cyndy, on the monastic lands of far western Lleyn, suggests the site of a former common field. Only 1.5 kilometres from Anelog the farm of Cyll-y-Felin (1728) contains some long, curving field boundaries suggestive of ancient and unrecorded enclosure from an open field. And the eye turns to the bleak windswept cliff top, above Bardsey Sound, where numerous long parallel field-boundaries seem to mark out the patterns of forgotten medieval systems of cultivation. Here perhaps we may locate the long lost hamlet of Trecarnen, the only settlement on the estates of Bardsey Abbey that remains to be identified.

SUGGESTED ITINERARY

The reputation of the Lleyn peninsula, like that of Cornwall, in the world outside Wales is one of sandy beaches, caravan sites, holiday cottages and 'marinas'. Like Cornwall, the interior of the peninsula still bears the marks of a long history, a history that is worth exploring in the landscape. If one approaches the peninsula from the north, by Caernarfon and the A487(T), it is rewarding to stop off and explore some of the features that lie close to the A499 and B4417 roads. First along the straight lengths of the A499 comes Clynnog-fawr. If the motorist heading for those family holiday resorts of Aberdaron and Abersoch can spare the time to halt, however briefly, at only one place, Clynnog-fawr is a 'must'. Here is one of the finest Renaissance churches in Wales and within the building we can see the outlines of the original Dark Age chapel of St Beuno. In the fields above the sea cliff, a few hundred metres to the west of the church stands the huge bare skeleton of a Neolithic burial chamber. At Llanaelhaearn (3844) the motorist takes to the B roads that lead to the furthest ends of the peninsula. The brooding cloud covered mass of Yr Eifl overwhelms the prospect to the north. If time allows and the weather is fine, it is worthwhile stopping to take the footpath that leads to Tre'r Ceiri, the Iron Age site and settlement, on the south-eastern summit of Yr Eifl

(3744). Here one can not only enjoy the whole landscape of the Lleyn peninsula with its distant prospects of lonely, isolated hills, each one rich with the evidence of prehistory, but also within the crumbling ramparts of the settlement there lingers a feeling of the Romano-British centuries. Beyond the ridge of Yr Eifl, visually among the most attractive mountain groups of the British Isles, the westward leading road turns towards the coast at Pistyll (SN3242). Pistyll, like Clynnog Fawr, was one of the traditional resting places for pilgrims making their way along the peninsular road to Bardsey in the Middle Ages. Here, on top of a bank above the road, three quarters of a kilometre to the west of Pistyll church, we find an eighth-century cross, a rough pillar stone with a ring cross, one of several monuments associated with the saints of the Celtic world that mark the Pilgrims' Road to the remote isle at the end of the peninsula.

Between Pistyll and Aberdaron B4417 passes through Nefyn, the one place on the northern coast of the peninsula that has experienced a number of efforts at economic and social transformation. Here was one of the rare late medieval boroughs of Welsh origin. The nineteenth century saw the abortive efforts to create an Irish packet station at Porth Dinllaen and the only resort of the northern coastline grew here in the nineteenth century—a resort that traded on the romantically Victorian comparison of the seascape towards The Rivals (Yr Eifl) with that of the Bay of Naples. The remaining kilometres to Aberdaron across a dull coastal plateau include Llangwnadl (2033), like Pistyll another important stage on the Pilgrims' Road, with a church dedication to Saint Gwynhoedl who lived towards the end of the sixth century. An inscription of the year 1520 on the north arcade of the church at Llangwnadl shows that the relics of this Dark Age saint were preserved here until the time of the Reformation. As the wide bay of Aberdaron opens before the modern petrol-driven pilgrim to Lleyn the road runs beneath the slopes of Castell Odo (1828), scene of the most important archaeological investigation in the peninsula of recent times. The site of Aberdaron's medieval parish church, a mere stone's throw from the high tides, summarises the role of this little resort through the centuries at the centre of a monastic estate and the place where one set sail for Bardsey, the object of pilgrims and the reputed burial place of 20,000 saints. But for anyone who wishes to explore in greater depth the landscape of south-western Lleyn and Bardsey Island the best key is Brenda Chamberlain's *Tide-race* (Hodder and Stoughton, 1961), a book that observes so many facets of this remotest part of Wales with the eye of the poet and the painter.

7. The resorts of the North Wales coast

The growth and character of towns is often a reflection of the needs of society at the time they came into being. Thus the castle towns of Edward I arose from his forays and ultimate conquest of North Wales and the attempt to anglicise the country. Similarly the resorts strung out all along the north coast date mainly from the second half of the nineteenth century when sea bathing became fashionable and seaside holidays were on the increase. For sixty-four kilometres, from Llanfairfechan in the west to Prestatyn in the east, a succession of resort towns sprang up within a few decades. A contributory factor undoubtedly was the coastal route chosen by Stephenson for his railway to the developing packet station of Holyhead. For much of its length the railway was in sight of the sea and even when it was forced inland to avoid headlands like the Orme, a branch line was constructed to the coast at Llandudno. Apart from the area to the west of the Conwy there was plenty of cheap flat land available for building so that resorts like Llandudno, Rhyl and Prestatyn could adopt a spacious design. Even at Colwyn Bay and Penmaenmawr, where the hills come down to the seashore, sufficient room could be found and here there was the additional advantage of contrasting inland scenery close at hand. The main disadvantage of this coast lies in its northerly aspect and open character which allow cold winds to blow in off the sea. In an age when the family car has become the main means of movement, the area is at present suffering from the lack of a good coastal road, even though improvements to the A55 are in hand. Persistent bottlenecks at places like Colwyn Bay and Conwy in the summer months highlight the dilemma of the local authorities who face considerable expenditure in order to overcome a seasonal problem, mainly caused by the day tripper.

Llandudno

A chance remark by Owen Williams, a Liverpool surveyor who came to a meeting of shareholders of the local copper mines, led to the founding of this premier resort. He commented on the fine site enjoyed by the sandy bay between the two limestone headlands and its immense possibilities. The idea was taken up by John Williams, the

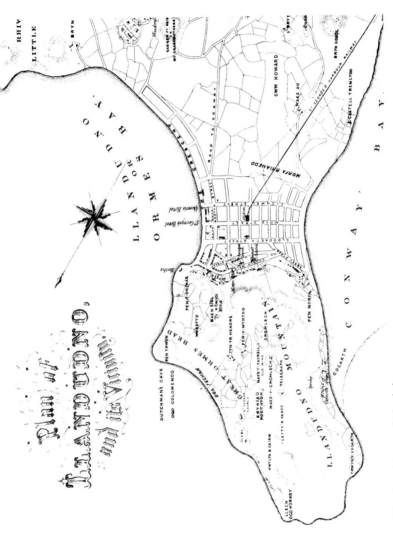

The planned layout of Llandudno

131

agent for the local Mostyn family who owned most of the land around. Up to that time there had been little development even though a fine new parish church of St George had been built under the east wall of the limestone mass of the Great Orme in 1840. Before any scheme could be put forward it was necessary to seek an Enclosure Award to establish the ownership of this large area of sandy wasteland and this was done in 1848. As Lord of the Manor, the Mostyn family acquired 344 hectares and therefore virtually controlled the whole area. At an auction held in Conwy in August 1848 much of this land was sold to developers, though there were restrictions written into the contracts and ground rent to be paid. It is this fact, more than any other, which determined the character of Llandudno as a resort and served to distinguish it from its rivals. One condition, for example, was that in certain parts of the town, building was to be restricted to substantial houses with wide frontages. Control was also exercised over many other aspects of the development so that initially, at least, Llandudno was as much a Victorian planned town as the better known examples of the industrial north like Saltaire. The whole plan was given official approval by the promotion of an Act of Parliament passed in July 1854.

The site of the sandy warren across the neck of the peninsula allowed a spacious layout. A broadly rectangular arrangement of streets was decided on at the outset. The only variant was The Crescent which followed the gentle curve of the bay. It was here that the finest hotels and other residences were built, including the imposing Queen's and St George's Hotels. A little farther along the gently sweeping curve of the bay as it ran towards the Little Orme was the Gloddaeth Terrace, named after the Mostyn estate on which Llandudno was being developed. It consisted of sixteen houses,

> built after the design of Mr Chater of Birmingham, in the Italian style of architecture. . . . The Crescent is beautifully situated; each house will be replete with every accommodation required by the most fastidious as a well-arranged marine residence; and in front of the entire range, there will be a private esplanade which will be turfed and laid out in ornamental parterres with a broad gravel walk in the centre of the promenade.

The resort nature of the new town of Llandudno led in time to the building of baths under the limestone cliffs of the Orme and a pier close by. Little by way of port development took place after the abortive attempt in 1836 to create a rival packet station to Holyhead here. The seriousness of this proposal is shown by the fact that the St George's Harbour and Railway Company was formed and proposals were put forward for a railway to run in a cutting through the town towards a harbour under the Great Orme. Nothing came of the scheme and when the railway did finally reach the town in 1858 it was only as a branch to the main Chester to Holyhead line. Efforts were now concentrated on making a rather exclusive 'garden city' type of resort. Gradually, year by year, it acquired more and more of the trappings of the typical Victorian seaside resort. In spite of the fact that many of the original large plots were never occupied and, in some cases less substantial houses built in their place, Llandudno managed to escape the worst excesses of garish vulgarity. There is no doubt that the original controls had a considerable influence.

Llandudno at the present time still retains much of its original character. The broad sweep of the Crescent, with its fine blocks of terraces, is perhaps the most imposing survival from the mid-nineteenth century. Its main rival is Gloddaeth Street, now extended to run right through to the west shore. Mostyn Street runs behind the Crescent and is now the main shopping and commercial centre. In spite of modern shop fronts, the early covered arcades of ironwork still survive in part. It was here that the town church of Holy Trinity was built, for the parish church of St George was some distance away. Although sporadic development has taken place towards the Little Orme, even the promenade is not continuously built up. Llandudno has not, as Murray's Guide of 1858 thought likely, become the Welsh Brighton, even though much favoured for retirement by the seaside.

Colwyn Bay

A little way to the east, around the limestone headland of the Little Orme the resort of Colwyn Bay began to grow about the same time as Llandudno. The parallel ends there for subsequent development at Colwyn Bay was much slower and took on a less orderly pattern. The beginning of the resort can be traced to the carving out of a new parish from the original Llandrillo in 1844. Even when the railway reached the area a few years later it led only to sporadic growth around the station. Unfortunately the railway authorities built a huge embankment along the coast which was later to shut off the town from the sea. Earth was dug out of a nearby pit, later termed the Ballast Pit, now used as railway sidings and a fairground and this too, has had the effect of dividing the town centre from the beach.

The real growth of Colwyn began after the estate of Pwllycrochan came up for sale in 1865. It had been in the hands of the Erskine family since the seventeenth century, covering the area of the present town and also the slopes of the hills inland. Following the sale in September 1865 immediate plans were made for developing the whole area. The manor house and garden of Pwllycrochan were acquired by Mr John Pender, while the remainder of the land was sold off in small lots 'to meet the great and increasing demand for marine residences on the coast'. Here lies the key to the present differences in the urban pattern of Llandudno and Colwyn Bay for whereas the former was planned and developed as a single unit, Colwyn Bay grew largely in a piecemeal fashion.

One of the earliest houses built, and one which still stands was Rhoslan on the Abergele road. Local limestone in large blocks was used in its building in 1870. It lies close to the most fashionable quarter of present-day Colwyn Bay, in an area which was developed after 1875 when John Pender sold his land to a Manchester syndicate The Colwyn Bay and Pwllycrochan Estate Company. This whole area to the south of the main coastal road was given a spacious layout. In the present townscape it contrasts markedly with the cramped setting of the older part of the town near the station, with its narrow streets

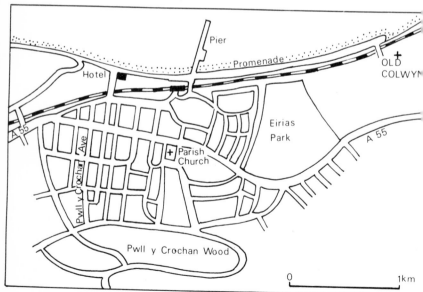

Colwyn Bay town plan

134

and haphazard growth. A series of parallel streets was laid out and the intervening areas infilled with large three-storey houses, each set well back from the tree-lined avenues. It is perhaps a sign of the times when they were built that brick, mainly the deep red from Ruabon, was the favoured material. The local limestone, used in the earlier buildings, was only used for the garden walls. The houses possess great individuality although a common design is the conical or pyramidal turret built as a corner projection. The original house of the Erskine family at Pwllycrochan still stands though now used as Rydal Preparatory School. It is still possible to appreciate its fine site overlooking Colwyn Bay, with the backcloth of the Pwllycrochan Woods, which are now owned by the local authority and threaded with paths.

While this rather exclusive and spacious development was taking shape inland the resort itself was growing apace. By 1875 the core area of the new town forming a triangle around the station, had been established. On the shore itself, beyond the railway, a stretch of promenade known as The Parade was laid out and extended to the Colwyn Bay Hotel. This massive building, which completely dominates the western part of the shore, stands symbolic of the Victorian atmosphere still very much in evidence in parts of Colwyn Bay. The great growth which took place in the last quarter of the nineteenth century led in 1887 to the town being given local government status. The name Colwyn Bay dates from this time, for previously it had been called New Colwyn to distinguish it from the village of Old Colwyn farther east along the coast. A new church, St Paul's, was started in the following year and given a prominent site near the town centre. Every respectable Victorian seaside resort could boast of a pier and Colwyn Bay was no exception. It was begun in 1899 and opened in June of the following year. The present pavilion dates from 1923, the original building having been destroyed by fire.

A little distance to the east (8678) lay the core of Old Colwyn, centred around the squat limestone church of St Catherine, built as a chapel-of-ease to the parish church of Llandrillo in 1837. At this time Old Colwyn could so easily have become the resort town but the releasing of 1,500 hectares of land of the Pwllycrochan Estate finally swung the balance in favour of New Colwyn. Although so close, the twin settlements have retained their distinctive identities, largely through the barrier formed by the Glan-y-For estate. The original house is now a civic centre and the grounds form Eirias Park, now a distinct asset to the seaside town.

Rhyl

In terms of size alone Rhyl could lay claim to being the premier resort of the North Wales coast. Its townscape is the least interesting of the seaside resorts although it would be wrong to dismiss it as without form or history. Unlike Llandudno or Colwyn Bay, there was no large estate here to provide some measure of control or stimulate planned development. Instead Rhyl was largely allowed to grow in a haphazard fashion, a fact easy to appreciate in the piecemeal and rather indeterminate setting of the present town. Rhyl also differed from the other North Wales resorts in that it had already established a reputation for holidays by the sea—the best in the Principality according to one observer—long before the railway came upon the scene in the 1840s.

The low-lying site on which the town was laid out was much less exciting than the comparable settings of Colwyn Bay and Llandudno. Lying as it does at the northern end of the Vale of Clwyd, the hill country is too far inland to form an effective backcloth. When the fashion of sea bathing was introduced in 1807 the area was little more than a sandy warren backed by marshland bordering on the lower course of the River Clwyd. Eight hectares of the common were set aside for building at that time but twenty-five years later the settlement was still small and within the old parish of Rhuddlan, the Edwardian castle town two miles inland (0278). The creation of cold and hot water baths and the building of a new Anglican church in 1835 acted as something of a spur to development but even then the actual coastal strip was neglected. By the time Rhyl became a separate parish in 1844 there was a nucleus of about forty shops, inns and hotels mainly in and around Quay Street (now Wellington Road, the main axial street of the present town).

It was the Rhyl Improvement Act of 1852 that led to initiating a sustained period of growth. A new waterworks, Town Hall, Market Hall and Convalescent Home were all built within a few years so that by 1861 the population had reached almost 3,000. The Chester-Holyhead Railway, which at this point ran within 1.5 kilometres of the shore, undoubtedly helped Rhyl to establish itself at this critical period in its growth. Land became available for building between the railway and the sea and a rough grid-iron pattern of streets was mapped out. The houses built were modest and formed long terraces running down towards the shore. In no way were they the counterpart of the development that was to take place on the Pwllycrochan Estate at Colwyn Bay. Rhyl, however, could boast that it was the first of the North Wales resorts to have a pier, built in 1867 at a cost of £23,000.

By the turn of the century the infilling of the land between the railway and the coast extended westwards almost to the mouth of the River Clwyd. The problem here was that the land was subject to periodic flooding and therefore unsuitable for housing. The solution was the creation of a pleasure park with a large lake. The adjacent sand dunes of the original warren had previously been levelled and converted into Rhyl Palace and Summer Gardens. This late-Victorian enterprise is still very much the core of the present day resort with its fun-fair and boating pool. An accident of history and geography, however, has meant that it is sited some distance from the town centre and railway station.

In contrast to this leisure development on the west side of Rhyl, the area to the east of the station was largely set aside for residential purposes. As in so many nineteenth century towns the growth stages find expression in the building of churches. Holy Trinity, a modest building dates from the time in 1835 when the town was still very small. The rapid growth of the 1850s is marked by St Thomas's built on an adjacent site in 1861 by Sir Gilbert Scott. Its sheer immensity, perhaps a symbol of the faith of the town fathers that Rhyl was destined to become a resort to be compared with Brighton or Blackpool, completely dwarfs the earlier church of Holy Trinity alongside. The phase of late Victorian expansion on the periphery led to the building of the church of St John in 1885 in a style typical of its period save for an unusual octagonal nave.

The present century has been one of consolidation rather than exciting new development. In terms of size it has stayed ahead of its rivals. Without too much difficulty it has managed to transform itself from a typical Victorian and Edwardian seaside resort, with all the trappings of arcades, ballrooms, waxworks and side-shows, to the needs of the present day car visitor. Its fine beaches and the reclaimed sandy warren behind, with its pools, pavilions and formal gardens, find favour with visitors from the industrial towns of Lancashire and Cheshire, as an alternative to Blackpool, Southport and Morecambe. Many ultimately retire here in their impersonal bungalow estates which have proliferated across the surrounding marshland in the last twenty years.

Prestatyn

Of the major resorts strung out along the coast of North Wales, Prestatyn can lay claim to having the longest history as a settlement. On the southern outskirts of the present town there is the site of a Roman bath (163818) while in later centuries it formed the northern limit of the Mercian frontier line of Offa's Dyke. Its medieval importance is reflected in the fact that the powerful Princes of Powys chose Prestatyn as the site to build a castle (072833).

Prestatyn shelters beneath limestone cliffs which form the northern edge of the Clwydian Range. It was from here in the nineteenth century that vast quantities of rock were quarried. At an earlier date lead mining was important with local families like the Mostyns participating in this relatively short lived period of prosperity. The hundred of Prestatyn alone produced over 3,000 tons of lead in the period of five years between 1742 and 1747. Prestatyn at this time must have been nothing more than a small village in the lee of the limestone hills with a motley collection of quarrymen's and miners' cottages. Even at the time of the census of 1811 it had a population of only 178. Somewhat surprisingly the fashion of sea bathing in the 1820s had a minimal impact on the fortunes of the village but with Rhyl only a few kilometres to the west, perhaps there was no room for two adjacent resorts to develop. Even the coming of the railway did not stimulate growth. To a certain extent it had the reverse effect in that it tended to isolate the village from the shoreline. Although two churches were built in the High Street in the 1860s they reflect the growth of the inland village rather than any expansion along the shoreline.

The main phase of growth at Prestatyn came much later than at the other resorts for it was not until the first quarter of the present century that any large scale development was attempted. As at Colwyn Bay and Llandudno it was the selling of an estate, in this case the Pendre in 1905, that triggered off the phase of expansion. Other small estates like the Penrhwlfa (1911), Plas Uchaf (1919) and Bryntirion (1922) were also put onto the market and led to considerable areas of land becoming available for building. In the case of the Penrhwlfa Estate, owned by Lord Aberconway, an attempt was made to control development. He called in the planner Abercrombie to produce a comprehensive scheme in 1912. Only superior houses with ground rents in excess of £25 a year were to be built and although the idea found favour at first and many of the more desirable hillside sites were sold, large areas were left undeveloped so that the present plan bears only the most superficial resemblance to Abercrombie's original proposals. Less control was exercised in the case of the other estates although for Plas Uchaf there was a restrictive covenant which only allowed the building of good class residences with an annual rental of over £18.

The housing explosion which took place as the former landed estates were gradually built up, had little impact on resort development. Apart from rows of houses close to the coastal road (A55) the coastal strip was shunned. One reason was that the land was low-lying, badly drained and suffered periodic flooding particularly during the winter months. What was unsuitable for housing proved attractive for camping and caravans and in the 1930s this form of holiday began to take root on the dunes bordering the shore, in spite of vigorous opposition from local residents and conservationists. The building of the Prestatyn Holiday Camp by British Holiday Estates, a subsidiary of the London Midland and Scottish Railway and Thomas Cook, finally resolved the issue as to whether Prestatyn should become a resort town. The impact of railway advertising was considerable and led not only to the popularising of this type of holiday in general, but finally put Prestatyn on the map as a holiday centre. The holiday camp atmosphere, self-contained with built-in amenities, did not affect the town on the other side of the railway to any real extent. Even a second holiday village which has been built in the last few years has had only a minimal impact. The shoreline has now lost its natural setting with the building of a long concrete promenade and groynes to retain the sand on the beach. The local authority has also built a swimming pool and other amenities in this coastal strip of Y Friff and it is clear that they intend to keep a grip on development so that Prestatyn can retain a somewhat exclusive air and not become too brash and commercial.

The railway still continues to provide the great divide between the earlier inland settlement and the resort quarter. Many of the features of the original village, the limestone cottages and inns, have now disappeared in the new shopping precinct and bus station, as Prestatyn attempts to move into the pattern of life of the latter part of the twentieth century. This recent addition to the town symbolises the duality of function which Prestatyn wishes to preserve, a shopping centre for local residents, many of whom have retired, and yet allow the resort some controlled growth now that at last it seems to have taken root. The great divide provided by the railway offers more than a hope that the plan will succeed and the duality of the town will survive the pressures of the last quarter of the century.

Each town merits detailed study by walking round its streets, appreciating the layout of the whole as well as the character and age of its individual buildings. At Llandudno a start can be made at the original settlement associated with the Celtic Saint Tudno set high and isolated on the bare limestone top of the Great Orme plateau (769 838). The route to the modern town lies to the south-east and on the way down passes some of the old lead mine workings which were worked sporadically over the centuries. At the foot of the limestone cliff in Church Walks lies the parish church of St George, built before the modern town was laid out. From the seaward end of this road, pass into Upper Mostyn Street and then into the modern shopping and commercial centre of the town in Mostyn Street. The later church of Holy Trinity, built for the developing town, occupies a prominent position in the centre. The best preserved buildings of the original early Victorian planned town lie along the promenade in St George's Crescent and Gloddaeth Crescent. Continuing along the shore of the bay towards the Little Orme it is easy to appreciate the restricted size of Llandudno and the undeveloped plots which have never been taken up for building.

From Llandudno the coastal road (A540) can be taken to Colwyn Bay. It passes the old, though much restored church of Llandrillo (833806), at the centre of the parish from which Colwyn Bay was carved. After entering the western outskirts of the town, the planned development of the original Pwllycrochan Estate, including the original house of the Erskine family at the top of Pwllycrochan Avenue (842787), can be studied. With its spacious development it stands out in great contrast to the original core of Colwyn Bay, centred in the streets which converge on the station (850790). The town church of St Paul's occupies a dominant position south of the main through road. Continuing eastwards along the main coastal road Eirias Park is passed (8578), on the site of the former Glan-y-For estate. At Old Colwyn (8678) the centre is dominated by the squat limestone church of St Catherine, a former daughter chapel to the main mother church of Llandrillo. Old Colwyn has still managed to retain something of its past character in its buildings which border the main road.

The walk around Rhyl can begin at the station (009812). The main survivors of the Victorian resort are found in the axial Wellington Road, dominated by the Town Hall. Nearby is the Market Hall (1906). Continue down High Street towards the shore and thence westwards along the West Parade to the Ocean Beach Amusement Park near the mouth of the Clwyd, a development which undoubtedly contributed to the popularity of Rhyl as a resort. The area between the West Parade and the present beach represents land of the former sandy warren which has been levelled and now forms a valuable asset to the resort. In stark contrast to the often garish development of the resort is Foryd Harbour, at the mouth of the River Clwyd where the small coasters still tie up and unload their cargoes of timber for the local sawmills. The area to the east of the station is almost entirely residential. Its growth stages can be worked out in the architecture of its houses and the dates of its churches.

The two distinct parts of Prestatyn are immediately seen from the footbridge across the railway (064831). Southwards from here lies the main shopping, commercial and residential quarters, with the new shopping precinct. The housing estates like Dawson Park occupy steadily rising land towards the limestone hills of the Clwydian Range. Resort development is restricted to the area north of the railway station and includes the holiday camps (053833) and (066837), a leisure centre which has been developed on the coast itself in the last few years (067840) on land that was once part of a golf course.

8. The Vale of Clwyd

THE EVOLUTION OF A BORDER REGION

The Vale of Clwyd extends for more than thirty-two kilometres, a lowland floored with warm red sandstones and boulder clays. To the east an ancient fault line defines the face of the Clwydian Hills; to the west the tangled tributary valleys of the river Clwyd are soon lost among the Denbigh Moors. The vale stands out as one of the most clearly defined tracts of the Welsh landscape. From the rampart of the Iron Age fort, Foel Fenlli, that crowns the abrupt western face of the Clwydian Range near Ruthin it is possible on a day of average visibility to encompass in a single view the whole valley plain.

Westward the land rises towards the heartland of Gwynedd. To the north the plain of the Clwyd widens into the desolate coastal lowland of Morfa Rhuddlan, in the Middle Ages an intractable marsh and today a wasteland of caravan sites. If the Vale of Clwyd seems to possess a strongly defined physical character, the same firmness of outline is lacking in the contours of its historical development. At so many stages of its development this lowland has been wanting in the political unity that seemed necessary for the emergence of a coherent social character. History has stamped this as a marchland tract—a place of centuries of border warfare and the meeting of Welsh and English ways of life. The dominant elements of the man-made landscape do not result from culture traits preserved over many centuries; so often they have been generated in short periods of conflict when the line of the river Clwyd has served temporarily as a frontier between Welsh and English, splitting the unity of the region instead of creating a political and social focus. The eighth century with the building of Offa's Dyke to mark the western frontier of Mercia brought the Anglo-Saxons to the very threshold of the Vale. In the closing years of the eleventh century much of north-eastern Wales became a marchland of the Earldom of Chester and for a time the Normans established a frontier along the line of the River Clwyd. Two centuries later Edward I's castle building at Rhuddlan represented a transient stage in the conquest of Wales, though it was not until Henry VIII's Act of Union in 1536 that this border lowland finally lost its insecure marchland character.

Relics of prehistoric landscapes

The uplands between the Clwyd and the Dee estuary preserve some of the most striking evidence of the presence of prehistoric man in Wales. There was much to attract early man in this region from the time of Palaeolithic hunters in the Ice Age to the final centuries of prehistory in the Romano-British Iron Age. The heavily faulted scarps of Carboniferous Limestone that enclose the lowland of the Vale of Clwyd contain caves that sheltered Palaeolithic hunting groups. Thousands of years later the rock shelters and caves of the limestone hills were used by Neolithic and Early Bronze Age farmers as communal burial places. The outcrops of the Carboniferous Limestone with their light and generally well-drained soils probably favoured prehistoric farming and settlement and by the time the Romans appeared on the scene in the first century AD their rich resources of

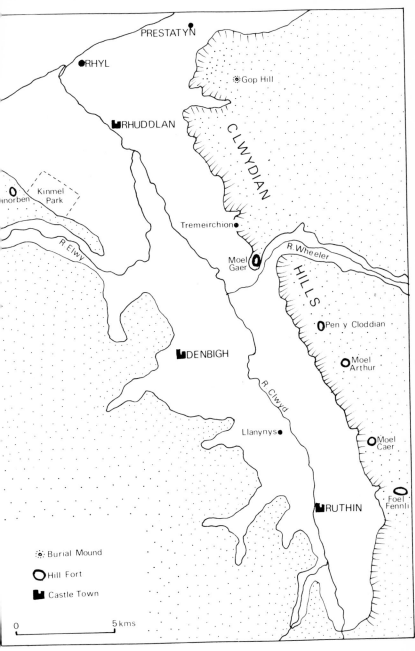

The Vale of Clwyd

lead were added to the economic attractiveness of the region.

It is impossible to sketch with any firmness of detail the geography of the major prehistoric periods in the Vale of Clwyd because of the incomplete nature of the evidence. The locations of settlements, the extent of woodland and the areas cleared for farming, and the precise patterns of the economy in the Neolithic and the Bronze and Iron Ages remain obscure. Only in the latter half of the last millennium BC when the fine series of ditched and ramparted enclosures, the Iron Age forts, had come into being along the high summits of the Clwydian Range do we begin to discern the outlines of a prehistoric geography, the spatial distribution of a vital element of a major cultural period. Of the many centuries that preceeded the Iron Age the great prehistoric landmarks of the Vale of Clwyd begin with the caves of Ffynnon Beuno, Cae Gwyn (085724), Cefn (022704) and Bont Newydd (015711). The two former sites lie in an embayment of the main Clwydian escarpment near Tremeirchion; the latter occupy the wooded limestone cliffs above the Elwy valley on the western flank of the Vale. These are key sites for the Palaeolithic period in Britain. When Ffynnon Beuno Cave was excavated in the 1880s it gave up the bones of hyena, bear, woolly rhinoceros and mammoth as well as tools of early Aurignacian type that had been sealed by deposits of boulder clay and sand laid down in the final advance of the ice sheet from the Irish Sea.

The evidence of the past never remains static. Until 1970 nothing was known in the Vale of Clwyd of the long period of prehistoric hunting cultures that followed the ending of the Ice Age. Then, when the site of the Norman borough at Rhuddlan was investigated in the summers of 1969 and 1970 there came to light the pit dwellings of a Mesolithic settlement. More than 10,000 flints were discovered, objects proving that this encampment of hunters belonged to the Maglemosian branch of Mesolithic cultures. In addition it was possible to obtain a radio-carbon date of 6789 BC (±86) from hazel-nut shells found at the site. The discovery of this important early occupation of the bluff above the right bank of the Clwyd, long before the techniques of the first farmers came into North Wales, illustrates the difficulties involved in the reconstruction of the regional geography of prehistoric times. The interim report that H. Miles published on the excavations of the early medieval borough at Rhuddlan at a place where a new school was about to be erected in 1970 provided much exciting material for speculation. In addition to the Mesolithic site and the firm evidence of its dating through the use of radio-carbon techniques, pottery of the Middle Bronze Age was discovered and, later still, Samian ware and coarse Iron Age pottery that suggested a focus of Romano-British settlement at Rhuddlan. It seems most unlikely that any continuity of occupation can be proposed for this strategic site at the head of the Clwyd estuary, but at least the site of Rhuddlan has asserted its importance in several periods before the masons of Edward I were to leave their indelible marks on the landscape in the years about 1280.

Evidence from the Neolithic and Bronze Age periods is as tantalising as the recent proof of Mesolithic settlement at Rhuddlan. There are no megalithic chambered tombs such as mark the sites of Neolithic communities in Anglesey in either the lowland corridor of the vale or on the surrounding hills. But at two adjacent sites, Dyserth Castle and King Charles' Bowling Green, overlooking the wide embayment of the Clwyd evidence was uncovered of settlements of farmers in the Neolithic centuries between 3000 and 2000 BC. In the same district where a rolling landscape of limestone hills rises above the line of ancient and long abandoned sea cliffs between Dyserth and Prestatyn we find one of the most striking and enigmatic objects of the Bronze Age landscape. Gop Hill (0880) is crowned by a mound almost 12m high and 91m in diameter. This is one of the most imposing mounds of prehistoric Britain, though doubtless some of Gop Cairn's grandeur is owing to the incorporation and shaping of the natural features of the hill. Despite an archaeological investigation of the 1880s that cut a vertical shaft and two galleries into the heart of the mound little is known about the Gop Cairn. No structures came to light inside the cairn and only a few animal bones were discovered. Even so, Christopher Houlder in a recent summary of the field monuments of prehistoric Wales has written that 'it may be in reality the most important of the many Bronze Age burial mounds of the region, indicating wealth or status such as might accrue from participation in the metal trade with Ireland along the North Coast'. Here we find a clue to the geography of the Vale of Clwyd in the Bronze Age when the region formed an important link in the trade between Wales, the Irish Sea and the lowlands to the east. It has frequently been suggested that the summit line of the Clwydian Range, rising gently southwards from the lower node of limestone hills behind Prestatyn, formed a corridor followed by traders in the Bronze Age. The Irish traffic in gold and copper objects probably made its landfall close to the site of Prestatyn. The trade-line along the Clwydian hills was later marked by a succession of Iron Age forts. It may even happen that the forts of Moel y Gaer (0970), Pen-y-Cloddiau (1267), Moel Arthur (1466) Moel y Gaer in Llanbedr (1461) and Foel Fenlli (1660) were raised on earlier occupation sites that date back into the Bronze Age. M. Bevan-Evans and P. Hayes in their report on the excavation of a Bronze Age cairn on one of the high spurs of Moel Famau have suggested that there might have been 'an earlier Bronze Age fort or settlement at Moel Ffenlli' associated with the burial site.

The most striking proof of the location of Bronze Age settlement on the fringes of the Vale of Clwyd has been obtained in the late sixties through H. N. Savory's excavations at Dinorben, one of the most closely investigated of Britain's hill forts that has yielded proof of more than a thousand years of occupation. Dinorben and its massive earthworks occupy the summit of an ancient cliff-line in the Carboniferous Limestone to the south-east of Abergele. Its topographical location in relation to the coastal lowland of the Clwyd is comparable to that of the prehistoric site at Dyserth Castle. Savory was able to show through the application of radio-carbon dating that the earliest rampart at Dinorben had been thrown up in the ninth century BC over the site of an open undefended Late Bronze Age settlement. The presence of Bronze Age man in the gentle limestone hills that flank the Vale of Clwyd to the west is also attested by a number of burial mounds in farms and park land.

Without doubt the most striking relics of the prehistoric landscapes of north-east Wales are the huge hill forts, a half dozen altogether, that crown the summits of the Clwydian Range. Little firm material evidence has been gathered from these magnificent sites to allow profitable speculation about their functions and origins. The most spacious of the hill forts, Pen-y-Cloddiau, has never been excavated. Its 26 hectares enclose part of a hill top at more than 400m above sea level and its northern flank is composed of complex earthworks of four successive ramparts and three ditches. Foel Fenlli, Moel y Gaer (Llanbedr) and Moel Arthur were all investigated as long ago as 1849. The only site that has been dug to the exacting standards of modern archaeology is Moel Hiraddug where Bevan-Evans conducted a rescue dig in part of its complex earthworks because the whole feature is doomed to extinction through quarrying for limestone. Consequently much remains to be discovered about the chain of hill forts along the Clwydian range. Until the present time, speculation has depended upon some acute field observations and the application of ideas drawn from similar but more fully explored Iron Age sites in Wales and the Marches.

J. Forde-Johnston in a field survey of the hill forts of the Clwyds has noted the commanding positions of several sites in relation to the gaps in the western escarpment. Foel Fenlli dominates the narrow defile of the Bwlch Pen Barras from a height of 511m. Further north, Moel Arthur enjoys a similar superiority of position over a minor col in the hills that provides a passage at 350m between the Vale and the Alun Valley. The important route of the Wheeler Valley opens into the vale beneath the steep slopes of Moel y Gaer. Such space relationships may have little meaning in the social geography of Iron Age times, though Forde-Johnston and others have argued that strategic motives and military considerations were perhaps uppermost in the intentions of the founders of these embanked enclosures. Apart from the obvious relationship of the hill top enclosures of the Clwydian Range to the cols and breaching valleys of the main escarpment, the 'forts' also stood as beacons along the ancient ridgeway that followed the crest of the hills.

Much evidence is still wanting to establish the hill forts above the Vale of Clwyd as a primary defence line in the long forgotten conflicts of the Iron Age. Apart from the patterns of rampart and ditch the only other substantial observations from the hill forts concern hut-platforms within the enclosures. Foel Fenlli and Moel Hiraddug both contain clusters of some two dozen hut circles and house platforms. The biggest fort, Pen-y-Cloddiau, has given up no such proof of occupation. A gathering of Roman coins from Foel Fenlli lies behind the suggestion that it acted as a market place during the Roman centuries. Theorists who find a strategic hypothesis insubstantial in understanding the closely-spaced forts of the Clwydian Hills lean towards explanations that relate their construction to the pastoralism of the Deceangli, the Iron Age tribe that inhabited this region of North Wales. In this view the camps were used for the overnight penning of cattle, sheep and goats to provide protection against predatory wild animals. The wide spaces between the multiple ramparts were designed for the penning of livestock while the hut circles suggest the foundations of shelters that were inhabited during the months of high summer while the community of a permanent lowland settlement exploited the summer pastures. It is not fanciful to suggest that these gatherings in the high hills might have provided the occasion for the trading of products from distant places; hence the perpetuation under the Romans of a market site on Foel Fenlli. Only further archaeological research can determine the truth in such speculations. The sites at present pose many problems.

The marchland character of the Vale of Clwyd first becomes evident with the Roman Conquest of Wales in the latter half of the first century. During the succeeding 1,500 years the corridor of lowland beneath the Clwydian hills becomes an arena where cultures of widely different characteristics merge, first a Celtic Iron Age society with Roman military organisation and later the way of life of Cymru with the social patterns of Anglo-Saxon and Norman England. In periods of sharp conflict when the power of Mercia or expanding medieval marcher lordships pressed westward a frontier line between Welsh and English was drawn through the Vale.

The Roman occupation outlines a pattern of political evolution that was repeated more than once in the succeeding centuries. The first probing of north-eastern Wales by Roman troops took place in AD 48, but it was not until AD 78 that the final conquest of Anglesey was achieved under Agricola. The Vale of Clwyd and the Flintshire hills, rich with lead ores, were within close reach of the Roman legionary base at Chester. This border country, the territory of the Deceangli—the tribe that built the lonely line of hill forts along the Clwydians, probably accepted Roman rule with little opposition. The basis of this view lies in the absence of Roman military works in the region. The chief Roman object in the landscape, apart from the lead mines of the limestone hills that have long since been obliterated by medieval workings, was the road that connected the primary military base at Chester with the fort at Caernarfon. Much of this road, recognised as Iter XI of the Antonine Itinerary, seems to be lost beyond recognition in the foothills of Flintshire and along the narrow plain of the Dee estuary, but beyond Holywell where it climbs westwards towards the Rhuallt gap in the Clwydian escarpment there is little doubt that the modern A55 trunk road follows the line of its ancient predecessor. Again, the Roman road is known for several miles to the west of St Asaph as the second class, B5381 road that leads to the Conwy valley. Until scarcely two centuries ago this route, probably on the line of a far more ancient prehistoric trade artery, provided the chief access from the east into the heart of North Wales. Even today, if one wants to savour the real Wales, it is infinitely preferable to the coastal trunk road with its multitude of caravans, desolate bungalow settlements, and stifling traffic jams, the last and worst of the invasions from the east. Somewhere between Chester and Caerhun, according to the Antonine Itinerary, lay the site of another auxiliary Roman fort, Varis. Archaeology has never been able to discover the exact location of Varis, though in all likelihood the fort was at St Asaph. All traces seem to have been obliterated in the growth of the little cathedral town.

The Vale of Clwyd as a frontier region

The centuries that followed the Roman withdrawal from Britain witnessed a perpetuation of the patterns of society and settlement that had become established in the Vale of Clwyd in Iron Age times. For instance, there are strong hints that the hill fort at Dinorben survived as a social focus into the Dark Age centuries and even into the post Norman period. As late as the fourteenth century Dinorben acted as a centre of local organisation when it was the site of the *llys* or lord's court for the commote of Rhos is Dulas. The hill fort, soon to be erased from the Welsh landscape by the advancing face of the limestone quarry, is the last symbol of a territorial unit that persisted from the pre-Roman Iron Age until the late Middle Ages. But there are other clues to the continuity of landscape history in this region. For instance, the tribal name of the Deceangli has survived several changes. In the centuries before the Norman Conquest it appears as Tegeingl, a name given to a tract of Flintshire that covered much of the Clwydian Range. Later the name changed to the English *Englefield*.

In a study of Llanynys (SJ 1062) Professor Glanville Jones produces even more striking evidence for the great age of the primary settlement pattern of the Vale. Llanynys, 'the church or parish on the island', occupies a site on a long mound with fertile, well-drained soils between the rivers Clwyd and Clywedog. It is a pattern that is repeated in the lower part of the Vale where the Clwyd is joined by the Elwy; there on a long low ridge between the converging rivers we find the site of St Asaph. Llanynys is the centre of a large primary parish that stretches westward into the confused hill country on the edge of the Denbigh Moors. Professor Jones believes that the core of the settlement, at the site of the present parish church, originated in a circular enclosure that contained the buildings of a Dark Age monastic community, a *clas* of the Celtic Church. The territory of the *clas* probably coincided with that of the parish that has survived down the centuries. In a brilliant synthesis of scattered evidence from documents and the field Jones has traced an expanding system of open-field cultivation from the original Dark Age monastic core. A handful of arable strips survived until the middle of the nineteenth century and even today some traces of this ancient system of farming may be discerned in the field patterns of Llanynys.

Llanynys is not the only place in the Vale of Clwyd where the presence of a former system of open-field cultivation has been recognised. A study of field-names, especially as they occur in the Tithe schedules of the 1840s, reveals that open fields were a common element of land use in many parishes along the Clwyd. The Tithe surveys for Tremeirchion and Bodfari both contain the terms *erw* and *llein*, names descriptive of the arable strips of open fields. Cwm, another large parish extending from the summits of the Clwydian hills across the vale to the river, was already a place of small, mainly square-shaped fields and scattered farms at the time of the Tithe Survey in 1840. But this early Victorian map still shows the relics of a few scattered strips and the accompanying Tithe Schedules bear witness to the former presence of open fields in the recording of such field-name elements as *erw, accar* and *quillet,* the latter a term that is used for the individual strip.

The lineaments of the present landscape in the Vale of Clwyd seem to contain elements that have survived over many centuries from the threshold of prehistoric times in the late Iron Age through the centuries of the Celtic Church and the later age of border conflict that culminated in the Edwardian conquest of Wales. But here, in this marchland, the earliest ground-plan of settlement has been largely concealed by the intermittent warfare and colonisation from the east between the eighth and sixteenth centuries. The earliest threat from the Cheshire and Shropshire lowland came with the westward expansion of Mercia in the eighth century. Two great Saxon earthworks, Wat's Dyke and Offa's Dyke, mark the frontier of Mercia with Cymru. Wat's Dyke traces a course through the foothills of Flintshire. The great earthwork of Offa, dating from the closing years of the eighth century, reaches the Irish Sea on the north-eastern fringe of the Vale of Clwyd at Prestatyn. The vale lay outside the territory that was opened up to English settlement in the centuries before the Norman Conquest. This view is borne out by the distribution of early English place-names in Flintshire. On the whole they are limited to the lowlands and foothills of eastern Flintshire; Wat's Dyke seems to have marked a frontier of colonisation in the expansive decades of Mercia during the eighth century. The high upland pastures of the Clwydian Range probably marked out a frontier zone between Welsh and Saxon, but for one place a shred of evidence survives to suggest that Mercia probed more deeply its natural frontier with Wales. The earliest reference to Rhuddlan, contained in the *Annales Cambriae* for the year 796, hints at the presence of a Mercian settlement on the right bank of the Clwyd. Again, Edward the Elder is recorded as the founder of a *burgh* at Cledemutha in 921. To the east and south of Edward I's planned town at Rhuddlan an earthwork, known as the Town Ditch, still survives. It encloses a space of some twenty-four hectares above the river-cliff of the Clwyd and although it has long been considered to form part of the defences of the Norman borough, the suggestion has lately been put forward that the Town Ditch represents the only surviving field evidence of Edward the Elder's *burgh* at the mouth of the Clwyd.

The Norman Conquest and the first half of the twelfth century witnessed the serious intrusion of the English into the Vale of Clwyd. It is evident that the Saxon foothold on the Clwyd estuary with its access to the important line of the Roman road leading westward into Gwynedd had been lost by the middle of the eleventh century. For instance, Rhuddlan briefly comes into the limelight of history in 1062 when an entry in the *Annales Cambriae* notes that 'the ships and the *llys* of Gruffydd ap Llywelyn were burnt by Harold'. Rhuddlan evidently sheltered the court of a Welsh prince. Anglo-Norman strategy in the conquest of Wales centred upon the site of Rhuddlan. In 1073, Robert, a kinsman of Hugh, Earl of Chester, raised a huge castle mound on a bluff above the river. On the landward side this circular motte, Twt Hill (0277) rises to a height of seven and a half metres; on the riverside it towers up to twenty-one metres. By the time that Domesday Book's surveyors were gathering their assessments of the resources of Norman England Rhuddlan had passed into the hands of the Earls of Chester. This greatest of medieval surveys shows that a borough was already in existence in 1086 for it notes that Rhuddlan had eighteen burgesses, one church and a mint.

From the middle of the twelfth century until the last quarter of the thirteenth century the fortunes of Rhuddlan illustrate the unstable character of the frontier between England and Wales; the Vale of Clwyd had become a dangerous marchland. In 1149 the castle and borough were captured by Owain Gwynedd and soon retaken into English hands by Henry II. After scarcely two decades they passed again to Welsh control and remained so for the greater part of a century. In 1241 Henry III's invasion of Wales foreshadowed the successful strategy of Edward I that was to be accomplished before the end of the century. He gained control of the coast as far west as Conwy, built a new castle at Dyserth and reinforced the defences at Rhuddlan. By 1256 Llywelyn ap Gruffydd had regained control of the Vale of Clwyd and the fortress town of Rhuddlan for Gwynedd. The

Edwardian Conquest of Wales began in 1277. Rhuddlan was reached in August of that year and the building of a new castle began in November, on a fresh site a few hundred metres downstream from the Norman motte. The urban history of Rhuddlan also saw the beginning of a fresh chapter when a new borough charter was granted in 1278 and the streets of a new town were laid out beside the castle to the north of the original Norman borough and, one suspects, of the earlier, mysterious late Saxon settlement.

The Norman town at Rhuddlan was completely abandoned after the creation of the Edwardian borough. For centuries the detailed pattern of its streets and the foundations of its timbered houses have lain hidden beneath the hedgerows and pastures that divide the town from Twt Hill. The recent excavations at Rhuddlan have revealed some of the outlines of the Norman borough. The line of the borough defences, enclosing some eight hectares within the larger space protected by the Town Ditch, has been traced. The foundations of the Norman church and of two timbered houses have also come to light. Rhuddlan presents a clear example of what must have happened in the history of many other medieval settlements—relocation on a new site adjacent to an existing town or village. The old borough of Rhuddlan was probably deliberately deserted about 1278. It is not hard to imagine that a largely Welsh population in the small town was dispersed to make way for a new core of English colonists.

The Edwardian Conquest introduced a fresh element into the political geography of the Vale of Clwyd. For the first time the frontier of English settlement was effectively pushed to the west of the river with the creation of two marcher lordships centred on the newly founded castle towns of Ruthin and Denbigh. The River Clwyd ceased to be a dividing line through the unit of the thirty-two kilometre long corridor of lowland. The three new towns, Rhuddlan, Denbigh and Ruthin, acted as markets, centres of English settlement, and centres too around which English ideas of land-holding and estate-building were to be put into practice. The Lordship of Denbigh was given to Henry de Lacy, Earl of Lincoln, who began building the castle on the crest of a limestone crag in 1283. Today we can still enjoy the site as one of the most romantically exciting medieval towns in the British Isles. The hill-top core of Denbigh possesses a sense of grandeur that is hard to match among the small towns of the border country. The original inner walled town crouches beneath the ruined castle and the gaunt sixteenth-century shell of the unfinished church that Robert Dudley, Earl of Leicester, planned as a cathedral. The Lordship of Ruthin was created at the same period of the Edwardian Conquest in the inner part of the Vale of Clwyd. The building of the castle began in 1277 on a ridge of red sandstone that rises sharply above the Clwyd. Ruthin, along with Rhuddlan, seems to belong to the first phase of Edward I's military strategy in Wales because the royal masons must have been at work in laying the foundations of the castle there at the time when others were working on the bluff above the Clwyd estuary. But Ruthin soon ceased to be of direct interest to the Crown as the advancing frontier of conquest was pushed to the Conwy valley and the highly strategic locations at the northern and southern entrances of the Menai Strait. With the creation of the Lordship of Ruthin the future of the castle and borough lay in the hands of the lords Grey, Earls of Kent. The foundation of the new borough at Ruthin was laid through a charter of Reynold Grey, granted in 1282.

Like Rhuddlan the new boroughs that marked the English advance into the heart of the Vale of Clwyd were not entirely fresh creations as settlements carved out of the wilderness. Both Denbigh and Ruthin used territorial structures that had long formed part of the Welsh way of life in the Vale of Clwyd. For instance, the marcher Lordship of Ruthin occupied the ancient territory of the Cantref of Dyffryn Clwyd. The site of the borough of Ruthin, on one of the many minor ridges that diversify the topography of the floor of the Vale of Clwyd, was already the most important place in Dyffryn Clwyd before the troops of Edward I overran North Wales. It was the site of the *maerdref,* the centre of government in the upper vale where Welsh princes had held their courts. Before the making of the borough there was already a settlement, a nucleated hamlet, at Ruthin. The Court Rolls of the borough in the fourteenth century show that the Welsh population was not scattered and that Welsh-speaking tenants remained on the land. In fact, a *Register of Tenants,* drawn up in 1324 when a new lord was taking over, shows that out of the hundred burgesses at Ruthin more than half of them were Welshmen.

Through the evidence that survives in fourteenth-century documents it is possible to trace the transformation of a Welsh market village into a medieval English borough. The *Register of Tenants* in 1324 shows that 24 out of 27 of the burgage holders in Well Street, were Welshmen. Here was probably the street of the pre-Conquest settlement. The quarter around the castle, on the other hand, was dominantly English. Across the river, in Mwrog, a dominantly English settlement seems to have arisen with almost three times as many English burgage holders as Welshmen. Ruthin held markets in the time of the Welsh princes and the stalls were laid out along 'the great street'. In December 1295 we see the marcher lord, Lord Reynold Grey, directing the laying out of the present market place. He ordered that 'a proper market was to be built near the pillory within six weeks'.

The task of the Edwardian Conquest and the work of the marcher lords of the thirteenth century was completed only two and a half centuries later, in Henry VIII's reign, with the Act of Union of 1536. The Tudor decades opened up a new period in the landscape history of the Vale of Clwyd. The open fields that belonged to almost every settlement were to dwindle away under the complex processes of enclosure, estate-building and the integration of farms that were made much easier by the introduction of the English legal system to Wales. The making of landed estates by the gentry was particularly active in the vicinity of the towns where merchants found the safest investment for their profits in the countryside. Most famous among the estate-builders of the Tudor period was Sir Richard Clough of Denbigh. Richard Clough came from a family of glovers in Denbigh, a family with no landed property. In the 1560s his position as Factor in Antwerp to the Royal Agent, Sir Thomas Gresham, was to bring wealth to Sir Richard. By 1566 he had accumulated several scattered properties in the townships around Denbigh. At the same time, in the late sixties, Sir Richard Clough was able to display his wealth and position in the building of two country mansions, Plas Clough and Bachegraig. Plas Clough still stands only 1.5 kilometres from Denbigh, beside the road to St Asaph. Its stepped gables, an architectural idea introduced from Flanders, make this the first Renaissance house in Wales. At Bachegraig, in a meadow close to the river Clwyd, Sir Richard Clough built a tall six-storeyed mansion after the design of the merchants' houses of Antwerp. It is said that masons and materials were imported from Flanders to make this merchant's base in the Vale of Clwyd. Clough died scarcely three years after the building of Bachegraig. This strange house, so out of keeping with its surroundings, lasted until its demolition in 1821. Thomas Pennant, a great recorder of Welsh topography at the end of the eighteenth century, visited Bachegraig and wrote that the outbuildings were meant to serve as warehouses 'to disperse his imports to the neighbouring parts'. Another traveller, Richard Fenton, wrote in his *Tours in Wales* that Sir Richard Clough's house was built 'with a view to future commerce' and that the development of this site 'half buried in woods', according to Pennant, was coupled with an ambitious plan to make the Clwyd navigable, perhaps by a sea canal, from Rhuddlan to Pont y Cambwll.

Kinmel Park, perhaps the grandest estate of the Vale of Clwyd, emerged from a long period of estate-building that began in the late Middle Ages. It lies partly on the limestone upland and partly in Rhuddlan Marsh and it grew by the purchase of lands in both Abergele and Rhuddlan. Early in the nineteenth century Kinmel Park was bought by Edward Hughes, the rich mine owner whose fortune had accrued from working the copper ores of Parys Mountain in Anglesey. Twice during the nineteenth century the great house in the park was rebuilt and the present mansion, designed in 1870, now serves as a girls' boarding school.

Sir Richard Clough's new houses at Plas Clough and Bachegraig not only introduced new styles and influences from the Continent into Welsh buildings, they also mark the start of a wave of rebuilding of farmhouses, barns, outhouses and other agricultural buildings that was to stretch into the middle of the nineteenth century. Bricks, first used at Bachegraig, were to replace gradually the traditional medieval materials of timber, laths and plaster. Along the Vale of Clwyd farmhouses were almost universally rebuilt in brick during the seventeenth and eighteenth centuries. Later, particularly between 1780 and 1850, another phase of rebuilding in brick saw the renewal of barns and outhouses. In the hills that fringe the Vale of Clwyd it has been shown that the movement towards rebuilding of farm properties came later than in the lowlands and limestone often replaced bricks as a building material.

The most dramatic changes in the landscape of the Vale of Clwyd have taken place in its lower estuarine part since the end of the eighteenth century. The reclamation of the extensive marshland, known as Morfa Rhuddlan, in the early years of the nineteenth century led to the enclosure of some 10,900 hectares of former grazing land. At times of high spring tides and when the Clwyd and its tributaries were in spate the lower parts of the valley were exposed to severe flooding. The ponding back of waters as far inland as St Asaph frequently isolated Rhuddlan from its communications with the west, a factor that has been cited to explain its failure as an urban settlement in competition with Denbigh. In 1794 the first step towards the reclamation of Morfa Rhuddlan was taken in a parliamentary bill for embanking the coast and enclosing the marsh. The thirteen-kilometre long embankment that contained the reclaimed lands of Morfa Rhuddlan together with the building of the Chester and Holyhead Railway in the 1840s prepared the way for the most striking change in the topography of the Vale of Clwyd, the development of a Victorian seaside resort at Rhyl. The Vale and its rim of hills, as we see the region today, are composed of a mosaic of landscape elements from several different ages. Between the prehistoric hill forts of the Clwydian Range and the shapeless caravan settlements of Kinmel Bay one can recognise formative elements from the Dark Ages, from the medieval centuries when the frontier role was uppermost to the period of economic expansion after the Tudor Act of Union.

SUGGESTED ITINERARIES

The Vale of Clwyd and its enclosing hills still form a borderland, a frontier zone, for the modern traveller journeying from England into Wales. Several main roads speed the motorist westwards towards his goals in the North Welsh coastal resorts, the mountains of Snowdonia or perhaps the Irish ferry port at Holyhead, but each trunk route provides a different transect of this region—a transect that can become much more worthwhile if a few stops and, perhaps, minor diversions are taken.

1. The least interesting approach to this region is by the traffic congested coast road, A548, with its occasional glimpses across the widening sands and saltmarshes of the Dee. Between Prestatyn, astride the northern end of Offa's Dyke, and Abergele, this route crosses the dull coastal strip at the mouth of the Vale of Clwyd whose lands were largely reclaimed with the enclosure of Morfa Rhuddlan at the beginning of the nineteenth century. For thirteen kilometres an ugly holiday conurbation, with Rhyl at its core, has cast a blight over this lowland. Here and there, as at Towyn (9779), a fleeting view inland reveals the spaciousness of the Vale of Clwyd and its boundary hills.

2. A5151 makes a much more interesting approach and crossing of the Vale between Holywell and Rhuddlan. There are some fine distant views of the higher summits of the Clwydian Range to the south. At the approach to Trelawnyd, a medieval new town, the road follows the line of Offa's Dyke and here too one comes close to that enigmatic Bronze Age earthwork, Gop Cairn. The descent to the lowland of the Vale of Clwyd passes through Dyserth (0579), site of a castle in one of the abortive medieval invasions of Wales. But the goal of any approach to North Wales by this route must be Rhuddlan when

time should be taken to explore Twt Hill (0277), the site of the Norman borough and the later planted town and castle of the Edwardian Conquest period. Crossing the Clwyd with a fine prospect of the castle high on a bluff across the river, the A547 road leads over the reclaimed lands of Morfa Rhuddlan to Abergele.

3. A more southerly crossing of the Vale is made by the A55T between Holywell and Abergele. Here the traveller is following one of the oldest lines of communication through the region, the Roman road that connected Chester with the fort at Segontium (Caernarfon). For some three kilometres across the Clwydian Hills the line of the modern road and its Roman forerunner coincide. The Palaeolithic cave sites in the limestone hills near to Tremeirchion lie 2.5 kilometres to the south of this road. Further along, on a low ridge between the Elwy and the Clwyd—a location typical of several settlements in the Vale, stands St Asaph (Llanelwy), a cathedral town and the likely place for the lost Roman fort of Varis. From St Asaph two roads open to the west. A55T continues past Kinmel Park, among the most successful examples of estate building in the post medieval centuries. An even more interesting route is the B5381 that winds through the unspoilt hill country inland from the coastal resorts. Some six kilometres from St Asaph it passes close to Dinorben, a hill fort that has revealed as much about the Iron Age as any single site in the British Isles.

4. A541 provides a different approach to the region. Instead of crossing the eastern backbone of upland it takes the Wheeler Valley and its gap through the Clwydian Range. At the entrance to the gap stands an accessible Iron Age hill fort, Moel y Gaer (0970) and not far to the south, by minor roads and hills tracks, one can reach the huge unexplored ramparts of Penycloddiau. Again, 1.5 kilometres to the north of the road and not far from the crossing of the Clwyd, secluded among woods and meadows is the site of Bachegraig, Sir Richard Clough's exotic mansion traces of which, alas, have all but vanished from the landscape. The road, A543, diverges from this route beyond Pontruffydd (0769) and leads into Denbigh, in its site perhaps the most eye-catching of all Britain's medieval new towns. Beyond Denbigh the A543 crosses the wild unspoilt landscapes of the Denbigh Moors to join Telford's A5 at Pentre Foelas for the descent into the Conwy Valley.

5. The 494T from Mold to Corwen and Bala presents the most characteristic cross-section of Dyffryn Clwyd, the southernmost part of the Vale. Foel Fenlli (1660), among the most exciting of the hill

fort sites astride the Clwydian Range lies scarcely 1.5 kilometres from the road as it descends towards Ruthin. At Ruthin one can pick out all the features of a planted town of the Conquest period—market-place, late medieval church and castle (now an hotel). 1.5 kilometres to the east of Ruthin at Llanrhydd (1457) is the church of the mother parish in which Lord Reynold de Grey's new town of Ruthin was to evolve in the closing decade of the thirteenth century. South of Ruthin as the A494T threads its way through the upper valley of the Clwyd an unexplored hill fort site lies to the south of the road astride the ridge of the Craig-adwy-wynt. It is more than a fanciful thought that this may form the prehistoric nucleus of settlement in Dyffryn Clwyd, a permanent base of the Deceangli who took their flocks and herds in the summer months to the high pastures of the Clwydian Range.

9. The Holyhead Road of Thomas Telford

Routes in North Wales are as old as the earliest settlements. That there were well-established trade routes during the Neolithic Period, perhaps 6,000 years ago, is shown by the distribution of the distinctive axe heads fashioned at this time from the granophyre of Graig Llwyd behind Penmaenmawr (7075). Finds of polished stone implements have been made from places as far apart as Land's End, the New Forest and the Firth of Forth. The exact routes of dispersal of this much sought-after material are not known exactly but it is most likely that the trackways mainly followed the high, less forested, plateau tops of the Denbighshire Moors as they spread out in all directions from the quarry centre near Penmaenmawr. The upland routes probably persisted throughout the succeeding Bronze and Iron Ages and may have determined the line of some of the Roman roads across this mountainous part of North Wales.

At this time a route which hugged the coast was not possible, largely because of the difficulties of rounding great buttress headlands like that of Penmaenbach (7478). The main Roman route westwards as it crossed Denbighshire ran from their centre at Varae (now St Asaph) to the crossing of the River Conwy at their fort of Kanovium (7770), a defensive site first established by Agricola in his campaign of AD 78. From here it climbed steadily to the col of Bwlch y Ddeufan

(7171) before dropping to the coastal plain near Aber. Apart from crossing the Lavan Sands at the northern entrance to the Menai Strait the final section of the route presented no problems as it made for the fortress of Caer Gybi, the present day Holyhead. As far as is known there was no Roman road further inland following the line of the Llwgwy and Ogwen Rivers from Capel Curig to Bangor, the line of the present A5 road. The minor fortress of Caer-Llugwy (7457), three kilometres east of Capel Curig, was located on a north-south route, the successor of the prehistoric track of Sarn Helen.

These early Roman routes, though paved and marked by milestones, at least in part, were not to play a major role in the later road system of North Wales. In medieval times the coastal headlands still presented a major difficulty and led in time to the opening of the Sychnant Pass road. To get round Penmaenbach and Penmaenmawr use had to be made of the foreshore and this, as Dr Johnson found, could be a harrowing experience. It was not until the latter half of the eighteenth century that an inland route through the mountains of Snowdonia was contemplated with the creation of the Turnpike Trusts. An Act of 1777 covered the section between Corwen and Cerrig y Ddrudion and Pentre Fan (8751). From the latter place the road ran north-west across the edge of the Denbighshire Moors before dropping into the Conwy Valley at Llanrwst. The present route of the A5 through Bettws y Coed and Capel Curig was not in being at the time for the natural obstacles like the steep drop into the glacial trough of the upper Conwy proved too formidable a barrier even to the builders of the turnpike roads.

The natural barrier presented by the rock step over which the River Ogwen drops 70m, was not successfully overcome until 1791 when Lord Penrhyn, the owner of the large slate quarry at Bethesda (6165) lower down the valley, built a road up the Nant Ffrancon and then on to his estate at Capel Curig (7258). The route he chose was along the western side of the valley along what is now a track connecting farms like Maescaradog (6362) and Blaen y Nant (6460). It then climbed steadily up and then along the southern shore of Llyn Ogwen. After crossing the low watershed at 312m between the westerly flowing Ogwen headwaters and the easterly flowing Afon Llugwy it kept to the southern side of this large, open through valley. The present road is not along this early route which is, however, still traceable in the field walls and towards Capel Curig it still forms a distinct track. Where it enters Capel Curig it crosses the Llugwy in an impressive stone bridge just behind the Post Office.

The influence of the Penrhyn family on the landscape of this part of Snowdonia was considerable. Apart from their large quarry, which ultimately led to the foundation of the settlement at Bethesda, their widespread interest found expression in other projects. One reason for building the road to Capel Curig was to develop it as a tourist centre at a time when the exploration of the mountains was in its infancy. To allow visitors to admire the picturesque, and particularly fine view of the Snowdon Range, Lord Penrhyn built an inn at Capel Curig. This was later to become the Royal Hotel—now the Coed Brennin Out-door Pursuit Centre—and established Capel Curig as one of the earliest of the tourist centres of Snowdonia. Lord Penrhyn's road went no further so that no through route to Bettws y Coed and beyond was contemplated at this time.

The turn of the century brought increasing pressure for the build-ing of an inland Holyhead route as an alternative to the treacherous road along the coast of North Wales. The Parliamentary Union with Ireland in 1801 acted as something of a catalyst to plans which might otherwise have lain dormant for many years to come. By 1805 a turnpike route had been established to connect Llandegai (5970) near Penrhyn Castle to Pentrefoelas (8751). With the fashioning of this link there was now a continuous route from Shrewsbury to Bangor and thence, after crossing the Menai Strait, on to Holyhead.

Even where the turnpike road was crossing country that was already provided with a track, like the section between Llandegai and Capel Curig constructed a short time before by Lord Penrhyn, it did not necessarily follow the same route. From Llandegai, for example, the turnpike road ran almost due south, hugging the west bank of the Ogwen as far as Pont Twr (626660). Part of this route forms the present A5 and then the B4366 past the Penrhyn Slate Quarries. From Pont Twr the original turnpike road crossed to the east side of the Ogwen and then continued under the steep crags of the Carned-dau, gradually climbing to surmount the Ogwen step. This section through the Nant Ffrancon again forms the route of the A5 but is different from the earlier Penrhyn road through the valley which ran on the other side. The turnpike road and the earlier Penrhyn road joined up once again around the shores of Llyn Ogwen but then departed from it by taking a new route much closer to the Afon Llugwy. This meant that it had to be built on an embankment as it crossed the marshy ground near the highest point of the through valley. The turnpike road still survives as a paved track about 2m in width. Minor streams were crossed by means of large flat slabs resting on low stone piles. When the Holyhead road came to be built by Telford this section was discarded and soon degenerated into the track it is today.

From Capel Curig eastwards the new turnpike was charting a fresh course for Lord Penrhyn's road did not cover the section to Bettws y Coed. At first it followed the line of what is now the A5 but after a kilometre it crossed over the river at Pont Cyfyng (7357) and then followed the north bank of the river past the Roman fort of Caer Llugwy. This section of the original turnpike still exists as a minor metalled road, rejoining the main A5 near Ty hyll (7557). From here to Bettws the road was along the line of the present route, past the Swallow Falls, where the River Llugwy drops over a rock step.

At Bettws y Coed, which was only a tiny hamlet at the time the turnpike was being built in 1805, perhaps the most difficult section of all was encountered. The road had to climb out of the deep glacial trough of the Upper Conwy Valley. To do this it followed the valley floor for about two kilometres and then began a zigzag ascent above what is now called the Fairy Glen until it reached the plateau around Dinas Hill. Once on the top its route was less hazardous although the gorge of the Upper Conwy around Glan Conwy (8352) was not easy to negotiate. At Pentrefoelas the turnpike linked up with the older road which was already providing a through route from Corwen to Llanrwst.

The completion of the turnpike had a considerable impact on opening up what had been a quiet corner of North Wales. The Post Office immediately began to use the road to carry mail destined for Ireland. The proprietor of the Capel Curig Hotel found that at certain seasons he was overwhelmed with guests who came to Snowdonia in search 'of the picturesque and awe-inspiring grandeur' of mountain scenery. Extensions were planned to increase the amount of available accommodation so that already Capel Curig was becoming one of the main tourist centres of the region. It was not long, however, before the deficiencies of the road were to become increasingly apparent. Lack of money had meant that the foundations of many of the critical sections were skimped and after heavy rains degenerated into muddy, rutted tracks. Snowdrifts also blocked the road during the winter months so that the mail coach often did not run for periods of several weeks. In time the deteriorating state of the road led to the withdrawal of the mail coach altogether.

It was this situation that ultimately led to the Irish Members of Parliament seeking and obtaining government aid. In 1810 Henry

Parnell succeeded in having the matter considered by a Parliamentary Commission. Thomas Telford, the most experienced and famous of the British road engineers, was called in to suggest improvement. Such was the impact he made that the name Telford Road is often used synonomously with the Holyhead Road. His report made it clear that improvements were urgently needed to certain dangerous sections and, if necessary, a new route altogether should be chosen. If the plan was to succeed there would also have to be some re-organisation over the control of the road which, at that time, was in the hands of no less than twenty-three turnpike trusts. Telford's report was accepted and in 1815 a grant of £20,000 was made towards improvements.

Telford lost no time in putting his ideas and practical experience to good use. Gradients were reduced to 1:20 as far as possible. For the first time adequate foundations of large stones topped with smaller rubble were provided and the whole upper road surface had a distinct camber to drain off surplus water. So successful was the Telford approach that in 1819 the Select Committee of the House of Commons was able to report:

> the great attention which Mr. Telford has bestowed to give the surface of the road one uniform and moderately convex slope, free from the smallest inequality throughout its whole breadth; the numerous land drains and where necessary, shores and tunnels of substantial masonry, with which water from springs or falling from rain is instantly carried off; the great care with which a sufficient foundation is established for the road, and the quality, solidity and disposition of the materials that are put upon it, are matters quite new in the system of road making.

Telford's approach to building the Holyhead or Parliamentary Road as it became known, was not simply an improvement of the existing route. In many sections he planned an entirely new line across country. Admittedly there were sections which because of the topography, like the gorge of the River Alwen at Glyn Diffwys (9944) allowed no alternative and here he was obviously content simply to improve rather than innovate. The vertical rocky sides of the gorge were cut back to create an artificial shelf 4m wide along which the road could run. A little further on he drove a new straight section for three kilometres across the marshy ground from Cerrig y drudion to Glasfryn (5091) in place of the former twisting track which ran a little to the north and which can still be seen to connect a string of farms. Telford was aware that if coach travel was to be speedy the road should be graded throughout and he went to considerable lengths to achieve this objective. Thus in order to climb the rock step at the head of the Nant Ffrancon (6460) he started the upward slope as far back as Tyn y Maes (6364) so that there is no steep gradient, as on the road which it replaced. Similarly from Bettws y Coed his road climbed out of the Conwy Valley with an even gradient for three kilometres before it reached the plateau top near Dinas Hill, a very different situation from the original twisting ascent out of the Fairy Glen.

In most cases the new sections of the road built by Telford led to a shortening of the route. Between Bettws y Coed and Capel Curig, for example, the twisting course of the old turnpike past the Roman fort of Caer Llugwy was replaced by a more direct road running along the north side of the valley. Similarly beyond Capel Curig, Telford drove his road right through the centre of the low col which formed the watershed between the opposing Ogwen and Llugwy rivers. Considerable embanking was necessary across the marshy ground which had earlier been shunned by both Lord Penrhyn and the Turnpike Trust when they made their roads. Even on lower ground Telford often chose an entirely new route. Between what is now Bethesda and Llandegai he forsook the Penrhyn road in favour of a new route on the west side of the Ogwen though not along the old line through the village of Llanechid (6268). This meant crossing the Ogwen River at Halfway Bridge (6068), so named from its situation midway between two toll houses. It was on this stretch of the road, close to the Penrhyn slate quarries, that the town of Bethesda grew up as an important quarrying settlement, perhaps an indication of the importance now placed on the through route which Telford had established. Although Lord Penrhyn had built a model village, Llandegai, near his castle the quarrymen found the distance too great and so gradually they formed a settlement taking its name from the first chapel built in the 1820s. This was later rebuilt in 1840 and when the population rose to over 5,000 in 1861, other nonconformist chapels added their imposing dimensions to what is essentially a single street village strung out along Telford's road. Over the years its character has not changed even though the quarry, one of the few active slate-working centres left in North Wales, employs fewer people than a century ago.

Today Telford's great road stands as a living monument to the meticulous care and attention to detail which he lavished upon it. Even after several decades of road improvement to cater for the ever increasing number of motorists who use it, especially in the summer months, it is not difficult to see the handiwork of the great road engineer. His retaining walls, built as buttresses to support the road as it climbed the valley side above the Nant Ffrancon, still form a classic piece of road engineering. Small lay-bys, which he built to hold stone for repairing the road, have the same function today as they had 150 years ago.

With the completion of Telford's design for the Holyhead Road, it still formed a turnpike and was to remain so until almost the end of the nineteenth century. Telford did, however, succeed in getting the number of turnpike trusts drastically reduced from twenty-three to five. Charges were made for all vehicles save the mail coach and local farmers carrying grain, implements and manure. Each year the various stretches of the road were let to contractors who made the highest bid at the annual auction. The price fetched was normally related to the income from tolls the previous year but this could vary considerably. The Denbighshire section of the road produced an income of £837 in 1883, the year before it was disturnpiked. Toll houses are still very much a feature of the present road. Many have disappeared in the course of the present century but the low, one-storey building, with its projecting porch to enable a good sight up and down the road, usually octagonal in shape, can be seen at many points on the Snowdonia section, as at Capel Curig, Ogwen Bank (626658) and Lon Isaf (602694).

SUGGESTED ITINERARY

The itinerary which follows covers that part of the present A5 from Llangollen to Llandegai (the junction with the A50 North Wales coast road) and still retains many features which it inherited in Telford's time. From Llangollen the road follows the south bank of the Dee, gradually climbing to the col near Dol Fawr (1843), the neck of one of the incised meander loops which are characteristic of this section of the Dee Valley. Just before Glyndyfrdwy (1542) it passes through a high level abandoned loop of the Dee. Three kilometres further on the road passes a mound, usually attributed to Owain Glyndwr but more likely the motte of a small Welsh castle. Corwen, a small market town in this part of the Vale of Edeirnion, is sited near the crossing place of the Dee with the main road continuing westwards along the valley of its tributary, the Afon Alwen. The route initially is of easy gradient but once the valley of the Alwen becomes more constricted, as at Glynduffwys (9944), an impressive piece of engineering was necessary to take it through the gorge section. The approach from the east was given an easy gradient by Telford who also found it necessary to carve out a shelf within the gorge to carry the road through into the more open upper valley. The country around Cerrigydrudion maintains this open aspect and is largely bare moorland, often marshy in places. Because of this the original road kept to a higher level, passing through farms like Ty tan y graig (9449). Telford's road was carried straight through this bleak area using an embankment to cross the ill-drained sections. In doing so it penetrates the watershed between the east and westward flowing headwaters of the Dee and Conwy. The through valley is wide and open with obvious signs of glacial deposition in the form of drumlins. At one time it was the site of a temporary lake (8950). At Pentrefoelas (8751), an old coaching station, the original road from Corwen struck out to the north-west in the direction of Llanrwst. Telford's Parliamentary Road however, had to enter now the upper section of the Conwy Valley and then by negotiating a series of gorges, especially around Glan Conwy (8352), it was cut into the side of the main valley in order to make a gradual descent to Bettws y Coed (7956). The river was crossed by a fine richly ornamented iron bridge built, in the same year as the Battle of Waterloo. From Bettws y Coed Telford's road ran up the valley of the Llugwy, past the Swallow Falls which later became a noted Victorian tourist attraction. Near Ty Hyll (7557) Telford forsook the old route which ran past the Roman fort and instead crossed to the north bank of the river before making Capel Curig (7257). Beyond this he again fashioned a new route through the open valley of the Afon Llugwy in preference to the earlier Penrhyn and turnpike roads. As elsewhere he preferred to cross marshy ground by a long straight embankment rather than taking a much more circuitous route. It is in the Nant Ffrancon that it is possible to appreciate most fully the gifts and skills on which Telford was able to call when needed. In order to surmount an almost sheer drop of over 70m he carried his road along the edge of the steep valley side with a graded descent. At times this meant extensive embankment on one side or cutting into a solid rock wall on the other. In order to minimise blocking by landslides of the loose scree he often had to build a protective wall on the inner side of the road. The route he chose through the Nant Ffrancon lay on the other side of the valley from the earlier Penrhyn road. On reaching the lower end of the valley he carried straight down the right bank of the Ogwen, a section where the quarrying town of Bethesda was ultimately to grow, until he reached Halfway Bridge (6069). There Telford built a fine stone bridge to cross the Ogwen river before carrying his road along the flat bench, now well above the incised gorge of the Ogwen, until he reached the coast road at Llandegai, the model village planned by Lord Penrhyn at the gates of his nineteenth-century castle (6071).

10. Towns of the Upper Severn Valley

The border regions or political marchlands of medieval western Europe were fertile ground for the growth of towns. The Rhine valley, where scores of kingdoms, dukedoms and powerful independent territories of the church had arisen with the demise of Charlemagne's empire, was rich with urban life. A multiplicity of political frontiers and local warfare encouraged the raising of castles. In turn these strong-points gave rise to markets and attracted merchants and artisans to settle within the aura of their security. Along the boundary of England and Wales, from the Dee to the outfall of the Wye, the Norman Conquest brought into being a marchland that was to provide the seedbed for scores of urban foundations between the eleventh and the fourteenth centuries. The landscape of the Welsh Marches—a landscape of little plains, secret valleys and benign hills—projects far to the west in the sterner country of Wales along the main river corridors. The Severn makes the most important thrust of the lowlands into the massif of central Wales. For miles above Welshpool it has provided a passageway for traders and invaders between the English Midlands and the coasts of Cardigan Bay. Bronze Age traffic seems to have used the hill trails above the Severn and centuries later Welsh cattle traders followed the same routes until the railways destroyed a trade network that had lasted for more than five hundred years. The Romans fully exploited the strategic value of the upper Severn corridor when they mounted their decisive campaign against Wales in the years about AD 70. Where the Severn's first important tributaries from the Plynlimmon watershed converge in the widening of the valley floor about Caersws the Romans established a legionary fort and a small civil settlement. Five Roman lines of communication converged on this fort at the centre of a tiny plain enclosed by hills on every hand.

The strategic values of the upper Severn are repeated in the years

166

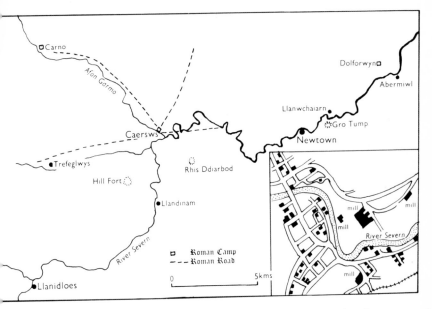

The upper Severn Valley around Newtown. Inset: woollen mills and spinning shops in nineteenth-century Newtown

that immediately followed the Norman Conquest. The reign of William I witnessed the first step towards the conquest of Wales with the creation of powerful marcher lordships focussed on the strategic centres of Hereford, Shrewsbury and Chester. The territories of the middle Severn fell largely to Roger of Montgomery who became the Earl of Shrewsbury in 1071. Roger de Montgomery's base for the extension of Norman power into Wales lay at Hen Domen or Old Montgomery (SO 2198). It is evident that at some time in the 1070s he had gained possession of the upper basin of the Severn around the long abandoned Roman fort at Caersws because Domesday Book, compiled in 1086, has a reference to Roger de Montgomery's territories in *Arvester*. It seems likely that this was the Welsh Cantref of Arwystli. In medieval Wales the cantref was the chief unit of regional administration. Each cantref consisted of a number of townships. Arwystli, for instance, contained all the headstreams of the Severn that gather together in the Caersws basin, and its eastern boundary was drawn across the main river valley three kilometres to the east of Caersws where the lowland corridor narrows temporarily towards the site of Newtown. For Roger of Montgomery the capture of Arwystli meant a deep thrust into Wales, just as the establishment of the fort at Caersws led the Romans towards the conquest of the Celtic west.

The most important phase of the Norman conquest of Wales belongs to the reign of William II in the closing years of the eleventh century. At the same time a military thrust into north-west England was to establish the northern march against the Scots. In central Wales the Earl of Shrewsbury was able to overrun the ancient princedom of *Ceredigion*, territories focussed on the southern shoreline of Cardigan Bay, from his base in the upper Severn. His forces then reached south-westwards into Pembrokeshire where his brother Arnulf de Montgomery was established in a new Norman lordship there. By the beginning of the twelfth century the foundations for 'a little England beyond Wales' had been established in distant Pembrokeshire from a springboard in the basin of the upper Severn. But by the middle decades of the same century the area of Norman power had contracted along the western fringe of the marches. In the Severn valley Arwystli saw the re-establishment of an independent local dynasty. Old Montgomery had become a lonely outlier of its marcher lordship rather than a supply base for the conquest and control of central Wales. For almost two hundred years the Severn from Welshpool to its headsprings above Llanidloes was to become a no-man's land in the political geography of the border country. As part of the decaying princedom of Powys it was subject to attack and territorial claims from the last remaining stronghold of Welsh power, Gwynedd—the kingdom whose geographical centre lay in Anglesey and Snowdonia. From the east the lands of the upper Severn were threatened by their aggressive neighbours of the marcher lordships and, in particular, the Mortimer family. In such conditions it is not surprising that these conflicting interests attempted to stake their claims to territories in the Severn valley through the building of castles. Consequently we find that nine medieval castle-sites are concentrated along the line of the upper Severn between Hen Domen and Llanidloes, a distance of scarcely thirty-two kilometres. Most of them, for instance Gro Tump (SO 1292) and the magnificent tumbled earthworks of Rhos Ddiarbed (SO 0490), display the characteristic motte-and-bailey construction that marks the Norman earthworks of the eleventh and twelfth centuries. Their origins remain largely obscure through a lack of documentary evidence, but it seems likely that the majority of these long-abandoned castle-sites were founded in the temporary occupation of Arwystli by Roger de Montgomery in the closing years of the eleventh century. It is possible that some may have been built at a later date, within the next century and a half, by Welsh lords in imitation of the English manner of castle building.

The Norman mottes of the upper Severn in Montgomeryshire have left no trace of their history except what can be read from an examination of their simple earthworks or inferred from a study of their sites and regional distribution. All of them lie to the south of the river. Gro Tump (SO 1292) with its crescent-shaped bailey and a motte that rises 12m above its deep encircling ditch stands on the very brink of the Severn's south bank. Rhos Ddiarbed (SO 0490) overlooks the Caersws basin and the approaches to the Afon Garno from a flat shelf 1.5 kilometres to the south of the gathering place of the Severn and its tributaries. Three-quarters of a kilometre to the north west of Rhos Ddiarbed another simple motte commands the same tract of country from an outlook 60m above the Severn on the steep flanks of the Cefn-nith ridge. The castle sites at Newtown and Llanidloes, now all but erased from the landscape, stood close to the south bank of the river. The location of all these defensive points on the southern rim of the Severn corridor suggest the uncertain character of the Norman thrust towards central Wales. The river, it seems, was there to provide an extra line of defence. Perhaps this locational pattern suggests a temporary frontier that recognised the Welshness of all that lay to the north of the river. The new castles that were raised behind this river-frontier represent the primary element in the incorporation of these territories into the Norman marchland. If Roger de Montgomery's efforts to absorb Arwystli into his marcher lordship had met with permanent success, it is more than likely that the present map of towns in the Severn corridor above Welshpool would have looked very different. Often the Norman castle mound became the nucleus of a market and a growing town within half a century of its raising. Rhos Ddiarbed might easily have become the focus of a flourishing urban settlement before the end of the twelfth century if the local lords of Arwystli had not regained control of their territories. The site of the future Newtown might well have been centred upon Gro Tump. But the medieval politics of the marches determined that the successful foundation of towns in the upper Severn Valley was not to begin until the close of the thirteenth century—at the time of the final conquest of Wales.

Dolforwyn and Newtown

The last quarter of the thirteenth century was a vital period in the urban history of the upper Severn. Along the river corridor above Welshpool two incipient boroughs, Dolforwyn (SO 1595) and New-town (SO 1091), competed with each other. Although the facts of local geography seem to supply a satisfactory explanation for the success of Newtown and the decline of its rival, it is far from certain that the final course of events lay in the immutable laws of the environment. Newtown spread itself across the flood-plain of the Severn, its chief axis Broad Street orientated upon the bridge to the north bank of the river. The advantages of Newtown's site astride the Severn corridor were underlined when it became the terminus of the Montgomeryshire Canal in 1819 and a new industrial quarter took root within reach of its wharves and warehouses on the north bank of the river. Dolforwyn lacked, from the very beginning, all the advantages of trade and communications that fell to Newtown from its location in the valley-corridor. This romantic hill top site steeply poised some 121m above the Severn's flood-plain near Abermule saw, in the 1270s, the foundation of one of the last castles by a Welsh prince. Here also Llywelyn ap Gruffydd aimed to hold markets and establish a town. Today from its silent grass-grown earthworks you can survey the long northern face of the Kerry Hills and Clun Forest, scoured with deep wooded coombes. Westwards the Severn draws the eye towards Arwystli and the wilder hills of central Wales. Dolforwyn was an excellent place from which to make a last stand for Welsh political independence as it brooded over Montgomery and the territories of the Mortimers that lay to the east. The very advantages of its site in the long forgotten strategic geography of the closing years of the thirteenth century seem to have doomed its extinction as a town. But can one be certain that the stubborn facts of geography—the unfavourable hill-top site and a benign location by the Severn—had the last word in the success and failure of Newtown and Dolforwyn? An examination of the events at the time of their foundation suggests that the complex politics of the relations between England and Wales at that period might have had much to do with the future shape of the urban geography of this part of the Severn valley. A Welsh victory in the year 1277 and the holding back of the territorial expansion of the Mortimers might have witnessed the growth of a new town at Abermule below the castle-crowned height of Dolforwyn. Newtown, then, would never have been, and contemporary geography would be just as wise in its explanations because the site of Abermule, at the junction of the Mule and Severn, could hardly be excelled as a meeting place for trade and markets. Let us turn to the events of the last part of the thirteenth century and see how they influenced the fate of Dolforwyn and Newtown.

For most of the thirteenth century the upper Severn valley formed an important zone of conflict in the political struggle between England and Wales. In 1255 the power of the northern Welsh kingdom, Gwynedd, expanded when Llywelyn ap Gruffydd became its ruler. Within three years he had been acclaimed Prince of Wales by a council of Welsh rulers and in 1267, by the Treaty of Montgomery, Henry III recognised Llywelyn's title as Prince of Wales and conceded to him the Cantref of Cedewain that included, on its southern margin, the Severn corridor above Welshpool. Llywelyn determined to strengthen his position in these newly acquired territories by the building of a castle on the hill top at Dolforwyn in 1273, a place that grandly surveyed the hostile marchland to the east. Beside the building of the castle with its rectangular curtain wall and projecting circular angle towers Llywelyn announced the foundation of a market town at Dolforwyn. It seems that this last act aroused the hostility of the English crown. On 23 June 1273 the Council of Regents discussed the matter and the Prior of Wenlock was instructed to deliver a personal letter of protest to Llywelyn that said 'we forbid you to erect *de novo* a borough or town or market'. Less than a month later Llywelyn ap Gruffydd replied asserting his right to build a castle and establish a market on his own land near Abermiwl. It could be argued from this contemporary reference to the developments at Dolforwyn that Llywelyn was intending to found a market town at a more logical site in the flood-plain of the Severn below the castle hill, a development, if it had been successful, that would have resembled the relationship between Castel Dinas Bran and Llangollen in the Dee valley.

The events that determined the fate of Dolforwyn were enacted on a much larger stage than that of the upper Severn corridor. In 1277 Edward I invaded Wales with three armies in a campaign determined to reduce the last stronghold of Gwynedd. Troops under the Earl of Lincoln and Roger de Mortimer advanced on the upper Severn to lay seige to the new castle at Dolforwyn. The seige lasted scarcely more than a week. A Welsh chronicler of the events says that the garrison was forced to surrender from a want of water, but reports from the English side of the operation suggest that a formidable military force was arrayed against the castle. Roger de Mortimer recorded that 'three good siege engines' inflicted severe damage, and after its capitulation the Sheriff of Hereford, Egidius de Berkely, claimed 'twenty-four shillings for the carriage of a catapult from Wigmore to "Dolvereyn" on Mortimer's instructions'. The chance of the growth of a new town at Dolforwyn now vanished. In 1278 the castle and all the lands of 'Ceri and Cydewain' were granted to Roger de Mortimer. Now the possessions of the Mortimer family stretched across the trough of the Severn far into the dissected hill country north of the river. A year later, in 1279, Roger de Montgomery took the decisive step that was to change the settlement patterns of the upper Severn; he obtained a charter for himself 'and his heirs forever that they may hold a market in his manor of *Thlanveyr, in Kedway*'. Soon Llanfair Cedewain was to be known as Newtown and the bold plans of a Welsh prince for the development of Dolforwyn were forgotten. For some decades the Mortimers occupied their castle on the hill top, even if only through the agency of a sleepy bailiff. But Dolforwyn was no competitor with New Montgomery among the strongholds of the Welsh Marches. A century later an *Inquisition post-mortem* of the possessions of the fifth Roger de Mortimer said of Dolforwyn 'which castle is ruinous and is worth nothing'.

The emergence of a new market centre at Llanfair Cedewain that was to become known as Newtown can be traced through the half century after the granting of the first charter to Roger de Mortimer. In 1279 there must have been a hamlet, called Llanfair Cedewain, in the great loop of the Severn where Newtown now stands. One element of Newtown's urban topography survives from this period in the ruined medieval church on the south bank of the river. At the time of the granting of the market charter this was a chapel within the mother parish of Llanllwchaiarn, 1.5 kilometres to the north-west on the further bank of the Severn (SO 1292). Soon after the granting of the market charter, perhaps even coincidental with it, Llanfair Cedewain was raised to the status of an independent parish. No documentary proof survives of the exact date of this first stage in the evolution of Newtown apart from a reference of 1291 that describes Llanfair as an independent rectory. At some time between 1279 and 1291 the growing importance of the settlement by the Severn had made it necessary to form a separate parish there. By 1321 the old name of the settlement is beginning to drop out of use because a document of that year refers to 'the new town in Kedewan'. In the intervening years since the grant of the first market charter one can be sure that the

13 *The former town church of Newtown sited by the banks of the Severn with its associations with Robert Owen*

outlines of a town had come into being at Llanfair Cedewain. Although no documents and little archaeological evidence remains to trace the process, we can still obtain some deep insights into the making of Roger de Mortimer's market town from a study of its topography. The main axis was Broad Street, focussed on the bridge across the Severn at its northern end. For the rest it is still easy to trace the formal grid-iron plan that is characteristic of the new urban settlements of the late Middle Ages in western Europe.

At the western end of the market town, in the grounds of Newtown Hall, stood the castle—a topographical feature that has given rise to much debate. Like the castle at Llanidloes the earthworks have all but vanished from the landscape. Half of the motte survives as a weathered D-shaped mound, while the bailey was contained in what is now the north-eastern angle of Newtown Hall's park. The date of the raising of Newtown castle is still obscure. In his excellent survey of the *Castles of Montgomeryshire* C. J. Spurgeon believes that the earthworks of the castle at Newtown were contemporary with the founding of the market. The remnant of the motte suggests that it was a low, broad-topped earthwork with a diameter of almost 42m and standing some 5m above its ditch. Gro Tump, on the other hand, lying only 1.5 kilometres down the Severn valley from Newtown Hall has a high standing mound that towers some 12m above its encircling ditch. It is like so many primitive Norman castle works of the late eleventh century. The change in style at Newtown Hall suggests a later period of castle building that could well belong to the end of the thirteenth century and the period of the making of the town. Beresford, on the other hand, in his study of the *New Towns of the Middle Ages* suggests that a castle was already in existence there at the time of the establishment of the market town. He believes that the presence of two castles—Gro Tump and Newtown Hall—close to the Severn, points to the importance of this crossing of the river. Here on the flat ground between the two castles and beside the chapel of Llanfair one could expect the establishment of a thriving market town.

Whatever the exact date of the foundation of a castle at Newtown, and such slender evidence that survives suggests that it was built to defend the newly founded market town in the last quarter of the thirteenth century, there is little doubt of the success of Roger de Mortimer's urban experiment in the Severn valley. Less than a century later, in 1365, the records provide proof of a flourishing urban community paying rents of £6-6-8d and whose markets and fairs yielded a yearly toll of £24. Alas, the documentary history of Newtown is far from complete and one of the most important steps in its progress as a settlement, the acquisition of a borough charter, remains totally obscure. Some local historians have argued that the first grant of municipal privileges dates back to 1321, the year when the name Newtown began to supplant the older Welsh name of the settlement, Llanfair Cedewain. The first borough charter has long been lost, but oral evidence from the seventeenth century suggests that it was granted about the middle of the fifteenth century. Certainly Leland, on his long itineraries in Henry VIII's reign in search of the antiquities of these islands, was able to describe Newtown as 'well buylded after the Welsh fashion'. By that time and through most of the seventeenth century its rectangular network of streets and lanes focussed on Broad Street, the place where the markets and fairs were held, contained a population of about five hundred. It was only in the years about 1800 with the expansion of the flannel industry and the opening of the Montgomeryshire Canal that population began to grow rapidly, reaching almost a thousand in the first census of 1801.

Llanidloes and Caersws

The foundation of a town at Llanidloes took place at the same time as the establishment of the markets and fairs at Newtown. Here a Welsh landowner secured the grant of a weekly market and two fairs a year from the English king. Owain de la Pole or Owain of Arwystli was one of those 'client lords' of the English crown when the first market charter was granted in 1280. Llanidloes seems to have prospered in the changed political geography of the upper Severn valley during the closing years of the thirteenth century. The power of an independent Wales vanished with the success of Edward I's campaigns in the north and the no-man's land of the Severn became firmly attached to England. Llanidloes, the planned market town, was the topographical expression of the new and permanent links of Arwystli with England. By 1293 there is documentary proof of a flourishing urban community there in an inquisition that records rents assessed at 59s-2d, tolls from fairs of £6 and another £5-6 shillings from the Saturday markets. By 1309 a survey of the estates of Gruffydd, son of the founder of Llandiloes, shows that the town had sixty-six burgesses. As in the history of Newtown no borough charter survives nor is there any direct evidence of the date when it was granted. The presence of sixty-six burgesses in 1309 suggests that Llanidloes had become a borough before that date, and it seems most likely that Owain's market was raised to the status of a town at some time in the last decade of the thirteenth century.

Just as Llanidloes came into being at the same time as Newtown so the topographical evolution of the borough closely resembles that of its urban neighbour a few kilometres down the Severn. An ancient church on the south bank of the Severn close to a traditional ford across the river is the only feature of the topography of Llanidloes that survives from the centuries before the making of the town. As you approach the church from the main axial street of the town, Long Bridge Street with its incessant summer traffic, you feel that you have passed into a fragment of Llanidloes that was disregarded in the planning of the new town towards the end of the thirteenth century. As at Newtown, the parish church plays no focal role in the regular grid-iron of streets. Instead the market hall, at the crossing of the main axes, provides the chief concentration of interest in Owain de la Pole's new borough. Llanidloes, too, only became a parish in its own right after the founding of the town. Previously it had looked down the Severn to a mother church at Llandinam.

The castle at Llanidloes presents problems similar to the castle-site at Newtown. As at Newtown, most of its features are now obliterated and its very origins are disputed. The site of the motte, at the south end of the long axis of China Street and Long Bridge Street, is covered by the Mount Inn and other buildings. In fact, the name of the inn which is rare indeed among the names of Welsh inns provides one of the few obvious clues to the site of Llanidloes' medieval castle. The castle bailey, lying to the east of the motte and stretching as far as New Street, has left scarcely any visual evidence of its former presence. Much of the land has been built over, but faint scarps and the curving boundary of the lane that joins Mount Street and New Street suggest its location. B. H. St J. O'Neil in his study of Llanidloes concluded that the castle mound was 30m in diameter rising only 3m above the surrounding ditch. Like the motte at Newtown Hall it formed a broad flat platform. He believed that the castle was thrown up at least a century before the founding of the market town, probably about 1160 when the territories of the upper Severn were once more in the hands of Welsh rulers after the failure of the Norman thrust to the west. If Llanidloes castle was in being before the end of the twelfth century it is not unlikely that the shelter of the bailey was used for trade and commerce. It certainly stood close to an important crossing point of the Severn where an ancient trackway from the west that followed the long ridge between the Clywedog and Severn came down to meet an eastern trail from the Kerry Hills. If this is the correct history of Llanidloes castle, the granting of a market charter to Owain de la Pole and the subsequent founding of the borough represents the recognition, in the changing political atmosphere of the late thirteenth century, of an already established trading centre. The narrow confines of the castle bailey were soon found to be too restrictive and the formal street plan of a new town was laid out in the 1290s—a town whose centre of interest became focussed at the Market Hall at the junction of the main axes of Long Bridge Street and Great Oak Street. Both castle and church lay on the edge of the new Llanidloes and ceased to exercise a dominant role in the fortunes of the town.

The lack of any conclusive documentary or archaeological evidence about the history of the castle at Llanidloes leads one into a realm of speculation. C. J. Spurgeon, in his recent and thorough survey of the castles of Montgomeryshire, came to the conclusion that Llanidloes castle was no older than the market town, and that it probably came into being 'as part of the defences of the new town of Llanidloes'. It must be agreed that the castle with its broad low motte closely resembles the earthwork at Newtown Hall which, given the same line of argument, was thrown up in the years at the close of the thirteenth century when the new urban settlement was coming into existence.

If a scarcity of firm evidence surrounds the early history of the two most successful towns of the upper Severn, Newtown and Llanidloes, the origins of Caersws remain even more obscure. Caersws lacks a medieval castle; instead the little settlement with its typical grid-iron layout of streets and lanes stands on the edge of a Roman fort at the junction of the Afon Garno and the Severn. Its location in the strategic geography of middle Wales is of the greatest importance, a site of far greater meaning than either of its two neighbouring Severn towns. The strategic value of the Caersws basin seems to have been exploited at several different periods of history. Scarcely 1.5 kilometres to the south-west Cefn Carnedd, an Iron Age fort, looks down from a height of almost 305 m on to the junction of the rivers. It is one of the possible sites of the battle in which the Romans took Caractacus prisoner during their advance upon Wales (SO 0189). The siting of the Roman fort and, a thousand years later, the throwing up of the earthworks of Rhos Ddiarbed (SO 0490) underline the continuing importance of this section of the Severn corridor. It is all the more suprising that the primary urban node of the region did not emerge here.

The evidence for the creation of a borough at Caersws before the sixteenth century rests on a sentence of Leland's in which he reports it 'as a former borough'. The field evidence survives too in the formal grid-iron pattern of roads that must have been laid out deliberately at some date to the east of the weathered grass-grown rampart of the Roman fort. One other fragment of information points to the late creation of Caersws long after the establishment of the basic settlement pattern of the region. It arose within the much older parish of Llanwnog. At this point one can only speculate about the beginnings of Caersws. The town probably originated in the second half of the thirteenth century and its location strongly suggests a Welsh origin. It seems highly likely that if the foundation of a town near Caersws had been in the hands of the Mortimer family the choice of location would have fallen on the earthworks of Rhos Ddiarbed, well-placed on the southern edge of the Severn flood-plain. The avoidance of Rhos Ddiarbed and the laying out of the town on the north bank of the river strongly points to a Welsh prince as the originator of Caersws. The fact that the settlement controlled one of the main routes into the mountain fastness of medieval North Wales suggests a political influence from that direction. Was Caersws perhaps a foundation of Llywelyn ap Gruffydd, ruler of Gwynedd, at some time in the two decades after 1255? Its failure as a market centre would be explained by the loss of Dolforwyn, the collapse of Welsh political power in the upper Severn and the subsequent successful rise of Newtown and Llanidloes.

The closing years of the thirteenth century were crucial in determining the outlines of the urban geography of the upper Severn. A different outcome of political events at that time might have seen the development of the two chief towns of the region at Abermule and Caersws.

SUGGESTED ITINERARIES

Each settlement can be made the object of a separate field study. Perhaps the most exciting of the places is Dolforwyn (1595), best approached through the maze of deep lanes from the west bank of the Severn near Abermule. The extensive view from the ruins of its thirteenth-century earthworks helps the understanding of this relic of medieval marchland geography.

Newtown is a fine example of urban geography, compact and also varied in the features that it has to display. Begin at the mother church of Llanllwchaiarn (1292). Go on to identify the medieval core of Newtown and its surviving elements; the castle-site at Newtown Hall (106915), the ruined church on the site of the medieval chapel near the Severn (109918), and between the formal street-plan of Roger de Mortimer's new town with its main axis and market, Broad Street, pointing to the bridge across the Severn. The first half of the nineteenth century was as important in the topographical development of Newtown as the years of its foundation about the beginning of the fourteenth century. It became the chief centre of the flannel industry and two industrial quarters were added to the medieval core. On either side of Broad Street, and especially around Severn Square, burgage plots that were once gardens have been taken over by factories. Now with the decline of the flannel industry much of this property is derelict or serving other purposes. On the north bank of the Severn another industrial quarter came into being with the completion of the canal from Garthmyl to Newtown in 1821. Here are canal cottages close to the river and in Commercial Street three and four-storeyed terraces in brick of the early nineteenth century in which the upper floors served a domestic industry. There is a textile museum in Commercial Street; the whole quarter still retains much of the atmosphere of its period of origin.

At Caersws the most impressive object in the landscape is the Roman fort, its western rampart obliterated by the line of the Cambrian railway. Of the medieval 'borough' that has left so little history we can make out the rectangular scheme of two axial streets and tributary parallel lanes. The chessboard squares of the burgage plots can be identified, some of them as hedged fields that probably escaped development from the first days of the town. The buildings of Caersws, cottages and farms, belong very much to the nineteenth century. The garish reds from the Ruabon brickyards date much of the place to the railway age. A visit to Caersws should be combined with an exploration of Rhos Ddiarbed, a twelfth century motte with two baileys to the south of the Severn that might well have been chosen as the focus of a medieval town.

At Llanidloes the basic elements of the town's topography should be compared with Newtown. The parish church, largely rebuilt and extended in the sixteenth century with material from the demolished Abbey Cwm Hir, occupies an obscure site near the river. Note the regular street plan and surviving Market Hall. There is a tiny industrial quarter, flannel mills that depended on water power, near the river. The castle has nothing to show, but it is important to view the site in relation to the layout of the town.

14   *The Market Hall of Llanidloes dating from 1609 and an indication of the former importance of this now small town of the Marches*

11. The Tal y llyn Valley

Few landscapes owe their present form to a single cause nor have they evolved over a limited period of time. It is true that certain major diagnostic features often stand out and can be readily appreciated. The effect of recent glaciation, for example, shows itself immediately in a U-shaped valley or a boulder-strewn terrain. Closer examination, however, will often reveal that the glacial episode is just one link in a complicated chain of events, perhaps the culmination of a gradual process of evolution which had been taking place over millions of years. Prior to the growth of glaciers there could have been a long period of uninterrupted river erosion and weathering when the type of rock found in the area exerted an important influence on the evolution of the landscape. Even the subsequent glacial episode did not wipe the slate completely clean so that the present scenery displays features which owe their origin both to river and glacial erosion. Man himself has contributed to landscape evolution by initiating changes through drainage schemes, forest clearance, cultivation or exploiting mineral wealth. All these natural and man-made influences are displayed with almost text-book clarity in the area of the Tal y llyn valley in Merioneth and the adjacent upland of Cadair Idris. The result is a scenically attractive region of diverse relief, with features on a scale which can be readily appreciated simply by walking over the ground.

Throughout the area the various rock outcrops have established a basic overall setting to the region. Three main rock types occur. The great north-facing escarpment of the Cadair Idris range, culminating in Pen y gadair (711130), is formed of a thick sill of granophyre. The summit ridge itself consists of a very resistant series of volcanic lavas and ashes. To the south-west of the Cadair Idris massif the second main rock type occurs. It consists mainly of a series of fine-grained mudstones which, because they offer less resistance to erosion, tend to coincide with the great trench-like feature of the Tal y llyn valley. Another series of mudstones, equally susceptible to erosion, occurs in the great hollow of Llyn Cau (7112). Scenic contrasts between these two dominant rock types are readily apparent in the field. When the upper part of the Tal y llyn valley is viewed from the col which leads across to the Corris valley (7369), the knobbly, broken slopes of volcanic rocks forming Craig Llwyd (7211) stands out in great contrast to the smoother, shivering and gentler terrain which coincides with the mudstone outcrops of Mynydd Pentre (7110). The third and final rock type found in the area, a relatively hard grit, dominates the country which forms the watershed between the Tal y llyn and the Dovey valley to the south. Slates also occur in this zone and in the past they have been worked in the upper part of the Gwernol valley around Bryneglwys (6905). All three rock types have been faulted and fractured in many places. The greatest dislocation occurs along the line of the Tal y llyn valley where a major fault zone occurs with the rocks let down on the northern side. The fault is probably rotational in character and has resulted in a lateral displacement of rock outcrops on the opposite sides of the valley. The faulting movements undoubtedly led to a shattering of the mudstone strata and this in turn made the work of erosion on the weakened beds much more effective. As a result the great trench feature of the Tal y llyn valley came into being.

River Development

Before snow began to accumulate around the higher peaks of the Cadair Idris range to signal the beginning of half a million years of the Ice Age, river erosion had been testing the weakness and strength of the various rock strata and taking advantage of the great line of

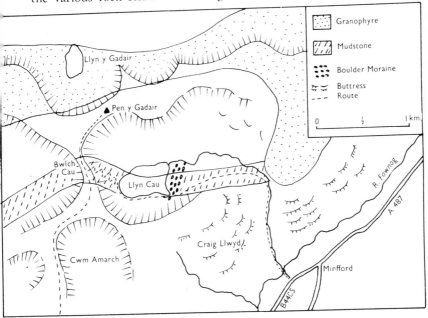

Geology and landforms of Cadair Idris

discontinuity formed by the Tal y llyn fault zone. At the outset there was probably a single major river flowing in a north-east to south-west direction from the western fringes of the Cadair Idris range. It followed the line of the present Dysynni valley from beyond Llanfihangel y Pennant (6708) to enter the sea near Towyn (5800) though, of course, it then flowed at a much higher level. This early Dysynni had a number of important left bank tributaries like the Gwernol (6607) and Eira (6708). By headward extension these drained right across the area now occupied by the Tal y llyn trough. At a slightly later date a parallel river to the Dysynni established itself a little to the south. This proto-Fathew river was able to cut back quickly once it reached the weakened rock strata of the Tal y llyn fault zone and in time it successively beheaded the tributaries of the Dysynni, beginning with the Dolgoch (6504) and then taking in the Gwernol and Eira headstreams. As the Fathew cut down, so the former routes of the Dysynni tributaries were left as high level cols or windgaps above the Tal y llyn valley. That of the Eira occurs at a height of just over 170m above Cedris farm (688084). The corresponding wind gap opposite Dolgoch is lower having a height of less than 75m in the col. This form of river capture is quite common where one river has an erosional advantage over another, even if the situation is quite temporary. The only tributary stream which has succeeded in retaining its course at the present time is the Gwernol. It continues to use the great gap in the watershed to the east of Abergynolwyn (6707) and in doing so causes the present river Dysynni to adopt a most curious twisting route which has aroused much speculation and many suggested explanations. None is entirely satisfactory and in full accord with all the known facts. Any explanation must take account of the events of the Ice Age which followed the pattern of river development outlined above. What the ice did as an active agent of erosion and deposition was to modify the pre-existing landscape to varying degrees. To some it also provides a satisfactory working hypothesis of the origin of the Abergynolwyn river gap, clearly a major breach in what was once a continuous watershed.

Glaciation

The Cadair Idris ridge, reaching to almost a 1,000m must have acted as a great area of snow accumulation at various times during the Ice Age. The snow, later compacted into ice, fed various glacier streams which radiated outwards from the highest ridges. The main glaciers

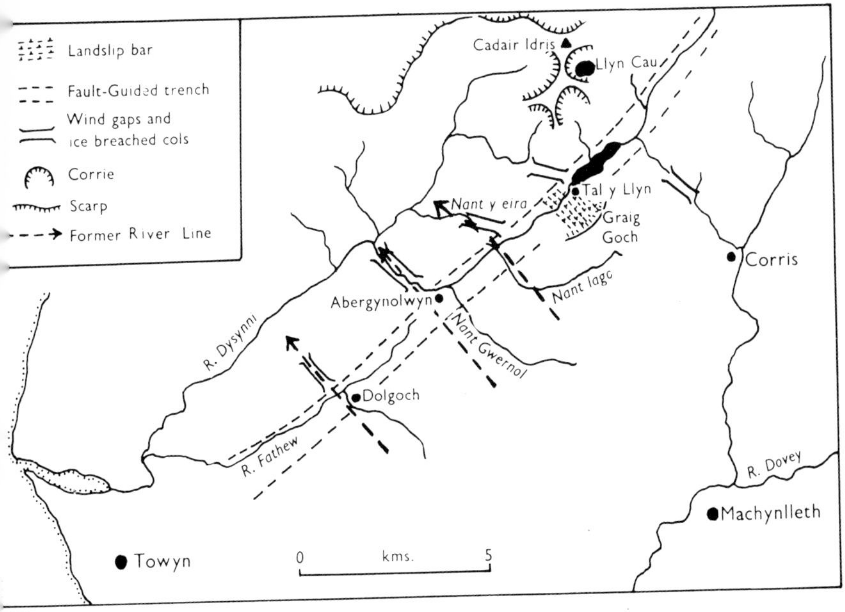
Landslip bar
Fault-Guided trench
Wind gaps and ice breached cols
Corrie
Scarp
Former River Line
Cadair Idris
Llyn Cau
Tal y Llyn
Graig Goch
Nant y eira
Corris
Nant Iago
Abergynolwyn
Nant Gwernol
R. Dysynni
Dolgoch
R. Fathew
R. Dovey
Machynlleth
Towyn
0
kms.
5

The features and drainage diversions in the Tal y Llyn valley

undoubtedly followed the lines of the pre-existing valleys of the Dysynni and Fathew and in doing so, must have deepened them considerably. Erosion under the glacier would vary in intensity and thus create rock basins like the one containing Tal y llyn lake. The tributary valleys of the Gwernol would also have contained glaciers but these would be smaller and therefore a less potent force in downcutting. This differential erosion in the main and tributary valleys has led to hanging lips at the mouths of the Gwernol and Iago (6907), although in both cases the river has cut down through them. In the case of the Dolgoch, the hanging valley step is marked by a series of picturesque falls (6504). The main valley glacier must have acted like a powerful rasp and being continually fed with fresh supplies of ice from the upper slopes, it had no difficulty in removing any side valley spurs of the original river valley. The net result is that the Tal y llyn valley today is a straight trough with unimpeded views right up to its head. The truncated spurs are clearly seen in places like Yr Allt (the cliff) on the western slopes of Mynydd Dolffanog (7310), particularly from the lower end of the lake when the sliced face is lit by the late afternoon sunshine.

An active glacier was, without doubt, a powerful and quick acting tool of erosion. Not only was it able to shape the basic features of the present Tal y llyn valley by down-cutting and side abrasion but it also led to secondary effects. The over-steepening of slopes formed of the rather incoherent mudstone beds quickly led to instablilty and the creation of gigantic landslides. A particularly good example occurs below Graich Goch (7108) when millions of tons of rock must have slid down into the valley below. At the present time it forms a great area of disturbed ground at the lower end of Tal y llyn lake in the vicinity of the Church (710094). The landslide also left a great gash in the face of Graich Goch whose edge now lies 300m back from the general line of the ridge top along this section. Amidst the jumble of rocks and other debris which blocks the Tal y llyn valley floor just below the lake, there are a number of solid rock outcrops, so that the valley constriction here could be partly formed of a rock bar. Ice has moulded the whole surface in places by depositing debris and then fashioning it into a succession of mounds and hollows. This would seem to indicate that the landslide occurred prior to the last advance of the ice down the Tal y llyn valley. Through the rock debris and the hummocky drift the River Dysynni has carved a narrow gorge and then deposited the excavated material in a large fan near Maen y Pandy Farm (7008). Below this point the valley again assumes a flat floor which at one time might also have been the site of a small lake which stretched almost as far as Abergynolwyn. The valley at this point is about 20m lower than at Tal y llyn lake, the two sections being separated by the morainic bar which presents a bold front downstream in the vicinity of Maes y Pandy Farm.

The most puzzling feature of this part of the Tal y llyn valley is the way in which the River Dysynni forsakes its direct route to the sea in favour of turning into the narrow gap west of Abergynolwyn. Various explanations have been given to account for this diversion, including river capture. In pre-glacial times there was undoubtedly some adjustment of the drainage pattern and we have already seen that such a process helps to explain the origin of some of the wind gaps which lie above the present floor of the Tal y llyn valley. While this is clearly an important aspect of drainage evolution, it is by no means the whole story. The events of the Ice Age, during which major landforms came into being, must also have played some part in the creation of the Abergynolwyn gap. One theory which might be applicable invokes the role of ice in breaching former watersheds. With a major glacier occupying the main Tal y llyn valley, any blockage which might impede its movement towards the present coastline at Towyn would lead to the upper layers seeking lateral escape routes. This process of glacial diffluence could lead to side glaciers passing through former high level cols across into an adjacent valley. For the Tal y llyn valley the cols of the former Gwernol and Eira tributaries could be used in this way. The ice actively eroded and lowered the cols and, in the case of the Gwernol, this downcutting went on to such an extent that after the ice had disappeared the river found it easier to use the new cut rather than its old more direct line to the sea. Other diffluent ice tongues could have moved across the other cols like that of Nant y Eira. One possible reason why the Gwernol route proved more effective was the larger catchment area of the upper valley east of Abergynolwyn where a huge ice field could have developed. With such a powerful ice stream coming from this direction the main Tal y llyn glacier could be turned away from its main south-westerly direction of flow and forced through the Abergynolwyn gap. Some confirmation of this is provided by the severely ice scarred southern side of the gap which would have to meet the full force of a deflected ice tongue. Whatever the true explanation of the origin of the gap and the resultant deflection of the River Dysynni, it has left the River Fathew with a much reduced drainage basin. At present the two rivers are separated by a low col at a height of just over 65m, close to Abergynolwyn station (671064).

Active erosion by ice went on in the higher parts of the area around Cadair Idris right up to the end of the Ice Age and even for a short time afterwards. Great corries, like that containing Llyn Cau (7112), were gouged out, possibly by a rotational movement of the accumulating ice. A band of mudstone which outcrops here made the task of the ice somewhat easier and helps to explain the great size and depth of the feature. The tarn of Llyn Cau, 50m deep, has been gouged out of solid rock but to some extent owes its present form to the great boulder moraine which was dumped across its exit. The fact that the corrie basin faces due east would help snow and ice to persist longer here than elsewhere. The influence which the varying degrees of insolation, depending on aspect, exerts on corrie development is clearly shown in this area. The south facing Cwm Amarch (7111), for example, is a much less impressive hollow than its counterpart, Cwm Gadair (7013) which has been gouged out of the north-facing escarpment of the Cadair Idris ridge.

Although in the geological time scale it is a mere yesterday since the Ice Age ended and the Dysynni established its present tortuous and unusual course to the sea, minor changes have continued to take place right up to the present time. The Tal y llyn lake has contracted in size as the outflow waters have cut steadily down through the landslip debris and thus lowered the whole lake level. There has also been some infilling at its upper end and at various places along its margins. As it is only 3m deep at most, any sedimentation which occurs will readily lead to a contraction of size. At one time the lake extended as far as Ty'n y Maes Farm (730111) as indicated by the present marshy valley floor. Another recent feature is the lake delta at the foot of Cwm Amarch (7110) which is gradually pushing out into the lake. Little extension is taking place at present for the stream has been artificially diverted to the west in order to prevent it flooding the pasture lands of the delta cone. This is but one aspect of the part played by man in controlling and fashioning the landscape. Over the centuries the clearing of woodland, the creation of walled fields and the draining of the marshy valley floors, have all combined to alter radically the original natural landscape. To many this makes the greatest immediate impact but a more thoughtful appraisal will show that the basic major landscape features of the area still reflect natural rather than man-made forces.

SUGGESTED ITINERARY

The main features of the Tal y llyn valley can be seen in passing from its head along its whole length to the sea near Towyn. Begin at the col known as Bwlch Llyn Bach (7513), noting the extensive scree slopes on both sides and the difference between the volcanic rocks of Craig y Llam (7412) on the left and the mudstones of Mynydd Gwerngraig (7413) to the right. The partially infilled valley gradually widens to finally open out at Minffordd (733116) where the A487 and B4405 roads diverge. From near this point it is possible to ascend to Llyn Cau and Cadair Idris. The path leaves the B4405 road, about 100m from its junction with the A487 and ascends by the side of the Nant Gadair through the knobbly terrain developed on the volcanic beds. The corrie basin of Llyn Cau is reached after an hour's walk. Note the low moraine across the entrance to the lake and the contrasting slopes of the corrie wall with steep crags formed by the volcanic beds and the surprisingly smooth skyline where the mudstones occur. This mudstone slope at the back of Llyn Cau can be ascended to reach the ridge south of Pen y Gadair and thence the main crest line of Cadair Idris. The return journey to the Tal y llyn valley can be made by skirting the west side of Cwm Amarch and making for Rhiwogof Farm (708100).

Complete the circuit by returning to the road junction and then proceed along the south-eastern side of the lake. Note the features on the opposite shore like the lake delta (717103) and the upper bench. At Tal y llyn church it is possible to study the details of the landslip topography and morainic mounds associated with the bar which lies across the valley just beyond the end of the lake. The main road (B4405) passes through the disturbed area until it finally opens out into the flat floored valley near Maes y Pandy Farm (704088). The abrupt edge of the morainic debris is seen clearly behind the farm. On reaching Abergynolwyn (677069) the minor road through the breached col, followed by the Dysynni, can be used. A good view point to appreciate its features lies at its eastern end (674073). Passing through the col a circuit can be made, first around the great volcanic buttress of Bird's Rock (6406) and then through the low col of Nantymynach (6405) to Dolgoch (650046). The hanging tributary valley here can be visited, with its famous falls, before a return is made either to Abergynolwyn or the Fathew valley followed to Towyn (5800).

12. The country between Llanidloes and Machynlleth

Mid-Wales is one of the few parts of Britain which still retains a feeling of emptiness. Great tracts of country in Powys are not served by metalled roads or even by tracks in some remote areas. In part this is an expression of the difficulties in penetrating hilly terrain which, although not particularly high, is lacking in through valleys of the type which Thomas Telford so successfully exploited for his coach roads elsewhere in the Principality. The valleys tend to end blindly in steep coombe-like heads so that each has given rise to its own distinctive cultural unit. The Dulas Valley near Machynlleth (8061) and the Pennant Valley south of Llanbrynmair (8797) are of this type, with a narrow road petering out at the last farm.

Any road which aims at crossing the plateau top must climb at the outset to make height and then keep to the ridges before descending, by an equally steep gradient on the other side. The road from Llanidloes to Machynlleth, in surmounting the watershed separating the Severn from the Dyfi valley, does exactly this. With its recent improvements it now forms a popular tourist excursion, especially to the impressive viewpoint overlooking the Clywedog reservoir a few miles from Llanidloes. There is more spectacular scenery around Dylife (8694) and expansive views across to Pumlumon (Plynlimon) in the west and the Cadair Idris range to the north. At first sight the route, with its difficult gradients, looks modern and certainly not older than the eighteenth century when the lead mines of Dylife were first worked to any great extent. A closer look at this plateau country between Llanidloes and Machynlleth however, suggests otherwise. The present road is probably following a prehistoric track which in later centuries was also used by the Romans in crossing from the Upper Severn Valley to the shores of Cardigan Bay. The siting of the Iron Age hill forts at Pen y Castell (9488) and Fan Hill (9388) certainly points to the existence of an ancient trackway across the hills. More convincing is the proof provided by the discovery of a Roman fortlet or signal station at Pen y Crocbren (8593), almost at the highest point of the route. When this was excavated in the early 1960s the turf fort was found to have a paved entrance and in it Roman pots, dating from the middle of the second century, were dug up. With the wide views it commanded in all directions the fort was probably used as a staging post and signal station. Whether or not the Romans knew about the lead deposits in the adjacent valleys is unknown, but in the absence of evidence from the fort itself this seems unlikely. The road started at Caersws (0392), an important Roman centre in the Severn Valley and for a while kept to the low ground skirting Trefeglwys (9790). This part of the route has long been known and is traceable on the map as field lanes and footpaths. There are even some standing stones associated with it. From Trefeglwys the probable route lay along the north side of the Tarannon valley to Llawr y glyn (9391) and then climbed up on to the ridge near the present hamlet of Staylittle (8892). The present road that runs to the north for two kilometres before turning west for Dylife was not part of the early route. Instead the early track continued in a mainly westerly direction from Staylittle and ran up to the ridge which would ultimately bring it to the eastern gate of the Pen y Crocbren fort. The exact route beyond is not known but in making for the Dyfi valley and the coast the present ridge top alignment seems most sensible. Thus far from being a modern route the present mountain road clearly has its origins in the distant past, certainly almost 2,000 years ago and possibly earlier still.

Prior to the building of the Clywedog dam and reservoir in recent years (9187), the road from Llanidloes passed close to the former rich lead mining area of Y Fan (9487). One mine, The Van, with its anglicised adaptation of the original Welsh name, was to produce great wealth from the bowels of the earth. It was by far the most productive and richest of a number of mines located on a lode which ran across this strip of country in a west-south-west to east-north-east direction for several kilometres. The existence of the lode had been known for a considerable time and sporadic working had taken place at various points along its length without a really rich strike having been made. But in 1862 the chance discovery of an exceptionally rich ore-bearing section completely changed the fortunes of the Fan valley. The ore was located about 60m below the surface at a point about 150m south-east of Van Farm. Even at the outset the great potential of the find was recognised and it was not long before the whole paraphernalia associated with ore mining—a dressing plant, washing launders, wheels and settling pits—began to appear. By April 1866 all was ready and the Van mine was able to despatch the first of many parcels of lead ore. A contemporary print gives a good impression of the scale of the enterprise, by far the largest mine in this corner of east Montgomeryshire. Those lucky enough to have bought speculative shares for about £5 a few years earlier now found that their capital had increased almost twentyfold. This first phase of prosperity was to last for just over a decade until in 1878 a world-wide drop in the price of lead caused the Van mine to reduce output. Production had been averaging between 4,500 and 7,000 tons of dressed ore a year but after 1880 the working out of the richer deposits, combined with competition from foreign ores, brought about a decline from which the Van mine never recovered. Even fresh discoveries in the late 1880s failed to carry production figures back to their former high levels. By 1890, a year in which only about 500 tons of dressed ore left the mine, the end of the era of prosperity was in sight. Consistent profits year by year were now replaced by considerable operating losses and by 1891 the mining company was £3,000 in debt, an all too familiar pattern repeated time and time again in the history of the metaliferous mining industry. The miners who had struck it rich only a few years previously now found themselves unemployed with only the memory of the period of prosperity when Van was a household name amongst mining speculators. Production could have ceased completely in 1891 but another company came in to try its luck. When a rich lode was struck in 1894 it seemed that their hopes were justified, as more than 2,000 tons of ore were raised in that year. The prosperity was short lived, however, for although there was ore to be won, the cost of extraction was greater and required much more capital. Ownership of the mine changed frequently but little happened to revitalise what was now recognised as a dying concern.

The end of the Van mines came in 1921 for even World War I had done little to promote production when, with foreign competition virtually removed, the fortunes of the workings would seemingly improve. The closure marked the end of a spirited venture which produced over 100,000 tons of dressed lead ore as well as quantities of zinc and some silver. In its heyday, in the 1870s, the fame of the Van mine was such that its name was used for many less successful mines, usually as a suffix or prefix. In both Merionethshire and Cardiganshire any chance find of lead immediately raised hopes that another Van lode had been located and it seemed natural enough to encourage the more foolish of the speculators by 'borrowing' the name that was known throughout the mining kingdom.

In the decade 1870–80, when production was at its peak, the Van valley presented a very different appearance from the solitude of today. The surrounding hillsides must have reverberated to the sound

15 *Ruins of the Van smelter and the former workers' cottages alongside*

of the crushing plant and at times a deep pall of smoke from the dressing plant must have covered the whole of the valley floor. As many as 500 men and boys were employed in the mine and the associated plant. Many were drawn from the surrounding hamlets and from the nearby market town of Llanidloes although inevitably there would be a sprinkling of 'foreigners' who were willing to work hard to reap the rich financial reward that was there for the taking. The prosperity of the mine was such that, unlike many other ventures in the county, it led to some permanent settlement. The mining company built cottages around the mine itself, alongside the already existing farms of Manledd, Llwynyllys and Y Fan. A school was started a little distance up the valley so that for a time at least there was a thriving community on the doorstep of the mine. The company also built a group of eighteen terraced houses lower down the valley, close to the Llanidloes to Machynlleth road, where there was also a post office, shop and two chapels and this really became the core of the mining township. There was never a sense of remoteness about the Van comparable with the mining settlements of the hills around Pumlumon. The mining company had in August 1871 opened a short branch railway, 10 kilometres long, to connect with the Cambrian Railway at Caersws. For the first few months it carried only the dressed lead ore but at the end of the year a rudimentary passenger service was begun. This gave the mining company easy transport of ore and in addition allowed the township a good link with the outside world. It was never really a success as a passenger line and by 1879 the company was only too willing to allow the Cambrian Railway to take it over. Perhaps for this reason the railway survived long after the mines were closed and it was not until 1940 that if finally closed and the track was taken up. Little remains today although the route is still easy to follow on the ground, a route along which the daily ore trains steamed to and fro through the pastures of the Cerist valley.

Tangible remains are still to be found in the vicinity of the Van mine itself. Like all similar sites it has an untidy air but one which allows some reconstruction of the atmosphere of bustle and noise, smoke and steam which once filled the confines of the narrow valley. The great spreads of grey waste, now submitting to the power of the bulldozer, occupy the bottom of the valley below the actual mine and form a great causeway across the lower end of the Van Pool. It has been suggested that the pool came into being as a result of the blocking of the valley by waste. Few mine buildings remain save at foundation level but the storage bins and brick supports for the washing troughs give some hint of the scale of the operation to remove the rich deposits of the Van lode. Higher up on the hillside, above the conifer plantation, are the remains of the mine site with its two ruined chimneys standing as sentinels over the waste lands below. The actual mine shaft is now filled in with rubbish and parts of the original winding gear. The raised ore was taken down to the dressing sheds on two inclined tramways, to await processing before being loaded into the ore trains of the Van railway. Water power from streams on the hillside above was extensively used and a contemporary print of 1870 shows the mine buildings with a large water wheel alongside. Although there is much desolation around, the original rural character of the site has not been entirely swept away for the surrounding farms, dating from before the time when the mine came into being, still survive as working entities. Some of the miners' cottages are still occupied and others form holiday homes. The Van community, unlike so many similar mining townships, has managed to survive to the present day as a quiet successor to the once thriving settlement.

From Y Fan the Machynlleth road begins its steady climb onto the plateau top at a height of about 300m. At Staylittle (8892), a small hamlet which once supposedly formed an isolated garrison settlement during the Civil War, the road drops down into the upper marshy and flat-floored valley of the River Clywedog. This upper valley section presents a setting which is in complete contrast to the deeply incised valley downstream, part of which has now been flooded to form the impressive Clwyedog reservoir (8891).

From Staylittle the main road continues northwards to the valley of the Twymyn and thence on to Llanbrynmair. The route to Machynlleth turns west near Dol-Bachog Farm (884937) and for the next few kilometres passes through one of the most spectacular pieces of scenery that Mid-Wales has to offer. Instead of climbing onto the ridge top and making for Pen y Crogbren, the line of the Roman route, the present road skirts the steep coombe head of the Afon Twymyn valley running away to the north. Bare slopes of shale, with hard teeth where the sandstone bands outcrop at different levels of the rock face, help to give this upper valley section its gaunt and constricted appearance. The setting is completed by the high waterfall where the headwater stream of the Twymyn tumbles over a sandstone ledge into the deep chasm below. After heavy rain the fall can be quite impressive considering the stream only rises a bare three kilometres away to the west. From the road at the head of the over-deepened valley (873939) the view to the north takes in the Pennant valley which soon widens as the hamlet of Pennant is approached (8797).

The imposing nature of the scenery of the Twymyn headwaters owes much to the character of the Silurian shales, grits and sandstones which outcrop here. The events of the Ice Age and the subsequent episode of river capture have combined to put the finishing touches to the setting. The original headwaters of the Twymyn followed the present easterly course past Dylife (8694) but instead of then turning northwards as they do at present, they maintained their easterly route to ultimately join the Afon Bachog near Dol Bachog Farm (8893). The mountain road now follows this dry col which was once the floof of the upper Twymyn valley. At this stage, the main Twymyn valley ended in a trough-like head near the present Pennant-uchaf farm (876952). During the Ice Age a considerable depth of snow would accumulate in this north-facing head of the valley and would be likely to persist because of the whole aspect of the site. Acting like a small corrie glacier it would gradually eat back into the headwall of the valley and cause it to retreat southwards. In time the ridge, which formerly separated the north-south Twymyn valley from the west-east Dylife valley, would be broken down and the capture of the Dylife headwaters completed. Although the exact sequence of events is not known in detail the present landscape does afford clues which help us to make a reconstruction of the possible evolution. Other tributaries, apart from the Dylife, point to a generally easterly flow for both the

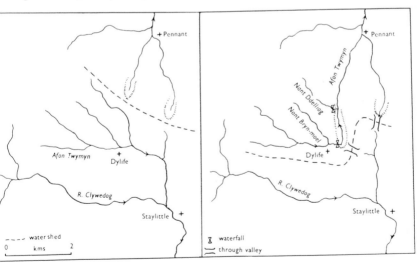

Drainage changes near Dylife

Nant Bryn-moel and the Nant Ddeiliog follow a general south-easterly direction. In the case of the Nant Ddeiliog, the present stream enters the main Twymyn valley in an upstream direction and tumbles over the valley side in an impressive waterfall. The fresh, rejuvenated appearance of the gorge below the Dylife road also points to a recent origin, an event which in time led to the complete disruption of the former drainage system and the creation of the 50m drop of the Ffrwd Fawr over a sandstone ledge to the over-deepened gorge below. As a result of this capture the old upper valley flow in the vicinity of Hirnant fawr farm (880938) is low and marshy. The beheaded Afon Bachog is now a misfit stream with a size out of all proportion to the wide valley it still occupies before joining the Clywedog near Staylittle.

Dylife, a kilometre to the west of the Twymyn gash, bears all the traces of an abandoned mining settlement, perhaps more so than Y Fan. It began its life of short-lived prosperity earlier than the Van mines for there are records of mining taking place here in the first part of the seventeenth century. As elsewhere mining activity was sporadic, with phases of high productivity (as in the 1770s) giving way to almost complete abandonment of the site until the chance location of a new rich lode brought back the miners and the inevitable speculators. The greatest period of prosperity was from about 1850 to 1880 when production approached 1,000 tons a year at times. Capital poured in and a 15m diameter wheel was built to drain the deeper workings. In place of primitive miners' shacks some attempt was made to found a proper community at Dylife with an inn, chapels, church and rows of terraced houses for the miners' families. After 1879 however, when there was a catastrophic drop in the world price of lead, the mines became uneconomic to work save by local adventurers who combined searching for ore with a little hill-farming on the upland pastures around. One difficulty which the Dylife mines had to face throughout their history was the transport of the dressed ore. Most of it moved down the upland tracks to Machynlleth and the Dyfi Estuary along what is now the mountain road, a difficult route even for pack-horse trains let alone waggons carrying a heavy load of ore. Derwen-las (7229), on the Dyfi banks, was the main outlet but as it lay more than 20 kilometres away from the mines in the hills, transport costs were always high and could only be justified when rich lodes of lead ore were mined.

By the end of the nineteenth century the life of the Dylife mines was nearing its end. The once thriving community with its chapels,

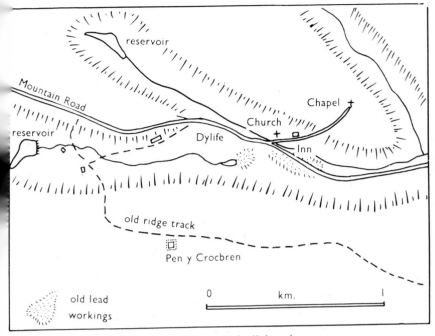

Features around Dylife on the Llanidloes to Machynlleth road

church, inn, post office and miners' rows was now dwindling rapidly as its means of support was steadily eroded away. Today an air of almost total abandonment pervades the area save for the Star Inn, which has recently been extended to take visitors, and some of the adjacent hill farms. The church has been in ruins for many years with only the original slate gravestones left to fight a battle of survival against the scrub and rank grass. In spite of the removal of the heart of the settlement the visitor can hardly be unaware of its former importance for great heaps of grey, dusty spoil fill the valley floor, the ruins of a former miners' row straddle the valley side a little upstream and there are the reservoirs which once ponded the water so necessary for the whole mining and dressing operation.

Beyond Dylife the mountain road climbs steadily until it reaches its highest point of over 500m on the crest of the col between Foel Fadian and Bryn y Fedwen (8395). From here, there are majestic views of the Central Wales Plateau with the massifs of the Arans and the Cadair Idris range rising above it. The rather featureless plateau top, often draped with a thick deposit of stony clay, gives way in places to youthful valleys where the headwater streams running down to the Dyfi have dug down deeply into the underlying shales and hard beds of flags. The road keeps to the plateau top by threading its way between the valleys. On its descent to the Dyfi it follows the ridge top and then the long spur which takes it into the valley of the Afon Dulas at Forge (7699). Its ridge top situation leads to extensive views over a countryside where man's shaping is seen at every turn. Spoil heaps from old lead workings dot the hillside around Rhoswydol Farm (8497) but in time these scars will disappear under a blanket of trees from a recently planted conifer wood.

Machynlleth, set within a nook by the side of the Dyfi valley, is a typical Welsh country town with sturdy stone grey buildings, rather drab when the clouds are low but mellowing in the summer sunshine. The main street of Maengwyn, wide and tree-lined, has served as the market place since the town was granted its right to hold weekly markets in 1291. It is here in the much restored building of the Institute and Library that Owain Glyndwr held his Welsh Parliament in the early years of the fifteenth century, an indication of the important role which Machynlleth played in Welsh history. The former Parliament house forms one of a motley collection of buildings of considerable architectural diversity yet because of the spaciousness of the former market place there is little to cause offence. The town plan is T-shaped with the other main street forming the cross piece. At the junction of the two main streets there is the dominating Victorian clock tower, perhaps symbolic of a re-awakening of the town following the arrival of the railway in 1865. The railway line was forced to take a route some distance from the town due to the hill of Pen yr Allt with the result that the station is $\frac{3}{4}$ of a kilometre away from the centre. This eccentric position led to some development on the approach road (the present A487) so that the town has a straggling appearance in this direction. The church lies in this quarter and although the oldest parts date only from the fifteenth century, its site could be much older, perhaps of great antiquity. That the town was laid out to some definite plan is suggested by its distinctive T shape and the allocation of narrow burgage plots each with a short frontage facing the main street but extending back for a considerable distance. In this respect Machynlleth is no different from many of the medieval new towns of England which came into being in the thirteenth and fourteenth centuries. The real contrast is with its near neighbour, Dolgellau, a town fashioned out of a maze of narrow streets which radiate from a tiny irregular market place, the whole arrangement suggesting haphazard growth without an overall plan.

SUGGESTED ITINERARY

The area between Llanidloes and Machynlleth, as outlined in the text, can be followed by taking the road crossing the bridge at Llanidloes (B4518). After a kilometre take the right fork to Van (9587). From the Post Office a short diversion up the Cerist valley leads to the lead-mining site. Return to the main road and then continue for 5 kilometres until the junction with the new road from Llanidloes is reached. From a viewpoint here (913889) there is an unparalleled view of the reservoir formed by the Clywedog dam further down-stream. Continuing along the mountain road, which ultimately drops into the upper part of the Clywedog valley at Staylittle (8892), the route then takes a left turn 2 kilometres further on towards Dylife, passing across the spectacular coombe head of the Twymyn and then through the grey wastes of the former lead-mining site. From Dylife a short walk up the hillside to the south leads to the Roman station of Pen y Crocbren (8593). Resuming the mountain road this now climbs steadily till it reaches its highest point of over 500m in the col three kilometres further on. This is an excellent place from which to appreciate the plateau-like character of much of central Wales with the upstanding massifs like Pumlumon, Cadair Idris and the Aran Range clearly visible on a good day. The road follows the ridge crest for some distance before descending along the back of a long spur to Forge (7699), a former quarrying and small industrial centre with woollen mills based on the local water power provided by the Afon Dulas. After crossing the common of Machynlleth, the road soon leads into the main street, Maengwyn, of the town.

FURTHER READING AND MAP REFERENCES

Introduction

Alcock, L. 'Castell Odo', *Transactions Caernarvonshire Historical Society,* 19 (1958), 2–7

Beazley, E. *Shell Guide to North Wales,* (1971), (Faber & Faber)

Challiner, J. and Bates, D. *Geology explained in North Wales,* (1973), (David & Charles)

Condry, W. *The Snowdonia National Park,* (1966), (Collins)

Dodd, A. H. *The Industrial Revolution in North Wales,* (1971), (University of Wales Press)

Jones, G. R. J. 'Post Roman Wales' in Finberg, H. P. R. (Editor), *The Agrarian History of England and Wales,* Vol. 2, (1972)

Jones, G. R. J. 'Early settlement in Arfon—the setting of Tre'r Ceiri', *Transactions Caernarvonshire Historical Society,* 24 (1963), 1–20

Jones, G. R. J. 'Anglesey Portrayed', *Anglesey Antiquarian and Field Club,* (1974), 109–117

Laing, D. *The Archaeology of Late Celtic Britain and Ireland, 400–1200 A.D.,* (1975)

Lewis, W. J. *Lead mining in Wales,* (1967), (University of Wales Press)

Lindsay, J. *A history of the North Wales Slate Industry,* (1974), (David & Charles)

Lynch, F. M. *Prehistoric Anglesey* (1970), (Anglesey Antiquarian Society)

North, F. J. *Sunken Cities* (1957), (University of Wales Press)

Sanderson, P. E. 'The importance of external factors in the development of the port of Holyhead', *Anglesey Antiquarian and Field Club,* (1963)

Thomas, C. (Editor), 'The Iron Age and the Irish Sea Province', *Council British Archaeology Report,* 9 (1972)

Watson, K. *North Wales—Regional Archaeology* (1965) (Cory, Adams & Mackay)

1. *Castle towns of Snowdonia*

Beresford, M. *New Towns of the Middle Ages,* (1967), (Lutterworth)

Brown, R. A. *The History of the King's Works,* Vol. 1, The Middle Ages, 1963 (H.M.S.O.)

Gresham, C. A. 'Tre Ferthyr and the development of Cricieth', *Transactions Caernarvonshire Historical Society,* 27, (1966), 5–13

Hughes, H. H. 'The Edwardian Castle and Town Defences of Conway', *Archaeologia Cambrensis,* 93, (1938), 75–92

Neaverson, E. *Medieval Castles in North Wales—a study of sites, water supply and building stones,* (1947)

Royal Commission of Ancient Monuments, Caernarvonshire, Vol. III, (1964), (H.M.S.O.)

Maps: 1:50000 sheet 115 (Caernarfon), 124 (Dolgellau).
1:25000 sheet SH 46 (Caernarfon), SH 67 (Beaumaris), SH 77 (Conwy), SH 53 and 43 (Cricieth and Harlech)

2. *Nant Ffrancon*

Greenly, E. The hanging valleys of Nant Ffrancon, *Geological Magazine,* 61, (1924), 189–90

Lewis, W. V. Glacial movement by rotational slipping, *Geografiska Annaler,* 31 (1949) 146–58

Seddon, B. 'Late Glacial cwm glaciers in Wales', *Journal Glaciology,* 3 (1957), 94–9

Seddon, B. 'Late Glacial deposits at Llyn Dwythwch and Nant Ffrancon, Caernarvonshire', *Proceedings Royal Society* B 244 (1962), 459–81

Unwin, D. J. 'The distribution and orientation of corries in N. Snowdonia', *Transactions Institute British Geographers,* 58, (1973), 85–97

Unwin, D. J. 'The nature and origin of the corrie moraines of Snowdonia', *Cambria,* 2, (1975), 20–33

Maps: 1:25000 SH 66.

3. *Tremadog and Portmadog*

Beazley, E. *Madocks and the Wonder of Wales* (1967) (Faber and Faber)

Lewis, M. J. T. *How Ffestiniog got its railway* (1968) (Railway & Canal Historical Society)

Richards, W. M. 'Some aspects of the industrial revolution in South East Caernarvonshire'. Part 1 'Y Traeth Mawr, Caernarvonshire', *Transactions Caernarvonshire Historical Society,* 4 (1942), pp. 62–75; Part 2, 'Portmadoc', ibid. 5 (1947), 71–87

Maps: 1:25000 SH 53, 54

4. *Aberffraw Sand Dunes*

Bagnold, R. A. *The Physics of Wind Blown Sand* (1941), (Methuen)

Hepburn, I. *Flowers of the coast* (1952), (Collins)

Landsberg, S. Y. 'The orientation of dunes in Britain and Denmark in relation to wind', *Geographical Journal,* 122, (1956), 179–89

Map: 1:50000 sheet 114

5. *Parys Copper Mountain*

Bingley, W. *North Wales; including its scenery, antiquities, customs and some sketches of its natural history* (1804), (Longman & Rees)

Cockshutt, E. 'The Parys Mountain copper mines in the Island of Anglesey', *Archaeologia Cambrensis,* 114, (1965), 87–111

Greenly, E. *The geology of Anglesey,* Vol. II, (1919), (H.M.S.O.)

North, F. J. *Mining for metals in Wales* (1962), (National Museum of Wales)

Rowlands, J. Copper Mountain, *Studies in Anglesey History,* Vol. I, *Anglesey Antiquarian Society,* (1966)

Thomas, T. M. *The mineral wealth of Wales and its exploitation* (1961)

Map: 1:25000 sheet SH 49

6. *Lleyn Peninsula*

Gresham, C. 'Townships in the parish of Llanystumdwy', *Transactions Caernarvonshire Historical Society,* 19, (1958), 8–38

Johns, C. N. 'The Celtic Monasteries of North Wales', *Transactions Caernarvonshire Historical Society,* 21, (1960), 14–41

Jones, G. R. J. 'Post Roman Wales', in H. P. R. Finberg (editor) *The Agrarian History of England and Wales,* Vols. I and II, (1972), 281–382

Jones Pierce, T. 'Bardsey—a study in monastic origins', *Transactions Caernarvonshire Historical Society,* 24, (1963), 60–77

Map: 1:50000 sheet 123

7. *Resort Towns*

Carter, H. *The Towns of Wales* (1956), (University of Wales Press)

Tucker, N. *Colwyn Bay—its origin and growth* (1953), (privately printed)

Maps: 1:25000 sheet SJ 08 (Prestatyn and Rhyl), SH 87 (Colwyn Bay), SH 78 (Llandudno)

8. *Vale of Clwyd*

Forde-Johnston, J 'The hill-forts of the Clwyds', *Archaeologia Cambrensis,* CXIV (1965), 146–78

Jack, R. I. 'The Cloth Industry in Medieval Ruthin', *Denbighshire Historical Society Transactions,* XII (1963), 10–25

Jack, R. I. 'The medieval charters of Ruthin borough', *Denbighshire Historical Society Transactions,* XVIII (1969), 16–22

Jack, R. I. 'Welsh and English in the Medieval Lordship of Ruthin', *Denbighshire Historical Society Transactions,* XVIII (1969), 23–49

Jones, G. R. J. 'Post-Roman Wales', in H. P. R. Finberg (editor), *The Agrarian History of England and Wales,* Vol. II, (AD 43–1042), (1972)

Jones, R. Gwyndaf 'Sir Richard Clough of Denbigh c1530–1570', *Denbighshire Historical Society Transactions,* XX (1970), 24–65 and XXII (1973), 48–86

Miles, H. 'Excavations at Rhuddlan, 1969–71', interim report, *Flintshire Historical Society Publications,* XXV (1971–2), 1–8

Savory, H. N. 'The excavations at Dinorben hill-fort, Abergele, 1961–9', *Denbighshire Historical Society Transactions,* XX, (1971), 9–30

Sylvester, D. 'Settlement patterns in rural Flintshire', *Flintshire Historical Society Publications,* XV (1945–5), 6–42

Sylvester, D. *The Rural Landscape of the Welsh Borderland,* 1969, (Macmillan)

Map: 1:50000 Sheet 116 (Denbigh)

9. Holyhead Road

Dodd, A. H. 'The roads of North Wales', *Archaeologia Cambrensis,* 80 (1925), 121–48

Pritchard, R. T. 'Denbighshire roads and Turnpike Trusts', *Denbighshire Historical Society Transactions,* 12 (1963), 86–109

Royal Commission of Ancient Monuments, Caernarvonshire Vol. 1, lxxi–lxxvi (1956) (H.M.S.O.)

Maps: 1:50000 sheets 115 (Caernarfon and Bangor), 116 (Denbigh and Colwyn Bay)

10. *Towns of the Severn Valley*

Beresford, M. *New Towns of the Middle Ages* (1967), (Lutterworth)

Davies-Pryce, T. 'The Fort at Caersws and the Roman occupation of Wales', *Montgomeryshire Collections,* XLII (1932), 17–67

Jones, E. V. *History of Newtown,* (1970)

O'Neil, B. H. St. J. 'The Castle and Borough of Llanidloes', *Montgomeryshire Collections,* XLIII (1934), 47–65

Spurgeon, C. J. 'The Castles of Montgomeryshire', *Montgomeryshire Collections,* LIX (1965), 1–60

Williams, R. 'Newtown: its ancient charter and Town Hall', *Montgomeryshire Collections,* XII (1879), 87–108

Williams, R. 'Dolforwyn Castle and its Lords', *Archaeologia Cambrensis,* I (Sixth Series), 1901, 299–317

Maps: 1:50000 sheet 136 (Montgomery and Llandrindod Wells), 1:25000 sheets SN98, SO09, SO19

11. *The Tal y Llyn Valley*

Cox, A. H. 'The geology of the Cader Idris Range', *Quarterly Journal Geological Society,* 81 (1925), 539–94

Cox, A. H. and Wells, A. K. 'The geology of the Dolgelly district, Merionethshire', *Proceedings of the Geologists' Association,* 38 (1927), 265–31

Linton, D. L. 'Watershed breaching by ice in Scotland', *Transactions Institute of British Geographers,* 15, (1951), 1–16

Howe, G. M. and Yates, R. A. 'A bathymetrical study of Llyn Cau', *Geography,* 38 (1953), 124

Watson, E. 'Glacial landforms in the Cader Idris Area', *Geography,* 45 (1960), 27–38

Watson, E. 'The glacial morphology of the Tal-y-llyn valley, Merionethshire', *Transactions Institute British Geographers,* 30 (1962), 15–31

Maps: 1:50000 sheet 124 (Dolgellau), 1:25000 sheets SH71, SH70, SH60

12. *Llanidloes to Machynlleth*

Lewis, W. J. *Lead Mining in Wales,* (1967), (University of Wales Press)

Morrison, T. A. 'Some notes on the Van Mine, Llanidloes, Montgomeryshire', *Industrial Archaeology,* 8, (1971), 29–51

Putnam, W. G. 'Excavations at Pen y Crocbren', *Montgomeryshire Collections,* 57, (1961), 33–41

Maps: 1:50000 sheets 135 (Aberystwyth), 136 (Montgomery and Llandrindod Wells)

INDEX

Numbers in italic type indicate illustrations